CMM® Implementation Guide

Choreographing Software Process Improvement

Kim Caputo

 **ADDISON-WESLEY**

An imprint of Addison Wesley Longman, Inc.

Reading, Massachusetts • Harlow, England • Menlo Park, California
Berkeley, California • Don Mills, Ontario • Sydney
Bonn • Amsterdam • Tokyo • Mexico City

This book is dedicated to my parents, Bailey and Evelyn Daugherty,
who instilled in me a life-long love of learning; the dedication extends to all who
encourage others in the process of learning, discovery, and development.

Many of the designations used by manufacturers and sellers to distinguish their products are
claimed as trademarks. Where those designations appear in this book and Addison-Wesley was
aware of a trademark claim, the designations have been printed in initial caps or all caps.

CMM® is registered in the U.S. Patent and Trademark Office.

The authors and publishers have taken care in the preparation of this book, but make no expressed
or implied warranty of any kind and assume no responsibility for errors or omissions. No liability is
assumed for incidental or consequential damages in connection with or arising out of the use of the
information or programs contained herein.

The publisher offers discounts on this book when ordered in quantity for special sales. For more
information, please contact:

Corporate & Professional Publishing Group
Addison Wesley Longman, Inc.
One Jacob Way
Reading, Massachusetts 01867

Library of Congress Cataloging-in-Publication Data
Caputo, Kim.
    CMM implementation guide : choreographing software process
improvement / by Kim Caputo.
        p.   cm.
    Includes bibliographical references and index.
    ISBN 0-201-37938-4
    1. Software engineering.   I. Title.
QA76.758.C354   1998
005.1'068–dc21   97-51575
                                                             CIP

Copyright © 1998 by Unisys Corporation. Published by Addison Wesley Longman, Inc.

Cover photo copyright © 1998 Glamour Shots.

All rights reserved. No part of this publication may be reproduced, stored in a retrieval system, or
transmitted, in any form, or by any means, electronic, mechanical, photocopying, recording, or
otherwise, without the prior consent of the publisher. Printed in the United States of America.
Published simultaneously in Canada.

ISBN 0-201-37938-4
Text printed on recycled and acid-free paper.
1 2 3 4 5 6 7 8 9 10-MA-0201009998
First printing, April 1998

Contents

Appendices

Foreword

Many, perhaps most, software projects have historically been late, over budget, and have had less functionality than expected, causing serious quality concerns. At the same time, software has become pervasive in modern society, and the power and complexity of software-dependent systems has exploded. Although we have many more powerful tools and methodologies today than ever before, it seems that the demand outstrips our ability to address software issues effectively.

Addressing the software challenge has led to many initiatives, including the application of Total Quality Management concepts to improving the processes for developing and maintaining software. Much of this work has been based on The Capability Maturity Model (CMM) developed by the Software Engineering Institute at Carnegie Mellon University. The Software CMM is a useful and powerful tool developed to provide guidance in software process improvement efforts. It is a generally applicable reference model that focuses on "what" rather than how.

Over the last decade, a network of process specialists has grown to exchange ideas and lessons learned about effective approaches to implementing software process improvement. Ultimately, improvement means changing the behaviors of organizations—a difficult task. Over a thousand professionals working on software process improvement from around the world meet annually at the Software Engineering Process Group (SEPG) National Conference. At the local level, Software Process Improvement Networks (SPINs) meet regularly to discuss improvement issues.

This book captures the lessons learned in real-world improvement efforts in a form accessible to everyone, many of which may have otherwise limited opportunity to learn from others. The author's guidance in using the CMM for defining, deploying, and improving processes will help many to attack software process improvement more effectively. The choreography metaphor should offer additional insight.

Software process improvement is not rocket science, but its relative simplicity does not mean it's easy. Caputo's *CMM Implementation Guide* is a useful resource to consider when embarking on the improvement journey.

Mark Paulk
Software Engineering Institute
Pittsburgh, PA
February 1998

Preface

Industry and Community

The software industry has experienced tremendous and unprecedented growth over the past 40 years, and our global and economic infrastructures are becoming more and more dependent on software. The software industry has been one of the fastest growing industries ever to exist. Along with it, a supporting industry has developed and grown into a strong international community: the community of SEPGs.

What Is an SEPG?

A Software Engineering Process Group (SEPG) is a team of software professionals with responsibility for driving and facilitating software process improvement efforts within a software organization.

This book was written by an SEPG member for SEPG members, with the intention of capturing the knowledge, tools, and techniques that we have found to be critical to our work. In this book, I have captured the things I wish somebody had told me when I first started in the SEPG business.

Goals of This Book

This book provides many thought-provoking ideas that are intended to help you be more effective in your software process improvement efforts. This book takes Humphrey's *Managing the Software Process,* Fowler and Rifkin's *Software Engineering Process Group Guide,* and Software Engineering Institute's *Capability Maturity Model* ® to a higher level of abstraction, a deeper level of understanding, and a broader level of application to build a foundation for a disciplined approach to software process improvement.

The goals of this book are as follows:

- To help SEPGs understand the image of successful improvement as represented by the guidelines in the Capability Maturity Model ® for Software (CMM ®) and explain concepts in insightful ways that will help you to make sense of what to do.

- To help SEPGs work as partners with their customers (the people in the software organizations: the managers and project teams).

- To help SEPGs understand how to drive and facilitate process improvement efforts to implement processes that their organizations are willing to accept and follow.

- To provide tools and techniques for SEPGs to use for driving and facilitating process improvements that lead to successful implementation efforts.

- To provide encouragement for starting and continuously optimizing software process improvement efforts.

Learning from Experience

At Unisys Corporation, when our first SEPG was formed there was not much guidance on how to do the work of an SEPG. There was a lot of information out there, but it took us two to three years to read it and translate it to our own situation. We had information about *what* to do, but it was difficult to derive the practical methods for *how* to make organization-wide software process improvements. We had to learn the hard way—from experience.

Who should read this book?

- If you are currently part of an SEPG you can benefit from these ideas, which encourage working toward continuous optimization. You can benefit from seeing the relationship between your experience and ours, recognizing a repeatable pattern, and focusing your improvement efforts to save time and effort. I expect this book to help existing SEPGs to be more effective and possibly more creative.

- If you are just starting an SEPG you probably don't have the luxury of a two- or three-year start-up phase. You can't afford to learn the hard way, but you can learn from the experience of others. You can benefit from our experience to save time and effort. By packaging this information and integrating it with practical experience, I expect this book to help new SEPGs to start their efforts and gain momentum.

- If your organization does not have an SEPG and has no plans to staff one but you are willing to champion improvement efforts, you might find these tools helpful. By starting a few small efforts and making progress, you will gain some short-term benefits, and you will begin to build an awareness of the focus that is involved in organization-wide software process improvement efforts. I expect this book to help process improvement champions to make the improvements that they can make on their own, but there may be global improvements that they cannot make on their own. If the champions want to convince senior management of the need for an SEPG and want to explain what the SEPG members would do for the organization, this book will be helpful.

A Choreographic Perspective

As I considered the source of inspiration for my work in software process improvement, I found a most unlikely source in my early life experience with dance and choreography. The analogy comes alive in this book. Dance is like producing software. Dancers perform the steps of the dance; software programmers perform the steps of the software process. Learning a dance could involve things such as reading the notation and interpreting the steps, or it could involve watching someone who has performed the steps before, trying to do the steps, trying the steps with the music, and making changes when something isn't working. Improving a process involves similar activities. As professionals, programmers are gifted and talented individuals, brilliant in their own right, who can collaborate to give a performance that does not diminish any individual performance. At least, this is our hope; sometimes the chemistry is wonderful, and sometimes it isn't.

Choreography involves movement of the body, guiding one or more dancers through certain steps and through changing rhythms while maintaining balance to create a peak performance for their audience.

Software process improvement involves the movement of an organization, guiding one or more individuals through certain activities and through changing conditions while maintaining balance to create a peak performance for their customers.

In both cases there is a need to understand how to move people's energy to continuously strive for excellence. Just as art is not done simply for the sake of art itself, but for the sake of enlightenment, entertainment, and encouragement of the audience, so software process improvement is not done simply for the sake of software process improvement itself, but for the sake of the customers whose lives are becoming increasingly dependent on software. We must learn to improve and create excellence for their sake.

How to Use This Book

Because this book is based on both theoretical models and practical experience, as you use the models you will encounter many of the same experiences described here. Some things may not apply to you right now, but they may apply to you later.

How to Use the Files on the CD-ROM

The CD-ROM contains templates, samples, and presentation materials that you can use to get started more quickly. However, please note that these materials are not intended for you to use directly but rather are intended for you to adapt to fit your organization. These tools will reduce your start-up time, but you must add your own finishing touches if you hope to succeed.

I am not suggesting that these materials are "silver bullets" or perfect templates. They fit the situation at the time they were used. If your situation is different, the materials won't fit as well. And your situation is sure to be different: a different day with different people (and remember that even the same people might be different on a different day).

These materials might be helpful to people who find it easier to start with something and make changes rather than start with nothing and create their own materials from scratch. There is a phenomenon called IKIWISI, an acronymn for "I'll know it when I see it." We often can't describe what we want, but we will know what we want when we see it. We will also know what we don't want when we see it. Both reactions provide valuable information for producing successful results. These templates give you something to look at so that you can consider what you want and what you don't want. Then you can create exactly what you need.

Acknowledgments

I gratefully acknowledge the following people who have had a significant influence on me and the writing of this book.

The choreographers whom I had the privilege to watch in rehearsals when I was young. They didn't know I was in the wings learning from them. Anthony Tudor, Eugene Loring, Agnes de Mille, Murray Louis, and Bela Lewitzky.

The choreographers and coaches who worked with me personally. They didn't know that what they taught me would one day apply to the software industry. Israel "El" Gabriel, Richard Adama, Olga Maynard, Jillana, James Penrod, Donald Bradburn, James Jones, Paul Shipton, and Paul Sutherland.

The "choreographers and coaches" at the Software Engineering Institute who didn't know that I was in the wings learning from them. Watts Humphrey, Stan Rifkin, Priscilla Fowler, Mark Paulk, Mike Phillips, Bette Diemel, Chuck Meyers, Suzanne Garcia, Jim Over, Tim Olson, and Roselyn Whitney.

The SEPG members, managers, and engineers whom I have had the privilege of working with personally, a cast too numerous to name here, but who participated in developing, reviewing, and implementing what I have written about in this book. This book would not be possible without their efforts.

Paul Goodwin and Rich Liechty who were my mentors, and Nancy Lynd and Alan Jones who were my peers in the early days on the first SEPG at Unisys Corporation, learning and discovering how to apply the CMM even before the CMM was documented. Laurie Patton and Vin Ludwig who were my teammates on the next cycle of improvement, whose support was instrumental in developing and implementing many of the process documents and files in this book. I am grateful for their support then and now.

Linda Lindquist who encouraged me to bring this work forward to be shared and leveraged with other SEPGs within the company. This led to the possibility of writing a book to further share and leverage these ideas. Linda is now at Xerox Corporation, but she worked closely with me during the early days, and I am grateful for her guidance and support during the early development of this book.

Jay Stockett, Larry Powers, Lance Callaghan, Paul Kraska, Gail Bertossi, Dave Parker, Frances DePonio, Dick Bland, and Joe Ringland, who were SEPG members at other sites in the company who were most actively involved in the sharing and leveraging, developing working relationships, and transferring knowledge and practice between SEPGs. I appreciate their enthusiasm and encouragement from the outside looking in, and from the inside looking out.

Lee Osterweil who founded the Southern California Software Process Improvement Network (SC SPIN) and to Debra Brodbeck, Leitha Purcell, Rick Hefner, Leia White, Kent Palmer, A. Windsor Brown, and Warren Scheinin, who continued to grow the SC SPIN after Lee's departure. (Lee planted the SC SPIN as a tree he never intended to sit under, and the others successfully took care of tending the tree.) This group provided me with access to other people in the software process improvement industry whose ideas stimulated or affirmed my work. Later the SC SPIN provided me with my first outside audience, giving me the encouragement and confidence to continue, and to reach further.

I would also like to acknowledge the contributions of three external reviewers who contributed much to help me improve my draft manuscripts: Michael Sturgeon of the Software Technology Support Center and Transitions Management, Inc.; Marek Wakulczyk of the Canadian Air Force and Small Bear Management Services; and Stan Rifkin of Master Systems, Inc., co-author of the SEI Technical Report, *Software Engineering Process Group Guide*, CMU/SEI-90-TR-24.

Michael Sturgeon for encouraging me to submit proposals to international conferences, such as the SEPG Conference and the Software Technology Conference, and attending and celebrating each successful presentation. Mike helped me develop my vision for this book, a vision that became much bigger than I first imagined. I am grateful for his understanding and support during the development of this book, especially for not letting me get stuck with my worst case of writer's block, and for always believing that I would make it to the finish line of this writer's marathon. Mike continuously encourages me to grow.

Marek Wakulczyk for his witty review comments and his encouragement and guidance that kept me thinking about how to keep the reader interested, and how to get more movement into the words. Marek helped me bring my draft manuscripts more into alignment with my vision, providing me with the outside perspective that I couldn't get when I was too close to the work. Because of the similarities in our approaches, Marek continues to be a remarkable mirror for me.

Stan Rifkin for his subtle yet powerful influence on my performance. Before I met him, his writing helped my SEPG to do the work. After I met him, his review comments helped me shape this book. Stan was my toughest critic when I was off balance, and my greatest fan when I struck the perfect balance. In my early drafts, I had the right idea but the wrong tone of voice in my writing style. Stan helped me find my voice, and then he encouraged me to use it, reassuring me to have confidence that others would hear it. Stan continuously builds my confidence in my own performance.

Carole Hollinger who supported me as my manager for a majority of the months that I spent writing the manuscript. Carole encouraged me when I got my case of writer's block, reminding me of the importance of fresh ideas, and telling me to stop worrying about what others will think and to trust that the readers will find the ideas they need.

Chris Harding who supported me as my manager as I completed this book. Though many people start to write a book, fewer finish it. Without his help, I might have remained one of the former instead of the latter, remaining incomplete instead of complete. I am grateful for his encouragement in helping me make the transition to a new beginning as a published author.

Special Thanks to my "supporting cast" from the Unisys Authors Sponsorship Program and Addison Wesley Longman, especially Peter Gordon, Dot Malson, Ellen Gwynn, Carla Freeman, Jim Senior, Helen Goldstein, Jacquelyn Young, and the anonymous reviewers.

Extra special thanks to my "supporting cast" at home, my husband Christopher J. Caputo, my children Curtis Caputo and Vanessa Caputo, my parents Bailey Daugherty and Evelyn Daugherty, and my other parents Ralph Caputo and Carol Caputo. Without their time, patience, and understanding, this performance would not have happened. I am especially grateful to my husband Christopher J. Caputo for reminding me that this book is just another performance, and that I have a life before, during, and after the performance. Thanks to him, I do.

1

Introduction: Performing Software Process Improvement

"Creative activity could be described as a type of learning process where the teacher and pupil are located in the same individual."

—Arthur Koestler

Practical Experience and Theoretical Models

To perform software process improvement, you need models and experience. Reading about it isn't enough to learn how to do it. You learn by practicing. When you practice, you learn more, and then you improve more. Even though much of this book is based on practical experience in improving the software process—my own experience and that of others—the work is strongly based on models that I have read about in the literature or have seen in presentations at local meetings or international conferences. Sometimes, exposure to the models came first and concept implementation followed; in other cases, the experience came first, and the models helped us to understand why our efforts were successful. In this book, I will share my experiences to help you understand the theoretical models from a practical point of view. You can use the ideas in this book to improve your own performance of software process improvement.

A Simple Pattern

When I began working in the first Software Engineering Process Group (SEPG) in my company, we started by reading about and trying to learn the tasks we needed to perform. It took time to absorb the information, but the tasks seemed simple enough. Essentially, the basic pattern is as follows.

- Understand the model for improvement (the Capability Maturity Model and the key practices contained in each Key Process Area).

- Understand the difference between your organization's actual practices and the desired practices from the model.

- Define the processes necessary to meet the improvement goals.

- Make sure the processes are followed and continuously improved.

A Complicated Movement

With experience we found out that it's much more complicated than that. Software process improvement is like dance. A dance movement seems easy to do until you get up and try to do it. Even something as simple as moving your arms in a circle while keeping your shoulders and hands relaxed is difficult at first. You think, "This is a lot harder to do than I thought it would be." It might look simple, but it is not easy. Similarly, with software process improvement, some concepts are easier to implement than others. Some concepts are difficult to discuss let alone improve. The CMM is complex, so there is always more to learn about it. There is always more to learn about the actual practices of the organization and more to learn about the needs of the organization.

Fortunately . . .
the CMM was developed from observations of what worked well in successful organizations as guidelines for what others can do to improve their work.

Unfortunately . . .
what works well for one organization does not always make sense to the people in another organization.

If you agree with Koestler's perception that "creative activity could be described as a sort of learning process where the teacher and pupil are located in the same individual," then the creative activity of an organization could be described as a sort of learning process where the organization works together and learns from itself. An SEPG helps the organization to discover what makes sense to the people in the organization, which leads to organizational self-awareness and self-actualization. This is the creative activity of an organization that creates software products.

The SEPG Function

An SEPG drives and facilitates the process whereby the organization learns from itself. Hypothetically, if communications were flowing clearly between managers and engineers and across functional lines, and if the people in the organization were working together effectively and were learning from their experience, then every individual in the organization would be performing the function of an SEPG. But that isn't the way life really is. With increasing complexity and increasing workloads, communication suffers. People begin to focus on their own personal perspectives, and they tend to forget how their work fits into the larger goals of the organization.

There are many gifted and talented people in the software industry who are very good at what they do, individually. And even though they are brilliant, if they focus exclusively on their own responsibilities, ignoring their shared responsibilities, they will step on one another's toes. When people lose sight of the "big picture" and focus on their part as if trying to avoid stepping on each other's toes, they communicate less and less with the rest of the organization. It is as though there were walls between people—"silos" or "stovepipes" in which communication flows only within departments and not between departments. They aren't dancing together anymore.

These gifted and talented people tend to forget that they share responsibility for the overall performance. But when they remember, they know that they must learn to dance together. They know that their part is important but while they are performing their part, they need to have a sense of where the others are standing and where they are going next so that everyone can move in a coordinated fashion. Each person needs to perform his or her part within the context of the big picture. If their efforts are well choreographed, they won't step on one another's toes. If they are going to dance together, they need choreography.

By devoting resources to an SEPG, the organization gives somebody the responsibility to take the time necessary to restore the big picture perspective. As the focal point for software process improvement, an SEPG can help the managers and engineers focus on an organizational perspective to enhance communication and increase control in areas of shared responsibility. However, the SEPG cannot develop an overall perspective without the involvement of the managers and engineers, just as a choreographer cannot create a dance without the involvement of the dancers. SEPG members work to understand the individual parts, learn how the parts are integrated, communicate what they have learned, and help the organization learn the next steps. The SEPG is responsible for choreographing software process improvement, supporting the organization as it works together and learns from itself.

Choreography as a Metaphor for Software Process Improvement

In the sixteenth century, choreography meant the writing down of steps. Today, choreographers create steps and organize the collaborative efforts of many designers, musicians, and stage technicians to create a dance performance. Choreographers work with dancers whose strengths and weaknesses inspire the creation of the steps. The steps may be created in full collaboration. The choreographer may suggest the desired effect for a certain part of the dance, and the dancers may suggest some movements. The choreographer and the dancers work together, developing the steps until everyone is satisfied with the results.

In my work I have seen a similar evolution in the approach to software process improvement. At first, software process improvement meant the writing down of steps. People developed flowchart diagrams and pages upon pages of process documentation. But today this work involves greater creativity, participation, and collaboration. As the software business changes, some of the old steps might not work as well in a new situation, so creativity comes into play to address new expectations. Software interacts with other system components, so the collaborative effort of many designers, engineers, and technicians needs to be organized. Customers' expectations of quality may suggest the desired effect for a certain part of the software process and the engineers and managers might suggest steps to create that effect, developing the steps until they are satisfied with the results.

Just as dance notation is not the dance—it is simply the method to capture what was done so that the steps can be repeated at another time—the process document only captures the steps and encodes them for enactment at another time. The dance notation is not the end product; the performance of the dance is the end product. Similarly, the process document is not the end product; the actual performance of the software process is the end product.

Whether it is dancing or software development, the actual process is written in the hearts and minds of the performers, and it is dependent on the communications, expectations, and assumptions that are shared by all the people who participate in enacting the process. When the process involves interaction or complex details, it helps to capture the process in writing. Process documents are useful for the following:

- Capturing intentions for reference, in case somebody forgets a detail or an agreement from an earlier conversation.

- Capturing expectations for activities and for developing time estimates and plans of what to expect when these activities are performed.

- Capturing expectations for communication documents, such as plans, reports, and engineering records, so that people know what to expect from one another and can compare actual results to expected results.

My work in software process improvement has been like choreography. When I work with managers and engineers, I describe the desired effect for a particular process, and they suggest the steps that they can do based on their strengths and weaknesses. I write the steps down so they can see what they have said, and together we work on refining the steps until they are satisfied. Then they begin to practice, and I help them learn to do the steps, so that in the end they improve their work and perform better than before. This work involves the creativity and collaboration of all who participate.

Other people in other groups have been able to leverage this work. Rather than create their own steps from the beginning, they have taken these process documents as a base and have made modifications to fit their needs. They have taken the choreography and have made it work for them. This adaptation work also involves the creativity and collaboration of all who participate. The participants are involved in making the modifications, and the changes account for their needs, their strengths, and their weaknesses. Because they have taken the steps that fit their situation and have modified the steps that did not fit, the improvement work has been less extensive, and it has taken less time to start practicing.

One Company, One Industry, One World, Many Cultures

Although my career experience has been solely with Unisys Corporation, my work has been applied to many cultures across the corporation and beyond. Unisys corporate culture is like a microcosm of the industry: not just one culture, but many cultures having different cultural roots. Unisys was formed by the merger of two major commercial corporations: Burroughs and Sperry. I joined "the Burroughs side," which typically had small development projects or larger projects with multiple interdependencies. When CMM-based improvement efforts began, this group had very few documented processes; most projects succeeded on the strength of the individuals and their dedicated overtime.

It seemed as if every project was done differently, and people had the flexibility to do whatever needed to be done. This made it difficult to recognize which tasks were being done the same way. Most people in the organization would say that there was no "process" for software engineering, so clearly at that time we were at the bottom of the capability maturity scale. People working on the smaller projects adapted quickly to software process improvement, but those working on the larger projects dragged their feet for a long time. Even with the same motivational pressure, it takes longer to organize the movement of a larger group. This is true in dance, too. It takes longer to organize and rehearse the movement of a larger group.

In contrast, when the CMM-based improvement efforts began, "the Sperry side" already had a lot of process documentation. However, that documentation was turning into shelfware as the business was changing. Because their processes no longer reflected their actual practices, these organizations were also at the bottom of the capability maturity scale. As their SEPG worked to upgrade or replace these documents, it was able to use some of the techniques in this book to bring the processes more in line with actual practice.

Another culture was added to the mix when Unisys acquired Convergent Technologies, a small business doing small software customization projects. When this group started to use the CMM, they had virtually no process documents. Their SEPG, which was staffed by just one person, was able to use the techniques in this book to develop processes, and this small, isolated group showed evidence of meeting all the Level 2 goals in just six months.

Furthermore, SEPG members from other government and commercial companies were also able to apply the techniques in this book in their organizations. Some of them learned these techniques from my presentations at local meetings or major conferences, and some of them developed similar approaches independently for their own organizations. At Software Process Improvement Network meetings, SEPG conferences, and Software Technology conferences, SEPG members typically discover that we face similar issues and develop similar solutions.

My experience is not isolated at all. It has been shared by others inside and outside my company. These techniques are transferable and flexible enough for you to learn to do what you can do, but you must discover what you must change to make it work for you. This effort is like learning a new dance and then adding your own style to make the dance yours.

The same ballet performed by different dance companies all over the world will not look the same. Even though the basic steps are the same, the culture and the unique talents of the dancers will affect the performance. Ballet emerged as an art form in France and Italy in an era when the epitome of dance was the ephemeral. Women danced like willowy spirits, lighter than air, escaping gravity on the tips of their toes for a few fleeting moments. But when ballet was brought to Russia, virtuosity was marked by strength and power. Dancers moved with strength, with leaps that seemed to defy gravity and hang forever in the air. As ballet developed in America, the emphasis was placed either on the individual character, with dancers developing emotional expressiveness, or on the athletic, with the dancers performing steps as a pure physical expression of the music. Now dancers from China and Japan display remarkable balance and control, balancing on one toe for what seems like an eternity. Each culture has its own unique style and its own admirable strengths. The performance is brilliant when each culture takes the dance and makes it its own.

But each culture also learns from the others, and the dance changes under cross-cultural influence. For example, French and American dancers learned to dance with more strength because of the Russian influence, and Russian dancers learned to dance with more expressiveness because of the American influence. Dance is a mutual adaptation in which we change the dance to make it our own, and as we change it we ourselves change. Software process improvement is also a mutual adaptation. In the software industry, many of us have taken steps in software process improvement and have made the steps our own, but perhaps many of us have not yet taken the more difficult steps of allowing ourselves to learn from each other and change under cross-cultural influence. It won't happen unless we share our experiences and our techniques. I am sharing my experiences and techniques, not to tell people to do it my way but rather to open the door for us to learn from each other throughout the industry and throughout the world.

Perhaps I am not the first to open this door, and I hope that I am not the last. This is an invitation to the dance.

What if You Don't Have a Choreographer?

Without an SEPG as a focal point, the organization tends to behave like a group of dancers without a choreographer. Somebody needs to work on the issues involved with getting these gifted and talented people to collaborate and develop shared priorities and shared goals. If choreography is everybody's responsibility, it ends up being nobody's responsibility. It is like saying that you have a lot of gifted and talented dancers who know how to dance, so you don't need a choreographer.

Most of the time, as the saying goes, "the right hand doesn't know what the left hand is doing." This makes it difficult for the people in the organization to work together and learn from their collective experience. Sometimes people think it best to keep their problems to themselves, to be responsible for solving their own problems. They do not see how organizational issues and problems are shared by others. They do not see that these problems are not likely to be solved in isolation. Before the formation of our SEPG, I worked with managers and engineers who thought that they should solve their own problems in isolation. Here are some examples.

Problem 1: Improvement Planning and Activities in Our Spare Time

The findings and recommendations report from our first assessment summarized the major issues found in our organization and provided recommendations for what to do to begin addressing those issues. The first recommendation was to form an SEPG to write an action plan and coordinate improvement activities. But the senior managers did not form an SEPG. They considered the issues, and they felt *responsible*. They felt responsible for allowing these issues to arise in their organizations, and they took personal responsibility for getting the issues resolved. They took ownership of resolving the issues, and they thought they should do it themselves. So these senior managers decided not to form an SEPG but instead to write the action plan themselves.

One year later, there was no action plan. A task force had been initiated to work on one recommendation, and a proposal had been written for another recommendation, but these actions were taken in the absence of a plan. It took a year of experience for the senior managers to prove to themselves that they could not make organizational improvement of this magnitude in their spare time.

Problem 2: Improvement Efforts Without Planning and Tracking

Meanwhile, even though the key issues from the assessment were not being addressed, improvements were happening throughout the organization. Every employee had received corporate training in Total Quality Management (TQM) techniques and was empowered to improve their work. Improvement was seen as a good thing and improvement efforts were rewarded. But there was a lack of communication between the managers and engineers. Improvements were coming from the bottom up—from the limited perspective of individuals—and not from the perspective of organizational impact. Even though the intentions were good, some of the results were not very good.

In some cases, a team of engineers would spend months devising a new process without informing the managers about their improvement ideas until they were finished. Then the managers were surprised. The managers' reaction was something like this: "Who told you to do this? You want me to tell my people that they have to do this? I'm not going to interrupt their work for this. I don't see the benefit of doing this." You can imagine the reaction of the engineers, who had spent months perfecting this process. In the absence of clear expectations, people were disappointed.

In other cases, the managers did not stop the improvements from being introduced. Eventually, too many things were changing, and it was difficult to remember what had or had not changed. It was like what happens in a dance rehearsal when, for a particular phrase of music, the steps have been changed so many times that the dancer can't remember which step to do. Her mind goes blank, and she either stops moving or fakes it and improvises. It's usually obvious when dancers become overwhelmed by too much change, but it's not so obvious in the software process. In our case, no one noticed the high number of changes until the organization was overwhelmed by it. The amount of change was generating confusion. People wanted some stability, some focus to the improvement efforts so that they wouldn't have to be reacting all the time. Without clear expectations, people were overwhelmed.

This was the environment when our SEPG began. We were chartered to write the action plan and coordinate improvement activities across the organization. The following underlying issues led to the formation of our SEPG.

- Senior management did not have time to devote to writing an action plan.

- People were spending time and resources on improvement solutions that management did not want.

- Improvement efforts were out of control.

In other words, this organization was ready for some choreography. People were ready for an SEPG that would provide focus on shared priorities so that people could work on what was needed and keep these kinds of problems from happening again.

How Many People Do You Need on the Choreography Team?

An SEPG can be staffed in various ways. In a large corporation it might be a full-time staff, but in a small business or small group it might be a part-time assignment for one or two people. (Some talented people can dance and choreograph at the same time, but it is rare.) SEPG techniques can be adapted to work for any staffing situation; however, the more you invest in time and resources, the more return you can expect, provided that the time and resources are spent wisely. It doesn't matter how you staff the SEPG, as long as you learn to spend your time and resources wisely.

It can be difficult to determine how many people you need to staff an SEPG, but it depends on how many dances you need your organization to perform. Choreographers have dance experience and understand how to dance, and SEPG members should have software development experience and understand the software process. By planning and managing the tasks of the SEPG, you can develop schedule and staffing estimates based on the work you want to complete. Instead of guessing how many people you need or using a rule of thumb (such as 1–3% or 2–5% of your total development organization), you can staff your SEPG according to the following:

- The work to be done

- The skills and knowledge of the staff

- The rate of change that you want, balanced by the rate of change that your organization can accommodate

Improvement Infrastructure

The people who needed to communicate in order to gain control over the improvement activities were senior management, the SEPG, and the process users (the people who do the work, use the process, or follow the procedures). Defining the working relationships among these people is known as defining an *improvement infrastructure*. An improvement infrastructure that we used at Unisys consisted of a Steering Committee, an SEPG, and Working Groups.

- The Steering Committee sponsors the improvement activities.
- The SEPG drives and facilitates the improvement activities.
- The Working Groups perform the improvement activities.

Table 1.1 describes these roles and provides an analogy with dance and choreography.

With this infrastructure, the SEPG's primary customers are the Steering Committee (senior management) and the Working Groups (small teams of process users), and the sec-

Table 1.1 Comparing roles for dance and choreography with roles for software process improvement.

Dance and Choreography	Software Process Improvement
Artistic Director	**Steering Committee**
• Determines which dances will be performed this season • Chooses the dancers • Commissions the choreographers	• Determines which processes will be improved this year • Chooses the Working Group members • Commissions the SEPG
Choreographers	**SEPG**
• Work in collaboration with the dancers to create the dance • Coordinate the details of realizing the vision of the dance • Coach the dancers and provide the support and motivation to perform the dance	• Work in collaboration with the Working Group to improve the process • Coordinate the details of realizing the vision of the improved process • Coach the Working Group and the process users and provide the support and motivation to perform the process
Dancers	**Working Groups**
• Bring their talents and experience to the task of defining what steps will be performed, determining what works and what doesn't work • Work in collaboration with the choreographers and other dancers to learn and improve the steps • Perform the dance • If necessary, coach other dancers	• Bring their talents and experience to the task of defining what steps will be performed, determining what works and what doesn't work • Work in collaboration with the SEPG and other process users to learn and improve the steps • Perform the process • If necessary, coach other process users

ondary customers are the other process users who will use the process improvements. The Steering Committee reviews improvement proposals and determines the expectations, or the charter, for each Working Group. The Steering Committee reviews the status and final results of Working Groups. The SEPG coordinates the activities by recommending charters for Working Groups, planning and tracking the Working Groups, and raising issues from the Working Groups to the Steering Committee. Often, one of the SEPG members participates as a facilitator on a Working Group. The SEPG role on the Working Group is not to tell people what to do but rather to understand and to contribute a big picture perspective. The SEPG also coordinates a review of the proposed improvement by other process users who were not part of the Working Group to ensure that others have a chance to be heard.

To best serve these customers, as the SEPG drives and facilitates the improvement activities it not only looks internally at the organization's current practice but also looks externally to discover what can be learned from others. Thus, the SEPG looks at what is happening within the organization as well as in the industry and in the world, keeping an eye out for new opportunities for improvement.

For an organization that is not familiar with the CMM, the CMM is an external force, something that is happening in the industry that represents a consolidation of many opportunities for improvement. By using the CMM as a set of guidelines for improving the software process, the organization will learn something new about what it does and about what it can do to improve. The organization will be expected to change. We used to think that people reacted to change by resisting it and that the resistance was like a brick wall that we could do nothing about. But now we realize that when we put the reactions in proper perspective, we can do something about them. We can respond to the organization's underlying needs. The most effective response is to involve people in creating their own success.

When a dancer is taught a new step, what reason would she have to resist learning it? Perhaps she doesn't want to fall or doesn't want to look bad in front of other people, but resistance is not a typical response for a professional dancer. Learning a new step is just part of the job, and she expects to learn new steps throughout her career. She isn't thinking about falling; instead, she's focused on discovering how to do the step. She tries to do it, and, if the first attempts are off balance, she tries again until she does it. Others may help her understand the step, but she must learn to do the step herself. If at first she doesn't understand the step, the choreographer helps her focus her attention on what it takes to perform the step: the position, the movement, the direction of the energy, and so on. The choreographer helps her focus on what she can do and encourages her to do what she has the ability to do. The encouragement makes a difference in her level of self-confidence, but the dancer is involved in creating her own success.

For dancers, there is a clear difference between rehearsal and performance, a distinction that is less evident in the software industry. In dance, mistakes are allowed in rehearsal; falling is allowed, even expected, in rehearsal, but falling is not expected in performance. If we took the same perspective in software, discovering defects in requirements, design, and prototyping would be expected and acceptable as if it were part of a rehearsal. We might expect a process in which defects are discovered and analyzed so that by the time we perform, the final product is nearly flawless.

Now imagine a scenario in which dancers would be under pressure to perform all the time, even in rehearsal. Imagine what would happen if somebody counted the number of times a dancer fell in rehearsal and posted it for everyone to see. Imagine the dancers being told that yesterday there were 100 mistakes in rehearsal, and now those mistakes must be eliminated. Now a dancer has good reason to resist learning a new step: fear. Fear of falling and fear of looking bad in front of other people create resistance. And now the dancer loses focus. When she should be concentrating on her next movement, she is thinking about not falling. Guess what happens when a dancer isn't concentrating on what she is doing? She falls!

In software, people tend to think of defects as bugs, failures, and faults that we count and eliminate one by one. We think we are performing all the time, and falling is not easily tolerated. We don't look at defects as part of a learning process. Then we put so much concentration on reducing defects that we lose our concentration and unwittingly create even more defects. We resist learning new steps because of fear; we do not know how the new steps will affect our performance, and we don't want to fall.

We might not be able to eliminate the fear, but we can focus and encourage people to do what they have the ability to do. The encouragement makes a difference in their level of self-confidence, but they must be involved in creating their own success. We could make it easier to change if we made it safer to fall and get back up and try again. Then resistance would not be associated with learning a new step. Learning a new step would be part of the job, and we would expect to learn new steps throughout our career. Instead of reacting to the chaos of change we could respond to the rhythm of change.

Envisioning, Encoding, and Enacting

If an organization expects to change what it does and expects to learn something new, the people in the organization will be involved in taking the actions that bring about these changes. People who have experience using the CMM for software process improvement efforts might notice a pattern, some familiar steps involved in performing software process improvement. It could be described as a simple pattern of three repeating steps.

- Envisioning: "We see what we are doing now and what we need to be doing."
- Encoding: "We decide what to do and document how to do it."
- Enacting: "We do it, and we improve our performance."

Of course, it's more complicated than that, but sometimes we make it harder than it has to be. The CMM provides a seed for organizational learning. It is a catalyst for starting this pattern of three repeating steps:

- Envisioning (specific to the needs defined in the CMM)
- Encoding
- Enacting

Repeat the cycle of steps:

  - Envisioning (generic for any needs)
  - Encoding
  - Enacting

Repeat the cycle of steps continuously.

Each of these steps typically begins with some degree of unfocused thinking and reactive behavior. When the change comes into focus, you experience a breakthrough and your thinking becomes clearer; you make sense out of your situation. When people focus, they can see how to respond and take effective actions to complete the step. Let's look in more detail at what might be typical of the experiences of people performing these three repeating steps.

Envisioning

In the initial envisioning step, the SEPG is given the task of improving the software process based on the Capability Maturity Model. SEPG members might think

- What is it that I'm supposed to do?
- What is the Capability Maturity Model?
- I don't understand it yet.
- How am I going to succeed at this task if I don't understand it?

Once the SEPG understands the CMM and tells the managers and engineers what it takes to apply it, the managers and engineers have the same reaction.

- What is it that I'm supposed to do?
- What is the Capability Maturity Model?
- I don't understand it yet.
- How am I going to succeed at this task if I don't understand it?

If the SEPG members don't focus, they might unnecessarily perpetuate this unfocused thinking with these reactions.

- They don't understand me.
- They don't understand what the CMM can do for them.
- They don't understand what I'm trying to do for them.
- They don't want to support my efforts.
- How am I going to succeed at this task if I don't have their support?

The SEPG members can turn this around with the following breakthrough idea: People want to succeed. They don't want their ability to succeed to be hindered by ineffective practices. They don't want to get stuck doing something that no longer makes sense to do. If they keep doing something just because "it has always been done this way," they won't be able to meet the expectations that result from changing environments and changing requirements. They need the capability to manage the necessary process changes that enable teams and organizations to continuously meet new challenges and new opportunities. You can use your understanding of the Capability Maturity Model to improve the software process to support the success of the managers and engineers.

When this breakthrough idea is understood, you can take effective actions with more focused thinking. Here are some focused actions that you can take to respond to the prevailing needs.

- Work to understand the Capability Maturity Model and related concepts of implementation cycles and culture change.

- Share your understanding with others and help others understand these concepts in their own terms.

Encoding

The second step, encoding, also typically begins with an initial period of unfocused thinking. During the first attempts to define processes, the managers and engineers might express one of the following:

- **Can't**—We can't define what we do. It's too complicated.

- **Won't**—Once we define it, people won't read it. People will ignore it.

- **Don't**—People don't do things the same way, so there is no process to define.

- **Aren't**—You aren't going to get this group of people to agree on what they want to do, or even what the process should look like.

- **Isn't**—It isn't possible to define the process perfectly, so no one will agree to follow it.

If the SEPG members don't focus, they might unnecessarily perpetuate this unfocused thinking by defining complicated documents that are perfect in every detail—and they will be kept busy for a long time reacting to yet another issue, yet another disagreement, and with more and more work to do. They will become frustrated with their apparent inability to please the managers and engineers. Even if the SEPG perseveres despite the issues, when the document is complete, the managers and engineers might react with self-fulfilling prophecies, as they claim that they

- **Can't** follow the process
- **Won't** follow the process
- **Don't** want to follow it
- **Aren't** going to agree with it
- And it **isn't** perfect yet!

In the encoding phase, the breakthrough idea is that people want to be heard and understood. The process document should capture what they say they want to do. When people see the words that they have been thinking or saying, they can focus on the consequences of those possibilities. The first draft of a process and a list of issues helps focus their attention. However, the first draft may reflect what you heard, but that might not be what they meant. They will not feel understood until after a few rounds of discussion and revision. You can use process documentation to show people that they have been heard and understood. The communication and discussion builds the real process, and that is more important than building the image of a perfect process document.

To move forward in the encoding step, here are some focused actions that you can take to respond to the prevailing needs.

- Keep to the essence of what must be captured. Don't clutter the process with text that no one will have time to read. Use simple, uncomplicated process formats that are easy to follow. Write the processes in terms that the process users understand.

- Define high-level processes that map to actual practices and low-level procedures for any critical details, optional tasks, or tasks that might be performed differently depending on the circumstances.

- Start building a process improvement cycle. Overcome the temptation to wait for absolute agreement and perfection. Do the minimum necessary to get started, and make corrections on the next cycle.

Enacting

After the envisioning and encoding steps comes the enacting step. Again, it begins with unfocused thinking. The managers or engineers who would perform the process will consider the personal costs and benefits of making the change. Their initial reaction might be any of the following.

- It's too much trouble. I don't have time to do things this way. I have a schedule deadline to meet. My management doesn't really want me to do this if it means I will miss my schedule deadline.

- Who else is doing this? If I do it, will I be the only one? If I don't do it, will I be the only one who isn't doing it?

- What if I have trouble with the process? Who will support me if I do it? Can I get help? What if it really doesn't work? Am I going to be stuck with it? Maybe it will just go away if I wait a little while.

As the managers or engineers consider the consequences, it may appear as if they might not adopt the processes. The SEPG members' reaction might be any of the following:

- What if no one will follow the processes? Would that mean the process documents are worthless?

- If the process documents are worthless, then all that time and effort spent on documenting the processes will be wasted.

- If the time and effort spent on this process is considered a waste, will people think all software process improvements are a waste of time?

The breakthrough idea in this step is that people want to see reinforcement and encouragement. They look to managers and peers for their reactions. They want to know whether the change will result in personal gain or loss. You can provide positive reinforcement to those who follow the desired practices. If those who adopt the desired practices early see the benefits of making the change and share information with others, then others will also be encouraged to change. As the practices are accepted, everyone experiences the intended benefits of making the change.

Once the breakthrough idea is understood, here are some focused actions that you can take to respond to the prevailing needs.

- Provide support to make it easier to adopt the process. Minimize the initial start-up effort as much as possible. If it makes their jobs easier, people will be more receptive to the change.

- Facilitate manager support and peer support. Make that support visible through discussion meetings or written feedback.

- Provide visibility of progress. Help people focus on their progress toward adopting the desired practices and help them notice that the practices are making a difference.

- Use a process improvement cycle. Make corrections to the things that don't work, and keep people encouraged that some things can be improved now, and some things can be improved later. Improvement is continuous, not an all or nothing event.

After envisioning, encoding, and enacting software process improvements using specific guidelines defined in the CMM, your organization will become more aware of the changing environment and changing opportunities that affect their products and processes. It will seem as if you are starting all over again with the same unfocused thinking that occurred in the initial envisioning step. The SEPG members will once again think

- What is it that I'm supposed to do?

- How do the changing environment and changing opportunities affect what we need to do?

- I don't understand it yet.

- How am I going to succeed at this task if I don't understand it?

Then once the SEPG understands what kind of improvement is needed and tells the managers and engineers what it takes to respond, the managers and engineers will once again have the same reaction.

- What is it that I'm supposed to do?

- How do the changing environment and changing opportunities affect what we need to do?

- I don't understand it yet.

- How am I going to succeed at this task if I don't understand it?

As before, if the SEPG members don't focus, they risk perpetuating the unfocused thinking.

- They don't understand me.
- They don't understand what the improvement can do for them.
- They don't understand what I'm trying to do for them.
- They don't want to support my efforts.
- How am I going to succeed at this task if I don't have their support?

The same breakthrough idea stops the unfocused thinking: People want to succeed. You can use your understanding of the managers and engineers, and your customers and their needs, to improve the software process to support their success. Then similar focused actions will help you respond to the prevailing needs.

- Work to understand the needs of the situation and people involved. Apply your knowledge of the CMM, implementation cycles, and culture change.

- Share your understanding with others and help others understand these concepts in their own terms.

As this new envisioning step completes, it is followed by another encoding and enacting step, and the cycle repeats again. The guidelines in the CMM help you to take the first steps because the CMM represents the changing environment and opportunities that put pressure on our industry as a whole. It represents the pressure on the industry to develop disciplined engineering practices and predictive management practices that lead to a higher probability of developing successful, high-quality products, on time and within budget. For organizations that have not learned to recognize their own unique changing environment and opportunities, the CMM is the catalyst to start the system of process improvement. The organization's initial awareness of the CMM exposes the organization to a representation of our industry's changing environment and changing opportunities.

Fast and Slow, High and Low

How quickly can process improvement occur? How quickly can your organization respond to its changing environment and changing opportunities? The rate of change depends on how quickly you can create a focus that the people in the organization can understand. You accelerate progress when you focus people's attention to take positive action in response to prevailing needs. As you go from unfocused thinking to focused action more quickly each time that the cycle repeats, eventually the cycle becomes faster and more natural. The cycle becomes continuously optimizing.

Continuous optimization is not the same thing as continuous acceleration. We don't want to rush or jump to conclusions that make things worse instead of better. So a little hesitation balances the tendency to rush, but too much hesitation might also make things worse instead of better. So a little acceleration balances the tendency to hesitate. Continuous optimization is a balancing act: making the right moves at the right time, overcoming unnecessary hesitation (not too slow) without unnecessary rushing (not too fast), and paying close attention to the prevailing needs of the changing environment, changing opportunities, and the needs of the people involved.

Continuous optimization is not the same thing as constant high performance. It doesn't mean that everything is always perfect. A dancer performing a perfect leap might appear to be defying gravity, remaining suspended in the air forever, but what goes up must come down. When she finishes one leap, she must prepare for the next, creating a new focus for the image she wants to hold in the air on the next leap. Preparing for the next leap, instead of defying gravity, she works with it. To jump high in the air, she must first bend her knees, moving her body in the opposite direction (down) to the direction she wants to go (up). She goes with gravity, and then she uses her muscles and her mind. If she tries to jump without bending her knees, she will barely get off the ground. The feet alone do not have enough leverage to lift the body. With a few running steps to gather momentum, bending her knees in preparation for the leap, releasing the muscles at the right moment, and lifting to hold the image in the air, it looks and feels as if she is defying gravity. But of course she is not actually defying gravity. She has learned how to dance with it.

At the beginning of a new step in software process improvement when things are unfocused, it feels similar to falling. And when something that was successful is not as successful in a new situation, it feels similar to falling. It feels as if things are going down instead of up. It seems as if we're not getting anywhere or that we're not moving in the right direction. But that's the way things are when you are between leaps. You can't stay up forever, and, when one leap is finished, you need to focus on the next leap. Gathering momentum to make a change requires some preparation steps, such as gathering information, understanding what people need, understanding new expectations, and learning what makes sense to people so that you can communicate clearly. These preparation steps might not seem to be actively moving the organization toward its goals, but without these steps the jumps don't get very high off the ground. These preparation steps are important, because they focus the energy so that focused actions can be effective. It might feel like falling at first, but it's just bending your knees to prepare for the next leap. After a while you get used to the way it feels. You learn how to dance with it.

2

Assumptions: Turning the Culture Around

"When one door of happiness closes, another one opens; but we look so long at the closed door that we do not see the one which has been opened for us."
—*Helen Keller*

Creating Movement

When you see a dancer moving with beauty and grace, you don't notice the effort exerted to create the movement, but the dancer works hard every day to make it look easy on stage. She learns how to create the movement and apply exactly the right amount of effort to make it look effortless. Even with something as simple as the basic "turn out" of the feet, what creates the movement is not always what you see and not always what you might expect.

When a new student attends a ballet class for the first time, she tries to imitate the teacher's turn out position with the heels together and the toes angled outward to point to the side. She sees the toes; she moves the toes. But the position is actually the result of hip rotation caused by muscles deep in the back. These muscles are inside the body, underneath layers of other muscles, so they cannot be seen or felt with your hands. These muscles contract to provide the strength and stability that a dancer needs as a foundation for every movement in ballet. Without the use of these muscles during each movement, the toes will slip out of position, or worse, the dancer might injure her ankle or knee by trying to force the turn out position.

I have seen many organizations attempt software process improvement for the first time by trying to copy the artifacts that are called out in the Capability Maturity Model. They think of the CMM as a checklist of documents. But if they don't know how a particular document relates to their work and if they don't see how it helps them, the change isn't likely to stick. If they don't understand why a document might be important, it either slips away or becomes the target of criticism.

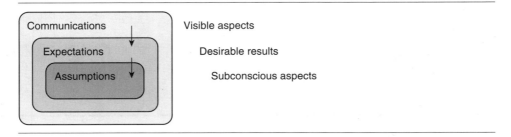

Figure 2.1   Communications, expectations, and assumptions in organizational culture.

Just as the feet are turned and held in place by layers of muscles, the documents are held in place by layers of organizational culture. The document is a visible aspect of communications within the organization. People have expectations about the document's content and results, and assumptions about the document's purpose and why it might be important. The organizational culture can be characterized by the three layers shown in Figure 2.1.

Communications, Expectations, and Assumptions

The communications layer includes the artifacts—the documents, data, and quality records—and the activities that produce the artifacts. These visible aspects are what people can see, hear, and talk about. Activities and artifacts are intended to bring about the desired results, and the vision of the desired results will influence and shape the activities and artifacts. The expectations layer includes the organization's goals or metrics, its values, and what it considers desirable behavior and desirable results. These expectations are based on certain assumptions that are central to the organization's culture. The assumptions layer represents the invisible aspects of the culture: the subconscious ideas that are typically not discussed. These assumptions are not discussed because people assume that everyone knows and everyone agrees that these things are so. These assumptions influence people's expectations, which in turn influence the activities and artifacts produced by the organization.

For example, a project plan document is an artifact of a planning activity. If the people in the organization share the assumption that is it important to plan the software development tasks before performing the tasks, then the project plan will be a desirable result. People will expect to see a project plan, will participate in planning activities, and will produce project plans. However, if they share the assumption that project plans are unnecessary paperwork because nothing ever goes as planned, then planning activities will be perceived as a waste of time. A forced expectation about producing project plans will not be supported by the underlying assumptions, and project plans will likely slip away or become the target of criticism until people understand why project plans might be important and useful to them.

Culture can be defined as a pattern of shared basic assumptions that the people in an organization have learned as they have solved the problems of relating to the outside world

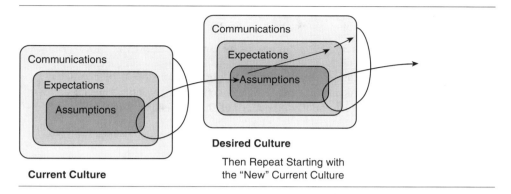

Figure 2.2   Changing the shared basic assumptions leads to changes in expectations, or desired results, which lead to changes in communications or actual results.

and of learning to work together. These assumptions lead to solutions that work well enough to be considered valid. These assumptions are taught to new members as the correct way to think, feel, and behave in relation to those problems.

Culture change can be defined as a change in the pattern of shared basic assumptions (see Figure 2.2). When something that worked once doesn't work anymore, the assumption underlying that solution may no longer be considered valid. So the thinking that takes place during a culture change is something like this: "We used to think this was true, but now we think something else is true. We used to put value on this behavior, but now we put value on some other behavior. This new behavior seems to work better for us."

As in the preceding example, an organization that at first did not put value on planning and did not expect project plans to be valuable might learn to find planning activities and project plan documents to be more useful than originally thought. Once this realization is shared, the expectation for all projects to have project plans will be supported. Shared assumptions and expectations and planning activities will hold project plans in place. Project plans will be produced because the documents will be desirable results supported by the subconscious aspects of the culture. In this example, people used to think project planning was a waste of time, but now people think project planning is valuable to them and to the organization. This is an example of one assumption, but culture is characterized by many assumptions, a pattern of shared basic assumptions.

For example, an organization's culture might be characterized by constant troubleshooting or fire-fighting, always operating in crisis mode, because of the underlying pattern of shared basic assumptions.

- If we put our best people to work on solving the problems, they will exert heroic efforts and save the project every time we get into trouble.

- We have no control over the occurrence of problems; all we can do is react to the problems when they occur.

- We don't have time to plan ahead; we must finish this project as soon as possible. We have enough to think about today. We can't begin to think about tomorrow right now.

- We reinforce these assumptions by rewarding effort and hard work.

At the other end of the spectrum, an organization might be characterized by its use of foresight or risk management, always continuously optimizing its performance, because there is a different underlying pattern of shared basic assumptions.

- We will have an easier time if we manage risks and prevent problems so that we won't get into trouble.

- We have no control over the occurrence of *some* problems, but we have control over other problems, and we can anticipate some problems before they occur. We can prevent or lessen the severity of some problems.

- If we plan ahead, we will have a better idea of what we intend to do, and we can direct our efforts toward those intentions with less wasted time and effort. We must think about tomorrow right now.

- We reinforce these assumptions by rewarding results and rewarding those who work smarter and not harder. (Note that the highest-paid dancer is not the one who sweats the most!)

These are extreme cases, but they illustrate the opposite ends of the capability maturity scale. Level 1 is characterized by operating in crisis mode, and Level 5 is characterized by continuously optimizing performance. If the assumptions for Level 1 are fairly well entrenched, it will be difficult to change them. In a stable culture, the prevailing attitude is "We think this is true." For culture to change, the attitude must become one that might be expressed this way: "We used to think this was true; now we think something else is true." For example, if crisis management is perceived as a successful way to do business, it will be difficult to change the assumptions. It will be difficult to persuade people to try something new, such as project management, risk management, process management, and other technologies and approaches that could lead to a more successful way to do business.

I have often heard people in a Level 1 organization talk as if they don't have any choice. They are stuck with the way things are. If people think they are stuck, they won't be able to move until they see things differently. When a dancer gets stuck in a position, it is because she holds her muscles in a fixed position. She must relax some muscles and flex other muscles to create the next movement. The same thing applies to people who get stuck in a perspective. To make progress, we must let go of some assumptions (relax some mental muscles) and adopt other assumptions (flex other mental muscles) to allow improvements to take place. We need to focus on the door that has been opened for us.

SEPG Activities: Visible and Invisible

Some of the SEPG's activities are easy to see; they are visible activities. Other activities are much more subtle; they are relatively invisible. Table 2.1 shows examples.

Table 2.1 Visible and invisible SEPG activities.

Visible Activities	Invisible Activities
Performing assessments to determine an organization's strengths and weaknesses	Redirecting organizational focus away from short-term gains toward long-term benefits
Developing action plans to address the organization's strengths and weaknesses	Redirecting management effort away from the crisis "problem of the day" toward future risks
Defining processes that meet the organization's needs Implementing processes and ensuring that the processes meet the organization's needs	Redirecting development effort away from cranking out "quick and dirty" code toward disciplined engineering techniques
	Expanding internal and external goals and measures oriented toward customer satisfaction
	Making it easier to continuously optimize processes so that problems are prevented, avoided, or addressed with long-term solutions instead of quick fixes

What Makes These Activities so Difficult?

Visible activities would be easy to do if they were not dependent on invisible activities. Stated more directly, software process improvement would be easy to do if it were not dependent on the culture change that it requires. But the dependency relationship is reciprocal, a bit like the chicken and the egg.

- Software process improvement requires culture change, and culture change requires software process improvement.

- Software process improvement brings about culture change, and culture change brings about software process improvement.

- Software process improvement provides a foundation for culture change, and culture change provides a foundation for software process improvement.

We typically focus on the visible activities: the pattern of assessment, action planning, process definition, and process implementation. This pattern of the visible activities works on the culture from the outside in and then from the inside out.

The assessment method works from the outside in. The assessors examine the artifacts and determine from them whether the goals for a Key Process Area are being met. For example, the assessors examine project plans and ask questions about the planning activities to determine whether the goals are being met for the Level 2 Key Process Area of Software Project Planning for Level 2, or perhaps for the Level 3 Key Process Area of Integrated Software Management. If a certain set of goals is being met, the assessors assume that the organization is successfully acting from the same assumptions held by other organizations at the same maturity level. Thus, if the organization is meeting the goals for maturity level 2, it is acting from the same assumptions as other organizations that are also at maturity level 2.

Action planning, process improvement, and process implementation work from the inside out by defining a new desired state, changing some of the shared basic assumptions, creating new expectations, and communicating changes in the transition that moves the organization to a higher maturity level.

If software process improvement is approached without regard to the underlying culture change, people try to make changes to the visible aspects only. They work on changing the artifacts as if they were trying to satisfy an "artifacts checklist." If the change to the artifacts works well enough to be considered valid, the underlying assumptions also change. "We used to think we didn't need this document, but now we think it has value." When successful, the change to the assumptions holds the artifacts in place. However, this approach will not succeed if the change to the artifacts seems artificial; the underlying assumptions won't change, and the artifacts won't become part of standard practice.

For example, if project plans are treated as unnecessary paperwork and nothing happens to change that assumption, project plans will not become part of standard practice. If, instead, problems are prevented because of good planning practices, the assumption changes, and the new assumption—that project plans have value—will help make project plans become standard practice.

To approach software process improvement with regard to the underlying culture change, consider the underlying assumptions and expectations affecting the culture. Typically, assumptions are not discussed. People don't talk about their assumptions, because they assume that everyone else knows the same thing and thinks the same way. So how do we talk about what we don't talk about? Let's look at the assumptions in a frame of reference, the CMM.

Assumptions in the Capability Maturity Model

The assumptions that support effective software process improvement are hidden in the CMM (like those muscles that you can't see or feel). The CMM does not state the assumptions directly, but you can discover them if you know where and how to look for them. I discovered these assumptions by studying the CMM from the outside in, looking at the key practices as the visible aspects, looking at the Key Process Area goals as the desirable results and expectations, and considering why this Key Process Area might emerge as an important factor (see Figure 2.3).

I once worked with a choreographer who said that there are only about seven or eight basic principles that underlie all the possible movements in dance; then when he found a new one, he called it number 9. I started thinking that maybe there are only seven or eight (or nine) basic assumptions that underlie all the possible practices in the CMM. Wouldn't it be a lot easier to learn and work from seven or eight basic assumptions than to work from 300 key practices?

Over several years of study and refinement, comparing the CMM with my own experience and with those of others, I came up with a list of seven assumptions. These seven assumptions are traceable to every Key Process Area in the CMM. There might be a couple more assumptions that I haven't yet found. Perhaps you might find number 8 and num-

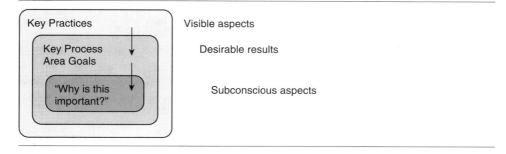

Figure 2.3   Discovering the assumptions by studying the CMM from the outside in.

ber 9 yourself. Or perhaps your experience might lead you to disagree with my list. You could come up with a different set of assumptions that makes more sense to you based on your experience. For now, let's consider these seven assumptions and see where they take us.

- Assumption #1: To build quality into products of large size and complexity, engineering discipline is required.

- Assumption #2: One person can't track all the details, and error detection is more probable when the work is examined by more than one person.

- Assumption #3: Our success is dependent on other groups and customers.

- Assumption #4: The organization uses process definition to transmit the culture's quality values.

- Assumption #5: The projects use process definition to incorporate the culture's quality values.

- Assumption #6: Process makes a difference in the quality of the activities and the quality of the products.

- Assumption #7: Surviving in a business world that is constantly changing requires constant adaptation and learning.

If you consider that all key practices of all the Key Process Areas in the CMM can be motivated from these basic assumptions, ask yourself these questions.

- What basic assumptions are motivating the current practices in your organization?

- Are your shared basic assumptions in alignment with these desired assumptions?

- Are your shared basic assumptions working for you or working against your good intentions, pushing you in the wrong direction?

- Do you need to turn the culture around?

When I presented these assumptions at conferences and seminars, I asked people what they thought about them. Typically they would think they are good assumptions and that it's hard to argue against them. They say it's like motherhood and apple pie; it's hard to disagree with common sense. So perhaps many people already agree with these desired assumptions. The trouble is that there are overriding assumptions that overrule the desired assumptions. I asked people to give me examples of overriding assumptions that were affecting their organizations, and the following list paraphrases some typical responses.

- Discipline always interferes with creativity.

- The schedule is fixed, the resources are fixed, the feature content is fixed, and we don't have any choice. The quality level is fixed, too. The quality level is whatever it happens to be on the delivery date.

- Managing requirements is a waste of time, because the requirements change too frequently.

- The sooner we get the software into testing, the sooner we can get the product out. We can test the quality into the product.

- If we define one common process and get everyone to follow it, it will guarantee the quality of the product.

- We don't have enough time and resources to follow the defined process.

- Our project is different. The process doesn't apply to us. The overhead will kill the project.

- Good people can do it without a process.

- We always hire qualified people, so we don't need any training.

You might recognize some of these overriding assumptions at work in your own organization. You might be wondering how to break through them. It would be easier if these assumptions were completely false and could simply be proved wrong. However, many of them derive from someone's personal experience, which has led to the conclusion that an assumption is true all the time, when in fact it might be partially true or true only under certain conditions. If personal experience is the foundation of someone's assumptions, you should acknowledge and respect that. It would be disrespectful to try to prove the person wrong. Then focus on discovering how both perspectives can stand together and maintain a balance.

Discipline and Creativity

For example, consider this assumption: Discipline interferes with creativity. This perspective treats discipline and creativity as opposites that cannot both exist at the same time. Choose one or the other, but you can't have both discipline and creativity at the same time. Or can you? Sometimes discipline interferes with creativity, but other times it doesn't. Sometimes discipline enhances creativity. Let's take a look at how these opposing elements might work together.

Software development is a creative activity. As people develop software products, they also *learn how* to develop software products. Sometimes people don't seem to learn from their mistakes, and it looks as if they are fighting the same crisis over and over. In other cases, people discover a pattern, something that works well, and they capture the pattern so that they can repeat it successfully next time. But sometimes what was successful before won't work this time, so the pattern must be altered to fit the current situation. Sometimes, with enough information, people can help keep projects on track toward their goals. Sometimes, with enough insight, people can create or use new methods that improve their results to meet or even exceed expectations.

I have just described what the creative activity of software development is like "sometimes" as if it were random chance. But if you look again, you will see a pattern of increasing discipline over the creative process.

1. Ad hoc process: Fighting the same crisis over and over.

2. Repeatable process: Discovering a pattern, and capturing and repeating it.

3. Defined process: Altering the pattern to fit the current situation.

4. Quantitatively managed process: Keeping on track toward goals.

5. Continuously optimizing process: Creating or using new methods to exceed goals.

Increasing the discipline over the creative process need not interfere with creative activity. Discipline allows people to harness the power of their own creativity. In any profession that strives for excellence, you will find examples in which undisciplined activity takes more effort than disciplined activity. This is most easily demonstrated in professions of physical activity, such as ballet or basketball, where you can see the exertion of effort. Compare the effort, precision, and quality of movement that you see in those who are constantly training themselves and are disciplined in their movements against those who are undisciplined in their movements. Rather than interfering with creativity, discipline allows more freedom to focus on creativity and on achieving the desired results. Creativity extends beyond software products to the process used to develop software.

Everything I stated about software development as a creative activity applies to software process improvement. Software process improvement is a creative activity. As people develop software, they also learn how to develop software process improvements. In the beginning it is more difficult to learn from mistakes, and it is harder to discover the patterns, but it becomes easier. Eventually people can discover their improvement patterns, alter their patterns, and use information and insight to help them succeed. The discipline over software process improvement increases to allow us to harness the power of creativity more effectively.

Foreground and Background

Just as discipline and creativity often appear to be opposing forces, the desired assumptions and overriding assumptions often appear to be opposing forces. If the desired assumptions are considered valid but are overruled by overriding assumptions, the overriding assumptions are in the foreground and the desired assumptions are in the background. When people discuss the desired assumptions, those assumptions are raised to the foreground. By sharing ideas, you create an opportunity to change expectations and act on the desired assumptions. You can then use the desired assumptions as a foundation for creating expectations for the desired culture that effectively supports software process improvement.

You can use the Assumptions Worksheet in Appendix A to capture and compare the current assumptions in relationship to the desired assumptions. In this way, you can identify the gap that needs to be closed by either changing an assumption or expanding the pattern of existing assumptions to include the desired assumptions.

Changes in assumptions lead to changes in expectations. If these expectations are communicated, understood, and carried out in practice, we should see activities being performed that are equivalent to the key practices in the CMM. The movement flows from the shared assumptions to the needs and expectations to the activities and results.

Tables 2.2–2.8 summarize the relationships among the assumptions, expectations, and activities.

The Most Important Assumption

Perhaps the most important assumption is that people want to succeed. Assume that people try to do their best at all times. Usually when it looks as if someone is doing something that doesn't work, it isn't because that person isn't trying to do his or her best. The person thinks it's the right thing to do and isn't aware of how everyone else might be affected. If people knew better, they'd do better because they want to succeed. People want to perform to the best of their ability.

Table 2.2 Assumption 1: To build quality into products of large size and complexity, engineering discipline is required.

The Typical Reaction	The Shared Expectations	Related Key Process Areas	Activities
"We need to consistently perform a well-engineered software process."	"We integrate all software engineering activities, we keep work products consistent, and we seldom deviate because it is too costly."	Software Product Engineering (Level 3) Requirements Management (Level 2) Configuration Management (Level 2)	• Use documented requirements as the basis for engineering activities. • Consistently perform engineering tasks that are defined and integrated. • Perform activities (such as peer reviews) to prevent downstream defects. • Review changes to requirements before incorporating changes to engineering outputs. • Identify engineering outputs that must be controlled, and record and report status and change activity for those engineering outputs.

Table 2.3 Assumption 2: One person can't track all the details, and error detection is more probable when the work is examined by more than one person.

The Typical Reaction	The Shared Expectations	Related Key Process Areas	Activities
"We need to formalize our evaluation activities."	"We use teams to review software work products so that the output of an activity meets the needs of downstream activities."	Peer Review (Level 3) Software Quality Assurance (Level 2) Defect Prevention (Level 5)	• Perform formal peer reviews to prevent downstream defects. • Plan and coordinate formal peer review activities across the organization. • Perform reviews and audits of products and activities to verify that they comply with applicable procedures. • Plan assurance activities and report the results to those who need to take action. • Perform defect analysis, identify common causes of defects, and take action to prevent the occurrence of specific defect types. • Plan and track defect prevention activities.

Table 2.4 Assumption 3: Our success is dependent on other groups and customers.

The Typical Reaction	The Shared Expectations	Related Key Process Areas	Activities
"We need to interact effectively with other groups and customers during development."	"We involve all interdependent groups, we resolve intergroup issues, and we involve customers to ensure that the right product is built."	Intergroup Coordination (Level 3) Requirements Management (Level 2) Software Subcontract Management (Level 2)	• Establish and maintain agreement with the customer on the requirements for the software product. • Define and review product-level system requirements with all affected groups. • Coordinate plans of all engineering groups. • Maintain an environment to support intergroup and customer communication. • Document customer acceptance criteria. • Select qualified subcontractors, establish commitments, and track and review the subcontractors' performance and results.

Table 2.5 Assumption 4: The organization uses process definition to transmit the culture's quality values.

The Typical Reaction	The Shared Expectations	Related Key Process Areas	Activities
"We need to pass on lessons learned, standards, and guidelines."	"We know what our standards are, we know what our project needs are, and we select and enact processes to meet both."	Organization Process Definition (Level 3) Configuration Management (Level 2) Process Change Management (Level 5)	• Identify established standards and translate them into a standard for the organization; build the standard into the processes. • Allow project members to define or alter processes to meet their project needs. • Collect process-related data to help current and future project teams make decisions. • Identify process documents and process-related data that must be controlled and keep these documents under control, recording status and change activity. • Define process improvement goals and plans. • Proactively, systematically, and continuously identify, evaluate, and implement process improvements.

Table 2.6 Assumption 5: The projects use process definition to incorporate the culture's quality values.

The Typical Reaction	The Shared Expectations	Related Key Process Areas	Activities
"We need to take advantage of lessons learned, standards, and guidelines."	"We know what our standards are, we know what our project needs are, and we select and enact processes to meet both."	Integrated Software Management (Level 3) Software Project Planning (Level 2) Software Project Tracking and Oversight (Level 2)	• Define or alter processes to meet the project needs and standards. • Integrate project management processes with processes defined for the project. • Develop estimates for the work to be performed, and define the plan to perform the work. • Establish the necessary commitments with all affected groups, and review any changes to commitments. • Perform the process activities, track and review actual performance against the plan, and adjust the plans based on actual performance status. • Collect and store project measures and processes for use by the organization.

Table 2.7 Assumption 6: Process makes a difference in the quality of the activities and the quality of the products.

The Typical Reaction	The Shared Expectations	Related Key Process Areas	Activities
"We need to gain more control over the process."	"We know what our process is, we measure it against a standard, and we take action to improve."	Organization Process Focus (Level 3) Software Quality Management (Level 4) Quantitative Process Management (Level 4)	• Assess the software process against a process standard and develop action plans to address findings. • Develop and continuously improve the software process, and plan and coordinate these improvement activities across the organization. • Define quality goals for the software products. • Establish plans to achieve quality goals and monitor performance, and adjust the plans, products, and quality goals to satisfy customer needs. • Define process performance goals for the project. • Measure process performance, analyze the data, and adjust the project's process to maintain process performance within acceptable limits.

Table 2.8 Assumption 7: Surviving in a business world that is constantly changing requires constant adaptation and learning.

The Typical Reaction	The Shared Expectations	Related Key Process Areas	Activities
"We need to develop skills and disseminate knowledge."	"We know our needs for skills and knowledge, we know which skills and knowledge we have, and we take action to obtain what we need."	Training Program (Level 3) Technology Change Management (Level 5) Process Change Management (Level 5) Defect Prevention (Level 5)	• Assess current skills and knowledge. • Develop and improve skills and knowledge through training program activities, and plan and coordinate training program activities across the organization. • Identify, select, and evaluate new technologies, and incorporate effective technologies into the organization. • Plan and perform pilot efforts before introducing the new technology into normal practice. • Continuously improve the software process, with senior management sponsorship and organization-wide participation. • Analyze defects and determine actions to prevent future defects.

3

Assessments:
Looking at Your Reflection
in the Mirror

"An activity becomes creative when the doer cares about doing it right, or better."

—John Updike

Frame of Reference

In almost every dance studio you will find a full-length mirror. Dancers practice their dance steps facing the mirror so that they can see their positions. They know in their minds what they should see, and they check to see whether they are actually achieving the correct position. They check the turn out position of the feet; they check to be sure the hips are aligned squarely; they check that the stomach is flat; they check that the arms are not tense; they check for the proper angle of the shoulders and tilt of the head to finish the quality of the body line. If something is out of place and they notice it, they correct it themselves. If they don't notice it, they will discover that something was out of place when they have trouble performing the dance steps. Even if they don't notice that they are having trouble with the steps, the teacher or the audience will notice.

If the teacher notices something out of place, she will have the dancer look in the mirror and will point out the area of the problem. Perhaps the dancer's arms were too tense, elbows too straight, and fingers strained instead of curved gracefully. The dancer might have been concentrating so much on the movement of her legs that she did not see what her arms looked like. Once the dancer looks at her arms in the mirror and notices what they look like, she usually can correct herself.

A dancer's level (such as beginning, intermediate, or advanced) is based on the dancer's self-awareness and ability to self-correct. A beginning dancer might not be aware of what the ideal position should look like, so she would not be aware of what to look for in the mirror. She could be off-balance and not know how to correct herself. As she learns to dance she becomes more aware of what the ideal positions are, and she learns how to correct herself more consistently. An advanced dancer not only knows the ideal position but also notices immediately when her body is even slightly off-balance, and she consistently readjusts her position. It appears to anyone watching her that she was never off-balance at all. When dancers know what the positions and movements should look like, they have a frame of reference. They can look in the mirror to determine their strengths and weaknesses. They can practice, and they can improve.

The Mirror

The Capability Maturity Model provides a mirror for reflection. By comparing your organization's practices with the practices in the CMM, you have a frame of reference for reflecting your organization's strengths and weaknesses. The CMM describes five levels of capability maturity, and each successive level indicates an increased capability to predict the results of using the organization's current software process. The five levels are usually depicted in a stair-step diagram with Level 1 at the bottom and Level 5 at the top (see Figure 3.1).

The Reflection

At each level we will see a reduction in the variability of the results so that the process is more stable, and we will see an increase in the capability to improve the process to meet new challenges. By reflecting on your organization's practices, you can see what needs to

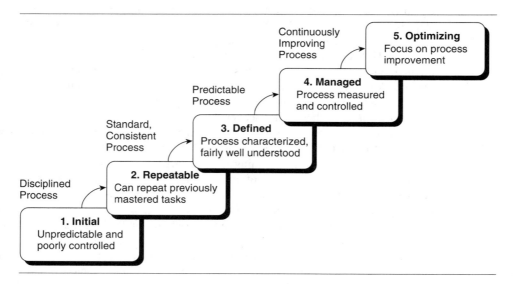

Figure 3.1   Maturity levels 1 through 5.

be done to improve, and those improvement actions will lead to higher levels of capability maturity.

When the people in an organization look in the Capability Maturity Model mirror for the first time, they typically see themselves reflected back as a Level 1 organization. This should not be surprising, because it is the first time they have looked in this mirror. They are only beginning the journey toward continuous optimization. But people hate to hear that they are Level 1.

Being told that you are at the bottom can be discouraging, and unfortunately the terminology doesn't help. Some people take the literal interpretation of the term *capability maturity* and think that Level 1 makes them look incapable and immature. However, *capability maturity* is a derived term that has a specific meaning. "Capability" refers to the ability to meet tolerance interval levels for measurable attributes of a process, and "maturity" indicates that this capability grows and improves with practice over time.

I take a positive perspective. We are all Level 5 organizations in training. Having a lower-level capability maturity means that an organization has little or no experience in improving its capability to meet its targets for cost, effort, defects, size, and schedule. Higher-level capability maturity means that an organization has experience in, and has been effective at, improving its capability to meet these targets. To gain a higher level of capability maturity you need experience, and you need to learn from your experience. The phrase *capability maturity* is not intended to imply whether people are capable or mature or whether organizations are capable or mature. A lower level of capability maturity does not imply that an organization is incapable or immature. Instead, it means that there is more to learn and more to be aware of before you can expect consistent performance from your software process. The learning doesn't stop at Level 5; even at Level 5 there is more to learn as you grow and maintain consistent performance.

Capability Maturity as Organizational Self-Awareness

If you look at the capability maturity levels as characterizing the degree of awareness that the organization has about its software process, then each maturity level indicates a significant increase in

- The degree of conscious effort to produce the results

- The degree of conscious effort to manage and control the effort to produce the results

- The degree of involvement from everyone in the organization in managing, controlling, and improving these efforts

As the organization increases its awareness about its software process, the organization becomes more aware of itself. It becomes increasingly capable of monitoring and changing its behavior, and that affects its capability maturity level. At Level 5 the organization becomes self-correcting and self-actualizing, able to direct its efforts toward increasing

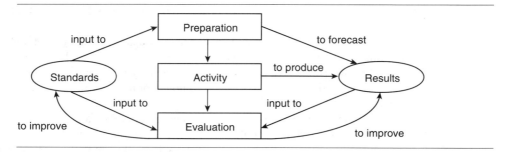

Figure 3.2   The ideal image of a Level 5 continuously optimizing system.

customer satisfaction and gaining new business, continuously modifying itself to adapt to the changing demands of its business environment.

Demonstrating What It is Supposed to Look Like

Typically, when a dance teacher is teaching a new combination of steps, she will demonstrate the entire combination to give the students an idea of the overall flow of the movement; then the teacher demonstrates each step in sequence. When people ask me to give them a brief overview of the five levels, I use the following combination of pictures to make it as concise as possible. I think this helps people to relate the CMM to their own work so they can understand it better. I use Figure 3.2 to demonstrate what the overall ideal image (Level 5) looks like conceptually, and then I demonstrate each of the basic components as a sequence of the levels from Level 1 to Level 5.

Looking at Level 1

At Level 1, we see an immediate focus on producing results (see Figure 3.3). The activities produce the results. People get the job done without giving much thought to the process involved. There are few if any indicators regarding the quality of the results, and most improvements occur as a result of individuals improving their individual performances.

What Happens at Level 1. At Level 1, everyone in the organization does whatever it takes to get the job done. Everyone does what he or she thinks is best. Unfortunately, what looks to be the best thing to do might not be the best thing to do in relationship to everyone else

Figure 3.3   Level 1, awareness of activities and results.

 "Just do it."

and everything else. Projects and processes operate with systematic effects, and singular effects have many side effects on the system as a whole. An optimization for one person might adversely affect everyone else. Something that looks like an improvement to one person might cause a system breakdown or might prove to be detrimental to the entire project.

A software process is categorized as Level 1 when it appears to be behaving with ad hoc effects. People find it hard to predict the results. Anything could happen, and it usually does, just when you least expect it.

Looking at Level 2

At Level 2, we see more conscious effort to manage the activities (see Figure 3.4). We see attention to preparation for activities and to evaluation afterward. More thought is given to positioning the activities to achieve the desired results and to correct the actual results if targets are missed. More improvements occur because of project-level evaluation activities.

What Happens at Level 2. At Level 2, project teams know what has worked well in the past. They use their experience and judgment to prepare for the activities and to evaluate the activities and results of their current and future projects. This level involves a lot more reflection—more thinking about the project and the results—than we saw at Level 1.

A software process is categorized as Level 2 when it appears to be behaving with repeatable effects. People in the organization are more aware of the process, and they actively reflect on their experience to help them prepare for this project. They also use their

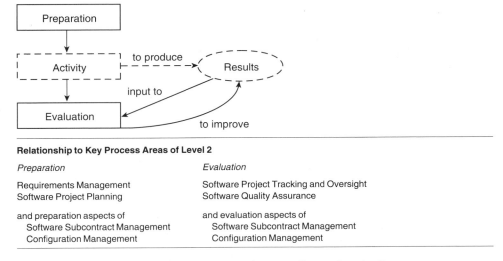

Relationship to Key Process Areas of Level 2

Preparation	*Evaluation*
Requirements Management	Software Project Tracking and Oversight
Software Project Planning	Software Quality Assurance
and preparation aspects of	and evaluation aspects of
Software Subcontract Management	Software Subcontract Management
Configuration Management	Configuration Management

Figure 3.4   Level 2, adding an awareness of preparation and evaluation.

 "Think before you act, and think after you act, just to make sure that you did it right."

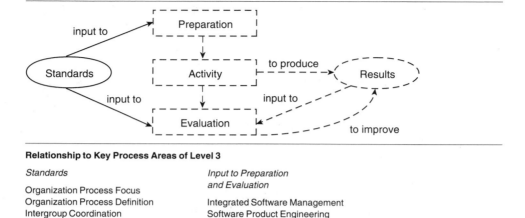

Relationship to Key Process Areas of Level 3

Standards	*Input to Preparation and Evaluation*
Organization Process Focus	
Organization Process Definition	Integrated Software Management
Intergroup Coordination	Software Product Engineering
Training Program	Peer Reviews

Figure 3.5   Level 3, adding an awareness of standards.

 "Use your lessons learned."

experience to help them distinguish good results from bad results. There is a shift in the cultural assumptions from "We don't have time to think" to "We don't have time not to think."

Looking at Level 3

At Level 3, we see awareness and involvement broadening to the organizational level (see Figure 3.5). We see attention to the definition of processes that capture lessons that can be used by every project team in the organization. These standards help project members to position their activities to achieve the desired results and correct the undesired results. More improvements are leveraged across the entire organization.

What Happens at Level 3. At Level 3, there is a greater focus on teamwork. People work together more effectively and contribute to developing knowledge that can be shared across the organization. Project teams take advantage of the organizational knowledge captured in the standard processes and guidelines, applying the standards as they prepare for activities and evaluate results. They take what they need and apply it to the current situation. Less effort is spent on reinventing the wheel, leaving more effort available to work on the more creative aspects of the project.

A software process is categorized as Level 3 when it appears to be behaving as a defined system. People are more aware of the systematic effects of their behavior, and they use their experience to help them define standards that help all project teams perform more consistently. They also define standards to help interdependent projects work together more effectively. There is a shift in the cultural assumptions from "This project is special and different" to "This project has some special needs, but we can learn from other projects and other projects can learn from us."

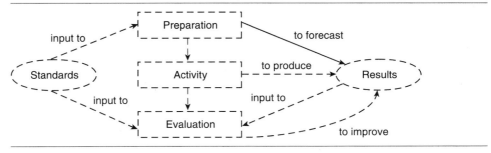

Relationship to Key Process Areas of Level 4

To Forecast Results

Software Quality Management
Quantitative Process Management

Figure 3.6   Level 4, adding an awareness of forecasting.

 "Predict the results you need and expect, and then create opportunities to get those results (create self-fulfilling prophecies)."

Looking at Level 4

At Level 4, we see more conscious effort to use information to manage both projects and processes (see Figure 3.6). We see attention to more-accurate positioning of the activities to achieve the desired results, and we see more-accurate correction. Most improvements are minor realignments instead of major recovery efforts.

What Happens at Level 4. At Level 4, the process is consistent enough that conclusions can be drawn from data about the process and performance results. People understand what the data means in relationship to their work activities, so they can use the data to make informed decisions. This includes forecasting results during preparation activities, setting goals, measuring the results, and anticipating changes that will affect the results.

A software process is categorized as Level 4 when it appears to be behaving as a quantitatively managed system. People apply foresight to their projects. People understand the meaning behind the information, and they analyze it to forecast possible outcomes. There is a shift in the cultural assumptions from "The data we collect is irrelevant" to "We can learn from the data and use it to make informed decisions."

Looking at Level 5

At Level 5, we see the entire picture (see Figure 3.7). Continuous attention is paid to recognizing when a process is no longer producing the desired results, and then changes are made to that process so that the resulting activities will produce the desired results. The results of the process have an effect on the process itself, thereby closing the feedback loop and completing the cycle of systematic effects. This produces a cycle of continuous optimization.

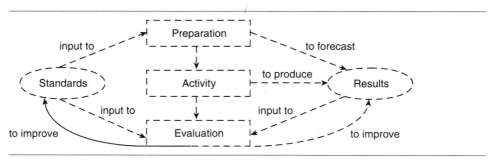

Relationship to Key Process Areas of Level 5

To Improve Standards

Defect Prevention
Technology Change Management
Process Change Management

Figure 3.7   Level 5, adding an awareness of continuous improvement.

"Create lessons learned, and use lessons learned to create more lessons learned, and use more lessons learned to create even more lessons learned, and use even more lessons learned to create . . . etc"

What Happens at Level 5. At Level 5, the organization improves itself consistently. People have the insight and information to know how results are produced and how to adapt their activities to ensure that they produce the desired results with the desired quality. They have the capability of being highly accurate in predicting their performance, and they can adjust their processes to accommodate a changing business environment. This capability opens opportunities for increased customer satisfaction and new business.

A software process is categorized as Level 5 when it appears to be behaving as a continuously optimizing system. People perform the process, produce results, and then use the results to improve the process. As the output of the system affects the system itself, the system becomes self-referential. The organization tells itself how to improve itself. It becomes self-correcting, continuously changing and renewing itself. There is a shift in the cultural assumptions from "We know how to perform" to "We know how to perform, but we can learn to perform better, and there is always more to learn."

Just as every dancer who involves her body and mind has the potential to learn to perform technically complex dance steps, every organization that involves its people has the potential to learn to perform at capability maturity Level 5. Just as a dancer can look at her reflection in the mirror to evaluate her strengths and weaknesses, an organization can look at its reflection in the CMM to evaluate its strengths and weaknesses. These pictures help you recognize what you see or don't see happening in your organization in general. If you know your overall strengths and weaknesses, you know what to focus on to improve, but you will also need specific information to determine specific strengths and weaknesses.

Assessment Techniques

You can use several techniques to identify your strengths and weaknesses. You can even create your own techniques. The following techniques have been used in my organization at different times to meet different needs. The important thing is to listen to the people who do the work and discover what they need.

- CMM-based appraisal method
- Interim Profile appraisal method
- CMM overview workshops
- Project manager interviews
- Great performance method
- Good performance method
- CMM Key Process Area checklist

The selection of an assessment technique depends mostly on who, what, where, when, and why factors, and the technique answers the question of how (see Table 3.1).

Table 3.1   Selecting a technique.

Factor	Questions	Options
Who	Who are you going to get information from?	• Sample of the organization • All project teams in the organization • A project team • Individuals • Project managers • Senior managers
What	What do you need to know?	• Current challenges and demands • Status relative to the CMM • Current issues and potential actions
Where	Where will you collect the information?	• Meetings • Questionnaires • Interviews
When	How much time do you have? How much preparation and follow-up activity is involved?	• 10 minutes • 60 minutes • 90 minutes • 1 week • 4 weeks • 12 weeks
Why	Why do you need this information?	• To identify process issues across the entire organization • To organize improvement activities • To measure progress and identify improvement action items

Select the technique that meets the needs of your current situation. What kind of results do you want, and how much effort are you willing to spend to get them? These techniques have worked for past situations, but there is no guarantee that they will meet the needs of your current situation. However, they could be a good starting point that you could adapt to suit your needs. Some of these examples are adaptations of our own. So take what you need, ignore what you don't need, and make it work for you.

CMM-based Appraisal Method

This method (see Table 3.2) was developed by the Software Engineering Institute (SEI), and can be performed only by trained assessors. Contact the SEI for more information.

As an intensive evaluation of the software process, the method helps people focus on their most critical issues relative to the CMM. A team of assessors will ask questions during interviews and meetings, review questionnaire responses, analyze documents and data, and report the key strengths and weaknesses relative to the CMM Key Process Areas. The report reflects what the assessors have seen and heard from the people in the organization. The assessors also provide a maturity level rating and a report of findings and recommendations for improvement. This method tells you everything you always wanted to know about your software process, and a few things you wish you could stay ignorant about.

Because these assessments are intensive and because major improvements are long-term activities, this technique is typically used only every 18 to 24 months.

Over the past few years, this method has developed into a repeatable, standard process, and it can be tailored to meet specific needs of your organization. The earlier form of this method, the Software Process Assessment, was used consistently to assess every organization within Unisys.

Our initial assessment experience was like a shock to the system. When the assessors presented the list of major issues in five or six key areas, the managers were shocked by what they saw as bad news. They were not surprised by the contents of the list, and they

Table 3.2   CMM-based appraisal method.

Factor	Need	Selections for This Technique
Who	Get information from	• Sample of the organization
What	Need to know	• Status relative to the CMM
Where	Collect information	• Questionnaire, meetings, interviews, evaluation of documents and data
When	How much time	• *For an organization of approximately 500 people, with five projects sampled:* one week for assessment with 5–8 hours for 45 participants, 60 hours for 7 assessors • As much as 12 weeks for preparation and final report generation for the assessors
Why	Purpose	• To identify process issues across the entire organization

agreed that these were indeed the key major issues. But it wasn't very pleasant to see all the major issues all at once.

The second assessment and subsequent assessments were slightly different. The expectations were higher, because improvement work was in progress. Even though there was a similar shock reaction to the issues, it was balanced by encouragement for the progress that had been made. So the shock was not as severe. It seems that the more an organization works on process improvements, the easier it is to accept the assessment of major issues objectively with fewer negative reactions. The report is simply information that you need to know in order to improve. You can't change what you don't know about; you can't change what you don't talk about. The assessment gives people a chance to talk about the process and about the major issues facing the organization so that they become known. Once the issues are known, improvements can begin.

This method is the most comprehensive but also the most time-consuming and most expensive method. I have seen organizations avoid the use of assessments because they know that they have major issues that would prevent their achievement of the next maturity level, so they choose not to spend the time and money to perform an assessment. This issue creates the opportunity for finding more cost-effective methods for gaining information to focus and direct process improvement activities.

Interim Profile Appraisal Method

This method (see Table 3.3) was developed by Roselyn Whitney when she was an SEI affiliate. She developed it because she needed a creative way to assess many organizations quickly with few resources. The method is documented in the technical report available from SEI. It can be performed only by trained assessors. Contact Process Focus Management for more information on training.

This technique helps an organization see progress between assessments. It is entirely questionnaire-based, and there is no evaluation of documents or data. It is assumed that the project teams know what is or is not being done for project management processes and software development practices. The questions from the maturity questionnaire that is used

Table 3.3   Interim Profile appraisal method.

Factor	Need	Selections for This Technique
Who	Get information from	• Project Teams
What	Need to know	• Status relative to the CMM
Where	Collect information	• Questionnaires
When	How much time	• One week for assessment with 1–2 hours for participants, 8 hours for 3 assessors • As much as 8 weeks for preparation and final report generation for assessors
Why	Purpose	• To measure progress and identify improvement action items

in the CMM-based appraisal method are also used in this method. The results of the method provide a profile for each project showing a graph for each Key Process Area, which are rated as not satisfied, partially satisfied, or fully satisfied based on rating rules for the questionnaire responses.

Our SEPG used this technique after the project management processes for Level 2 had been introduced, and the results showed progress in the areas that had received the most attention and showed a lack of progress in the areas that had received the least attention. The method shows progress, but it does not give any detailed information about specific strengths and weaknesses. However, the Interim Profile results can be used to focus on the areas that need more attention, and the results can be a springboard for further discussion by the project managers and project teams. When a specific area is problematic for all or most projects, the data might also indicate organizational issues.

CMM Overview Workshops

This method (see Table 3.4) was developed for internal use at Unisys. The presentation materials are included in Appendix B and on the CD-ROM.

This technique is a presentation with structured group discussions. It provides an opportunity for people to reflect on how their experience relates to the expectations given by the Key Process Areas. This method was developed as a follow-up to an assessment, but it can be used at any time. When used with the management team, this method helps to set realistic expectations for what needs to be done. When used with a project team, it also fosters communication and teamwork.

The facilitator presents an overview of the CMM and a summary of the Key Process Areas. Then the participants discuss what they do currently that fits the purpose and scope of the Key Process Area as well as the issues they see in meeting the goals of the Key Process Area. The ideas are captured and reviewed to identify recommendations of what could be done to address those issues.

Project Manager Interviews

This method (see Table 3.5) was developed for internal use at Unisys, but I have seen similar variations described at conferences over the past few years. The questionnaire and results graphs are included in Appendix C and on the CD-ROM.

Table 3.4   CMM overview workshops.

Factor	Need	Selections for This Technique
Who	Get information from	• Management team or project teams
What	Need to know	• Current issues and potential actions
Where	Collect information	• Team meetings
When	How much time	• 2–4 hours
Why	Purpose	• To organize improvement activities

The questions were adapted from the maturity questionnaire that is used in the CMM-based appraisal method, but the questions are not used to score an organization's or project's maturity level. The questions were changed to help project managers understand the relationship between their work and the goals of the CMM. At first, using the original maturity questionnaire questions, the SEPG members found that the terminology in the CMM is like Latin; it's a common language, but nobody really speaks it. So the SEPG would have to interpret the questions before the project managers could understand the intent and be able to answer questions accurately. Because the project managers were really answering a translation of the questions, we saved time and reduced confusion by adapting and translating the questions. The original maturity questionnaire is necessary for industry comparison, but the terminology can be a barrier in practice. When the questions are stated in familiar terminology, it helps people understand where they are and helps them make progress.

Using this questionnaire, members of the SEPG personally interview each project manager to give the project manager a chance to reflect on actual practices. The project managers identify any documents or data that they have as evidence of satisfying the question. If there is nothing to satisfy the question, the interviewer asks them what issues they face and what action could be taken to bring them closer to satisfying the question.

The result of this method is a score of the number of questions answered yes and a list of action items for every question answered no. The SEPG then helps the project managers make progress toward closing those action items as soon as possible. Any issues that are beyond the scope of the project manager's responsibility are raised to senior management for resolution.

A typical use of this technique would be to gather questionnaire responses monthly for about three to six months following the introduction of project management processes for Level 2. Monthly progress is shown graphically as the number of questions answered yes. We typically see an increase of yes answers each month until all questions are answered yes by all project teams.

Our experience with this method was very positive with respect to the progress made by the project managers both in understanding the CMM goals and in implementing improved project management practices. However, the reaction to the measurement graphs was mixed. In one organization the graphs had a positive motivational effect. As some project managers made good progress, other project managers were encouraged to make

Table 3.5 Project manager interviews.

Factor	Need	Selections for This Technique
Who	Get information from	• Project managers
What	Need to know	• Status relative to the CMM
Where	Collect information	• Interviews with questionnaires
When	How much time	• 30–60 minutes
Why	Purpose	• To measure progress and identify improvement action items

similar progress. They found that it was easier than they thought. However, in another organization the graphs were not as well received. These project managers thought that senior management was putting too much emphasis on the charts and that the goal was to answer yes to every question just to satisfy senior management. They put their focus on the charts and not on the tasks, but they still did the tasks. In the end, progress was made by both organizations. The graphs turned out to have a motivational effect on both organizations.

Great Performance Method

This method (see Table 3.6) was developed for internal use at Unisys. The questions worksheet is included in Appendix D and on the CD-ROM.

This technique is a generic set of three questions that helps people focus on their relationship to their customers and suppliers. These questions were adapted from *Flight of the Buffalo,* by James Belasco and Ralph Stayer. Our SEPG used this technique after a reorganization to get an idea of what the new management was most interested in for sponsoring improvement initiatives. The SEPG members personally interviewed representative managers, asking these three questions:

- What is great performance for your customers? (This means not just meeting their needs, not mediocrity, but rather what would be considered great from you.)

- What do you want, and what can we do, to provide you with great service? (This means what would be considered as great from us to you.)

- What must we do to help you achieve great performance for your customers? (This means linking the two together. What do you consider to be great performance from us that would help you achieve what would be considered great performance from you to your customers?)

The first question asks the SEPG customer (the manager or engineer) to consider what the software customers would think of as great performance from the manager or engineer. The second question asks what the manager or engineer expects from the SEPG and how the SEPG can contribute. The third question focuses on what the manager or engineer requires from the SEPG and what the SEPG must contribute for the manager or engineer to contribute to their customers' success.

Table 3.6   Great performance method.

Factor	Need	Selections for This Technique
Who	Get information from	• Sample of the organization
What	Need to know	• Current challenges and demands
Where	Collect information	• Interviews, three questions
When	How much time	• 3–60 minutes
Why	Purpose	• To organize improvement activities

These questions are intended to get managers and engineers to think about what they really want regardless of limitations. Sometimes people don't say what they really want, because they assume that there are limitations that prevent them from getting what they really want. But if we knew what they really want, we might be able to find a way to eliminate the limitations to give them what they really want instead of just what they will settle for.

We used this technique at a time when people were very busy and didn't have a lot of time to talk to us. We developed these three questions and told them that we would take only three minutes of their time and would stop by their office to get their answers in person with one-on-one interviews so that they wouldn't have to formulate any written responses. To our surprise, even though we told them we would take only three minutes, once they started talking—once they were actually listening to what they were thinking—they didn't want to stop at three minutes! Most of the people we interviewed talked for a full hour. If we had told them that we were going to take an hour of their time, they wouldn't have talked to us at all. But by their own choice, they took extra time to discuss the questions because it was important to them.

Setting the expectation that we would take only three minutes sent an underlying message that we were looking only for the few most important things from their perspective. We were not looking for an exhaustive list of everything we could possibly do for them. We were looking only for what was most important to them, what would make a positive contribution, and what would make a difference.

We analyzed the information by sorting it into broad categories and looking for recurring themes, and most of the broad categories could be directly related to Key Process Areas from the CMM. Then we looked for driving actions that could drag other actions along with them, actions that would give us the most bang for the buck. This resulted in a short list of requirements for the SEPG to initiate improvements to address the few most important needs of the organization.

Variation: Good Performance Method

This variation on the preceding technique helps people focus on their relationship to their customers and suppliers. This technique (see Table 3.7) was used in a meeting with a project team that was interested in getting assistance from an SEPG member. When this project team was asked the great performance questions, they rejected the questions. Their response was "We are so far behind that we can't even think about being great. That's too

Table 3.7   Good performance method.

Factor	Need	Selections for This Technique
Who	Get information from	• Project team
What	Need to know	• Current challenges and demands
Where	Collect information	• Meeting, three questions
When	How much time	• 60 minutes
Why	Purpose	• To organize improvement activities

much of a challenge for us. We'd be happy if we could just do a little better. But don't ask us about great performance. That's impossible."

Words can get in the way sometimes. The team's negative reaction to the phrasing of the questions could have ended the communication then and there. Fortunately, because we responded positively and rephrased the questions, they were able to communicate positively. The rephrased questions were as follows.

- What would be good performance for your customers, or at least better performance in comparison to the current status?

- What do you want, and what can we do, to provide you with good service?

- What must we do to help you achieve good (or better) performance for your customers?

This project team refused to think idealistically, but they were willing to think realistically. They were able to relate to these questions because they were closer to their real lives and their real work. These questions resulted in getting them to think about what they really wanted instead of just what they would settle for.

CMM Key Process Area Checklist

This method (see Table 3.8) was developed for internal use at Unisys. The checklist is included in Appendix E and on the CD-ROM.

This method is used as part of the quarterly review meeting with senior managers. The senior managers review the checklist of CMM Key Process Areas and consider the following questions.

- In which areas are we satisfied with our current performance?
- In which areas are we not satisfied with our current performance?
- Which areas are most important to the achievement of our business goals?
- Which areas need the most immediate attention?

Then follow-up actions are assigned for investigation or improvement of those areas in which there is dissatisfaction and a need for the most immediate attention.

Table 3.8   CMM Key Process Area checklist.

Factor	Need	Selections for This Technique
Who	Get information from	• Senior management
What	Need to know	• Current issues relative to the CMM
Where	Collect information	• Meeting
When	How much time	• 10–60 minutes
Why	Purpose	• To generate interest in initiating or continuing improvement projects

4

Improvement Cycles:
Dancing with the Rhythms

"Always will I take another step. If that is of no avail I will take another, and yet another. In truth, one step at a time is not too difficult. I will persist until I succeed."

— *Og Mandino*

Finding the Steps: Implementation Life Cycles

In a ballet rehearsal, the orchestra conductor works with the dancers and choreographers to find the right tempo for each musical phrase. If a step does not look or feel right, it is usually because the music is being played too fast or too slowly. If the movement is too slow it looks labored and heavy, so the conductor picks up the tempo and the orchestra plays faster. If the movement is too fast it looks messy and rushed, and the dancers cannot complete the movements with accurate positioning and pure lines. The conductor slows the tempo and the orchestra plays more slowly.

The performance tempo is derived as a consensus of everyone: dancers, choreographers, conductors, and orchestra members. The pulse of change is like the beat of the music. The dancer performing to live music matches the rhythm of the movements to the beat of the music. But the dancer is not simply following the music; rather, the dancer joins with the music, becomes part of the music, and indeed makes music.

The cycle time for software process improvement is derived as a consensus of everyone: engineers, SEPG members, managers, and perhaps even external customers, who want to be satisfied with our results. It might look as if the manager is controlling the tempo, but everyone involved has an impact on cycle time. Typically, the people involved in software process improvement feel that implementing process changes takes too long; the movement is too slow and labored and they want to do it faster. What can be done to speed it up? If you know the steps of the process improvement cycle and if you understand the rhythms of change, perhaps you can learn to go faster.

Implementation Life Cycle Models					
Technology Transition Stages					
Awareness	Understanding	Definition	Installation	Adoption	Institutionalization
Software Process Stages					
Requirements	Design	Code	Test	Run-Time Modules	
IDEAL Approach (Initiating, Diagnosing, Establishing, Acting, Leveraging)					
Initiating Leveraging	Diagnosing	Establishing	Acting		
PDCA (Plan Do Check Act)					
Plan		Do	Check	Act	
DUME (Define Use Measure Evaluate)					
Evaluate		Define		Use	Measure
OODA Loop (Observe Orient Decide Act)					
Observe	Orient	Decide		Act	
TQM (Total Quality Management) 7-Step Process					
Identify Customer/Supplier Relationships	Determine Customer Needs/Expectations	Define Work Process	Identify Candidate Change	Implement Change in a Controlled Environment	Evaluate Effects of Change	Change Process Permanently
Envisioning		Encoding		Enacting	

Figure 4.1   A comparison of the steps in several implementation life cycle models for software process improvement.

What are the steps that your organization uses to perform software process improvement? Maybe you already have a defined process for software process improvement, or maybe you are doing something without knowing the steps, or maybe you are just beginning and are trying to decide which steps to take. The basic pattern of the steps is likely to be similar to the following activities.

- Get information on the Key Process Areas.
- Plan and develop a framework.
- Define and document processes.
- Pilot and evaluate processes.
- Require the use of processes.
- Practice, assure, and correct processes.

The implementation life cycle models in use in the industry have similar steps (see Figure 4.1). They basically follow the same pattern, with a feedback loop to continue with the next improvement. If you compare the steps of each model, they do not all start from nor end in the same position as all the other models, but they are all continuous loops. I have aligned the steps of each model as closely as I can to the three steps of envisioning, encoding, and enacting to make the correlation between the different models more evident. For example, from this perspective, the Leveraging step of the IDEAL approach and the Evaluate step of the DUME model are correlated to the Envisioning step as it repeats on the next cycle of improvement.

Performing the Steps with the Music

This pattern of steps supports the learning process involved in adapting to process change and technology transition. Technology products enhance the capability of human activities. Consider the Key Process Areas of the CMM as technologies that either are or are not currently being performed effectively in your organization. Learning to perform with new technology (learning to put the key practices into *actual* practice) is like learning to perform the steps of a new dance. First you learn the steps, and then you learn how to put the steps to the music. Then you practice the steps until the movements are well coordinated with the music.

Finding the Music: The Stages of Transition

What does the music sound like? It sounds like what you hear people saying as they move through the stages of transition. As an organization's commitment to a new technology increases over time, the organization experiences the stages of transition shown in Figure 4.2. You can identify these stages by observing the behavior in your organization. There are common activities performed at particular stages, and there are common questions you will hear in discussions (see Figure 4.3). These observations identify the current stage.

Measuring Progress by Stage of Transition

By listening for the questions, you can identify the current stage, predict what might happen next, and determine what to do about it. By observing what you see and hear in real life, you can identify your current stage of transition. You can measure progress as the movement from one stage to another over time, by what you observe about the past and present, and what you can foresee about the future.

- **Past:** You can look back and identify where you have been and see how far you have come. People stop asking the old questions when they find the answers. Then they start asking the new questions.

- **Present:** You can make observations about what is happening today that will identify your current stage of transition.

- **Future:** You can look ahead and see where you are going. You can anticipate what must be done to get through the upcoming stages of transition.

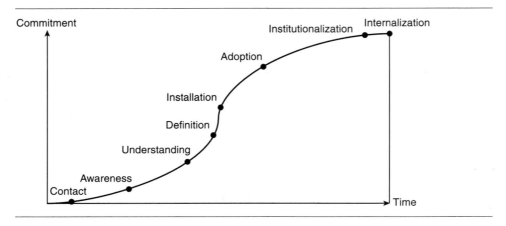

Figure 4.2 The stages of transition between end-point states of contact and internalization.

(Note: This figure is an adaptation of a similar figure from *Software Technology Transition,* a tutorial presented by Stanley M. Pryzybylinski, Priscilla J. Fowler, and John H. Maher of SEI. They showed the stages as contact, awareness, understanding, trial use, adoption, and internalization, applied to a learning curve. These stages are taken from "Building Commitment to Organizational Change," by Daryl R. Conner and Robert W. Patterson, and a similar figure and explanation appears in *Managing at the Speed of Change* by Daryl R. Conner.)

Questions	Stage	Key Activities
What is it?	Awareness	Get information and training on the Key Process Areas.
What does it mean to us?	Understanding	Plan and develop a framework.
How will we do it?	Definition	Define and document processes.
Will it work?	Installation	Pilot and evaluate processes.
Are we using it?	Adoption	Require the use of processes.
Is it good enough?	Institutionalization	Practice, assure, and correct.

Figure 4.3 Stages of technology transition: What you hear, where you are, and what to do when you hear it.

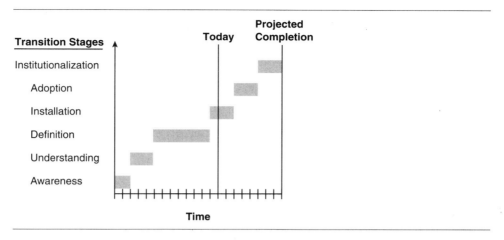

Figure 4.4   Using the observations of the stages of transition over time. See where you are today, see how far you have come, and predict future efforts.

This concept gives you a context for where you are during the transition. You can see where you have been, where you are, and where you are going. This is how you can measure your progress over time. Figure 4.4 shows an example of a group that just started the installation stage. Looking at process improvement in this context helps you manage the effort and results.

Finding the Tempo: The Pulse of Change

To encourage continuous process improvement, imagine that the end of one cycle is actually the beginning of the next cycle. The cycle begins at the point of contact with a new technology or a new process improvement. The cycle continues until the change becomes part of the way the organization does business. The cycle begins again with the next new technology. With the image of a cycle, we can now consider *cycle time* (see Figure 4.5).

Accelerating Cycle Time

Relative to the cycle time for process improvement or technology transition (see Figure 4.6), the length of the circle's circumference represents the cycle time.

- **Normal cycle time:** The medium-length circle. The normal length of time in which you could expect to complete the transition.

- **Faster cycle time:** The shorter-length circle. If actions are taken to shorten the length of time, the cycle can be completed faster.

- **Slower cycle time:** The longer-length circle. If no acceleration actions are taken and if issues are not addressed, the deceleration causes the transition to take longer with a slower cycle.

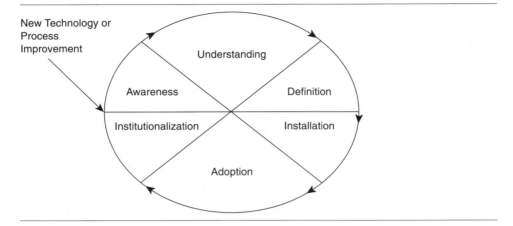

Figure 4.5   A cycle for continuous process improvement. Cycle time is like musical tempo. How fast or how slow are the steps being performed?

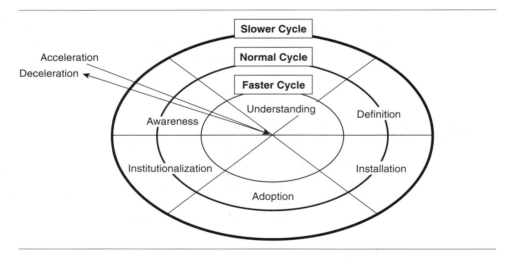

Figure 4.6   To shorten cycle time, additional effort must be applied. Lack of effort or inefficient activity lengthens cycle time.

The right tempo is ordinarily a natural rhythm, but that does not necessarily mean that the tempo must be comfortable all the time. For dancers, a more challenging tempo will display their virtuosity. Tempos that are faster than normal display the dancer's speed and agility, whereas tempos that are slower than normal display strength and precision. By pushing the limits, choreographers challenge dancers, and dancers challenge themselves.

- How fast can we do this without losing our balance and control?
- How slow can we do this without losing our balance and control?

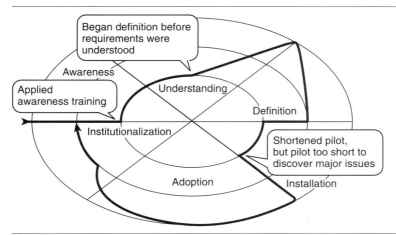

Stage of Transition	Actions	Effects
Awareness	We wanted to accelerate through the Awareness Stage, so we applied awareness training. In that way, people would become aware of the concepts more quickly than if they had been left to discover the concepts on their own.	Faster
Understanding	About halfway through the Understanding Stage, we began to work on definition before the requirements were understood.	Slower
Definition	The lack of understanding caused a lot of rework for us in the Definition Stage.	Slow
Installation	We shortened the pilot test in the Installation Stage.	Faster
Adoption	The pilot test was too short to discover major issues, and these unresolved issues caused more resistance in the Adoption Stage.	Slower
Institutionalization	As the major issues were addressed, we eventually settled into the final stages of the transition.	Back to Normal

Figure 4.7   Examples of acceleration and deceleration.

 "What could go right, and what could go wrong."

We challenge the people in our organization to improve at an increasingly accelerated rate, and we push the limits to go faster than normal without losing our balance and control.

A Hypothetical Example

The tempo changes during the performance. It is not constant but rather is dynamic. Sometimes it accelerates, and sometimes it decelerates. Figure 4.7 is a hypothetical example illustrating acceleration and deceleration.

What is Really Going On? From my observation, I conclude that this hypothetical example in Figure 4.7 is not really hypothetical but instead represents what normally happens to us when we live through this experience, and normal cycle time as depicted in Figure 4.6 is as mythical as the mythical man-month. (This is an allusion to the mythical man-month described by Fred Brooks. It takes nine months of labor for one woman to have a baby, but if we put nine women on the project for one month, they can't deliver. The project takes nine months of labor—nine man-months, but it is a myth that the effort can be subdivided and still produce the same result. The myth falls apart for software projects as well, even though we sometimes act as if it were possible. Likewise, we often expect projects to be performed according to normal cycle time, even with all of our experience to the contrary.) When we stop believing in the myth that everything is supposed to go smoothly with normal cycle time, we can begin to respond appropriately to the current situation and prepare for the next step. With practice, we learn to decelerate when approaching a new step and accelerate through the step. With practice, we manage to go faster without going out of control.

Studying the Dynamics

After studying the pattern of several organizations going through technology transition for the CMM Key Process Areas, I've concluded that the curve is not smooth after all. It feels more discontinuous than continuous, especially when you're approaching a new stage of transition (see Figure 4.8).

Progress seems to slow or stop as you approach the next step. These are the times when people are the most unsure of what the results will be and what the effects will be on them personally. The momentum can be disrupted a little or a lot depending on how much uncertainty people are experiencing. The greatest potential for disrupted momentum is just before adoption, and that's why this gap is depicted as a chasm rather than just a crack. At this chasm, silent veto could completely stop the change. Silent veto describes the situation when managers appear to be in agreement with the change, but they allow themselves or their engineers to keep doing things the old way, never actually implementing the changed process. They don't say that they won't do it, but then they don't do it, so the change is

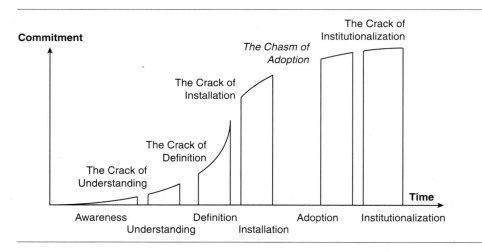

Figure 4.8   The cracks and the chasm where commitment levels drop and progress could decelerate or stop. Technology transition is discontinuous.

never really adopted in practice. Although the risks are higher as you approach the cracks and chasms, if you watch what you are doing, and if you know what to look for and listen for, you can avoid stepping into a crack or falling into a chasm.

The chasm of adoption is analogous to a dancer's stage fright. The dancer who is about to perform in front of an audience for the first time might feel anxious about how her performance will be received. She might feel unprepared, thinking that she did not get enough rehearsal time, that she is still not comfortable with the steps, or that she might forget some of the steps. So whatever can be done to increase her confidence as she prepares will help to reassure her that she can perform well. If she feels well prepared and comfortable with the steps, she will have the confidence to step out on stage and perform. Of course, she might be perfectly well prepared but get stage fright anyway. How does she overcome it? The music starts, and she goes on stage. She hears her cue, and she starts dancing because it's time to do the steps. Even though she's nervous at first, as she concentrates on the dance the stage fright seems to disappear.

Silent veto is like silencing the music. The dancers never get their cue to start, so nobody moves. If there really hasn't been enough rehearsal time, if there really is a lack of preparation, then a delay might be in order. But if everything has been done to prepare for the performance, there's no sense in waiting for the stage fright to subside before beginning. Stage fright doesn't subside until you get yourself on stage and begin performing.

In our experience with the software process improvement efforts of several groups, we discovered that each stage of transition has its own characteristic stage fright (see Figure 4.9), and there are certain actions that help prepare for performance in each stage.

What to Listen For	Translation	Action
We don't have enough time/resources for it.	Now we're understanding what is *really* involved in this change.	Reduce the scope and time/resource requirements.
There's no consistent focus.	We can't start definition with so many mixed messages of what to do.	Identify desired state, current state, roles, and approach.
The problems aren't fixed yet.	We're not ready for installation or adoption.	Fix the most important problems.
How do we get everyone to use it?	We think silent veto may sabotage adoption.	Provide assistance and feedback to users, share success stories.
Is it working, or do we need to change it?	(When they ask this question, you have institutionalization.)	Evaluate results, initiate improvements.

Figure 4.9 Focusing action at each stage of transition: what you hear, where you are, and what to do when you hear it.

Confidence

Do the people in your organization seem to be confident that the changes brought about by the software process improvement efforts are going to be effective and worthwhile? Do they seem to be more confident in the beginning and then appear to lose confidence in the efforts over time? And do they regain their confidence as more progress is made?

This, too, seems to be a recurring pattern. It's much easier to work when confidence is high, and it's much harder to stay focused when confidence is low. Sometimes software process improvements stall or even stop when confidence is low. But is it low confidence that stops the work, or does the work stop because people stop trying? It's harder to work through the period of low confidence, but when the work for that stage is complete, the progress that is made helps increase the level of confidence. Figure 4.10 shows what hap-

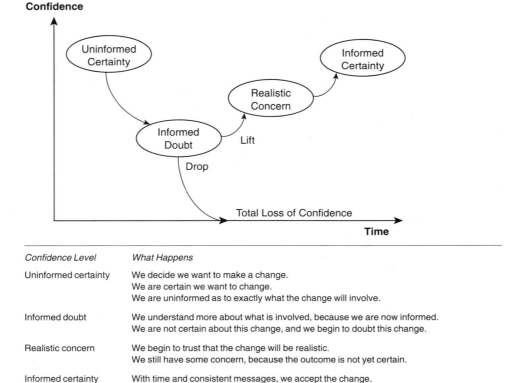

Confidence Level	What Happens
Uninformed certainty	We decide we want to make a change. We are certain we want to change. We are uninformed as to exactly what the change will involve.
Informed doubt	We understand more about what is involved, because we are now informed. We are not certain about this change, and we begin to doubt this change.
Realistic concern	We begin to trust that the change will be realistic. We still have some concern, because the outcome is not yet certain.
Informed certainty	With time and consistent messages, we accept the change. We are informed by witnessing our experience of the change. We are certain the change is realistic and acceptable.

Figure 4.10   Confidence in a change over time: high and low confidence levels.

pens to confidence over time. Beginning with the high confidence level of uninformed certainty, the confidence level drops as people experience informed doubt. Here, if confidence continues to drop, it might result in a total loss of confidence, but if people work through the doubt and lift their spirits again, confidence can be regained. As confidence grows, it is lifted through a medium-level realistic concern and then to the high confidence level of informed certainty.

Confidence Levels and the Stages of Transition

The fluctuation of confidence levels might appear to be unpredictable, but, if you are paying attention to the stages of transition, the pattern is predictable. This pattern occurs twice for each transition cycle as in Figure 4.11. The pattern repeats with variable highs and lows and thus can be represented as a smooth sine curve as in Figure 4.12. The confidence levels are the points on the curve. The stages of transition are the arcs of the curve. Movement through each stage results in a different point on the sine curve and thus a different level of confidence.

Put it all together, and we've got rhythm. The tempo might fluctuate with the rise and fall of the dynamics, but what we want is for the rhythm to keep going and not to stop. We don't want people to lose confidence. We want continuous process improvement. If the loss of confidence is overwhelming, there is a risk that the rhythm might stop (see Figure 4.13).

Some organizations have made it all the way through the curve to improve their actual practices. Other organizations have never created an action plan before a reorganization or reassignment of senior managers occurs. Still other organizations have defined processes that are never fully adopted, because a reorganization occurs just as they are beginning to install the processes. From my observations, it seems that when you're trying to introduce a change of the magnitude of CMM Key Practices, you will get one of these three outcomes within one reorganization, and then you start all over again.

But that's what it looks like at Level 1. With repeated successful attempts, the drop in confidence is not as steep as before. People develop a more confident attitude toward change, and, although they experience informed doubt, they have more confidence that they can succeed again. This is a matter of practice over time, so it also is a matter of maturity. With practice, time, and experience, the confidence interval narrows (see Figure 4.14). As an organization experiences successful change, capability maturity increases people expect their improvements to be successful, and their confidence contributes to their success. Eventually we expect that we can succeed at whatever steps we are asked to perform.

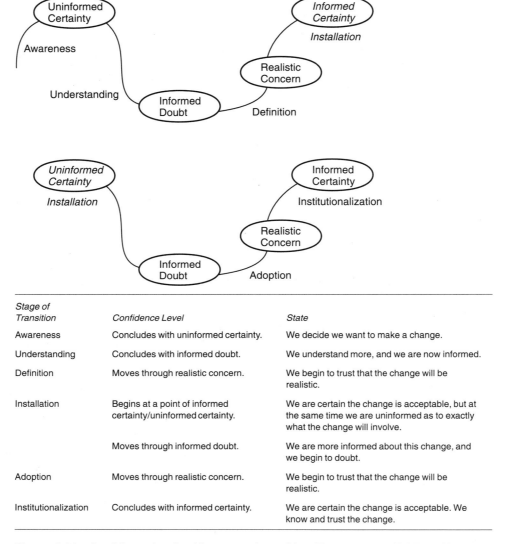

Stage of Transition	Confidence Level	State
Awareness	Concludes with uninformed certainty.	We decide we want to make a change.
Understanding	Concludes with informed doubt.	We understand more, and we are now informed.
Definition	Moves through realistic concern.	We begin to trust that the change will be realistic.
Installation	Begins at a point of informed certainty/uninformed certainty.	We are certain the change is acceptable, but at the same time we are uninformed as to exactly what the change will involve.
	Moves through informed doubt.	We are more informed about this change, and we begin to doubt.
Adoption	Moves through realistic concern.	We begin to trust that the change will be realistic.
Institutionalization	Concludes with informed certainty.	We are certain the change is acceptable. We know and trust the change.

Figure 4.11   Confidence levels with stages of transition. Two patterns of high and low confidence superimposed on one cycle of the stages of transition.

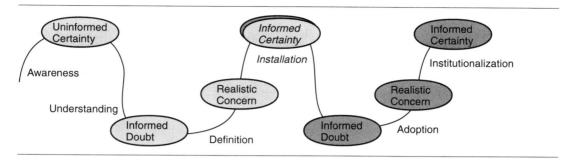

Figure 4.12   Keep the rhythm going for two beats to make a successful change.

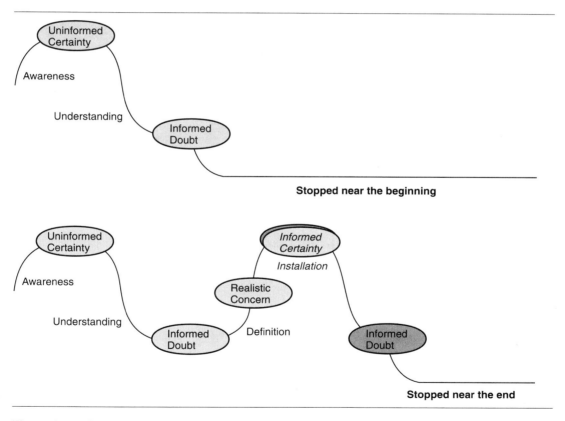

Figure 4.13   Sometimes the beat stops, so you must start over again.

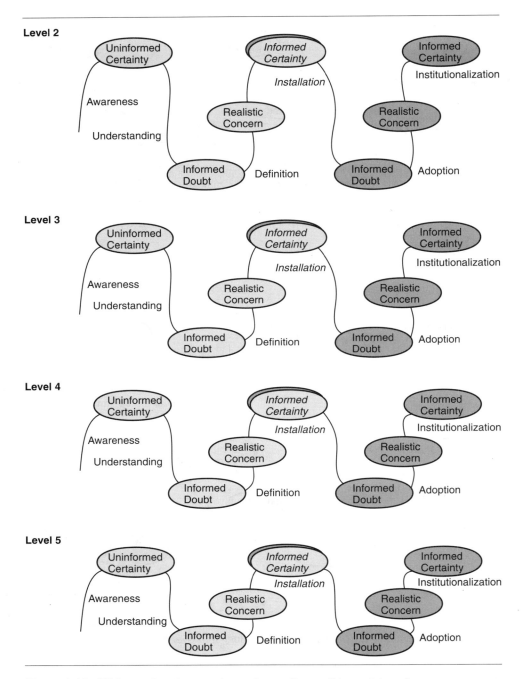

Figure 4.14 With practice, time, and experience, the confidence interval narrows.

Using Feedback to Manage Change

Use the results of your observations of the stages and confidence levels to determine the next appropriate action. Instead of assuming that the next action is predefined, you can use feedback to determine the next action. Instead of getting stuck thinking that low confidence stalls or stops progress, work within the parameters of varying confidence levels and take appropriate actions that will help lift the confidence level.

Putting the Steps to the Music

You can take the steps you are performing for software process improvement and map them to the rhythm. You can do this for the steps of any of the implementation life cycle models shown in Figure 4.1. Figure 4.15 shows an example of the steps of the IDEAL approach in relationship to the rhythm. Some steps perform the work of the transition, and other steps increase confidence in the change. This is how the IDEAL approach relates to what really happens during technology transition. By observing the intent of the IDEAL activities in relationship to the stages of transition and confidence levels, we can put the steps to the music. We can perform the steps with appropriate timing and effort. The idea is to keep moving without missing a beat. Complete the step when the purpose of the step is achieved, and move to the next step.

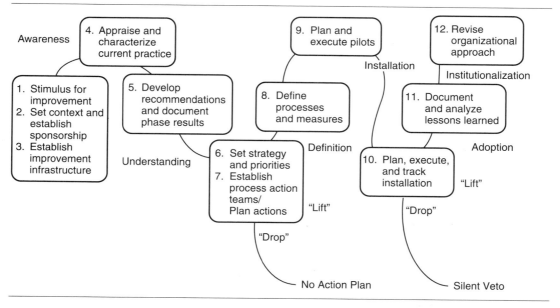

Figure 4.15   Correlating the steps in the IDEAL approach with the stages of transition and fluctuating levels of confidence.

Estimating How Long it Takes to Complete a Process Improvement Cycle

Progress depends on two interdependent factors: the work to be done and the willingness to make the change. Improvement tasks and activities will have a positive effect, completing the work to be done. Doing nothing to improve will have a negative effect. Similarly, momentum and a driving force for change will have a positive effect on people's willingness to make the change, but doing nothing to raise confidence will have a negative effect on progress. When estimating how long it takes to complete a process improvement cycle, people typically consider the first factor—the work to be done—but forget to consider the second factor—the willingness to make the change. If you focus only on the first factor and put all your emphasis on activities and effort, you could lose sight of the results. Progress does not equal effort spent.

I have seen people spend 12–18 months writing a process that no one wanted to follow. They did not pay attention to the second factor. They were not prepared for the fact that other people might not agree with their improvement ideas, and they didn't prepare for doing what it takes to gain the necessary cooperation. They were frustrated when the effort was over, because it appeared to be a waste of time. I have also seen people pay attention to both factors and spend one month writing a process that was quickly adopted with the visible commitment of senior management and the facilitation support of the SEPG.

How long does it usually take for a Level 1 organization to get to Level 2? It depends. But now we have a better idea of what it depends on. Rather than set a goal to reach Level 2 by the end of the year, we can use project management techniques to plan the necessary activities, and we can use risk management techniques to prepare for low confidence during the transition. (Examples of the use of these techniques will be given in the chapters and appendixes that follow.) Rather than run blindly, we can perform the implementation effectively.

Here are some things to consider when you're estimating the length of time to complete a process improvement cycle. First, consider the work to be done.

- Is the change minor, major, or drastic?
- How many people or groups are affected?
- How many people must agree, and how close are their opinions likely to be?
- How much time is available to discuss and review the process?

Then analyze the willingness to change.

- How much do the affected people want the change?
- How much does senior management want the change?
- How beneficial is the change perceived to be?

Progress will accelerate if you perform the improvement activities and create the momentum and driving force for change. Progress will decelerate if you do nothing to improve and do nothing to raise confidence in the change.

5

Action Plans:
Preparing for Movement

"Do what you can, with what you have, where you are."

—Theodore Roosevelt

Preparation, Action, Finish

Every dance is a chain of movements. The dancers start from where they are and gather their energy in preparation to move in a certain direction with a certain finishing position in mind. The dancers learn the dance by visualizing the steps before they perform them and by memorizing the sequence of movements. They envision the dance movements before they begin to practice.

Software process improvement is a chain of movements. The organization starts from where it is and prepares to move to a higher level of capability maturity with Level 5 in mind. An assessment defines the starting position. Start from where you are. An action plan helps people envision the expectations for what they are going to do and where they will finish. Begin with the end in mind. Writing and executing a successful action plan entails three challenges:

* Making it easy to visualize the finishing position
* Making it easy to understand the sequence of steps
* Making it easy to move from one step to the next

Visualizing the finishing position helps people focus on what they want to accomplish. Understanding the sequence of positions helps people see themselves making progress.

Making it easy to move from one step to the next helps keep people from getting stuck. Do what you can with what you have.

In the overall context of the three basic steps of envisioning, encoding, and enacting, the action plan is part of the envisioning step. The action plan is an approach for envisioning what will be done in the encoding and enacting steps. At first, the action plan is based on the CMM; when the cycle is repeated, the action plan is typically expanded based on the organization's broadening awareness of the changing environment and opportunities.

This chapter describes several experiences with action planning, focusing on what worked well, what didn't work well, and how the action plan might evolve over time to meet the needs of the people in the organization.

Action Plan Problems

An action plan considers the *current state* as the starting position and defines the *desired state* as the finishing position. An action plan describes the actions that we plan to take as a *transition* from the current state to the desired state (see Figure 5.1). There must be a relationship between the current state and the desired state, or else it isn't clear which actions to take. Here are some examples of some of the problems we have experienced with action plans.

Problem 1: Focus on Desired State with No Relationship to the Current State

When I started on the SEPG, the goal of our first action plan was to address all the findings and recommendations of our assessment and define all the tasks necessary to get to Level 2.

We set out to write "the perfect action plan." We studied the literature (this was before the CMM was published), and we created a plan with all the tasks that had to be done. We edited; we reviewed; we made sure we covered everything. But we didn't make sure we involved the senior managers. They had tried for a year to write an action plan in their spare time, and they were tired of it, so they sent us away to do what we could with it. They wanted us to go away and come back with the perfect plan, right? Wrong.

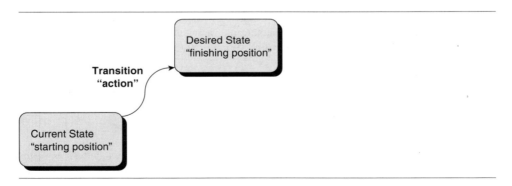

Figure 5.1   Movement has a starting position, action, and a finishing position.

We came back with a 63-page plan with 70 tasks divided into two parts and eight phases, including deliverables, interdependencies, and priorities for every task. It was a lot of work. We satisfied the goal, but we didn't satisfy our customers (the senior managers, managers, and engineers). They were overwhelmed. They were thinking about how many resources it would take to staff an additional 70 Working Groups. They were thinking that this was overkill for an action plan. They were unwilling to commit so many resources to so many tasks. But at least we had their attention now, and if this wasn't what they wanted, at least now we could start listening to what they really wanted. This plan was never put into action. Success rate: 0%.

What was wrong with this action plan? With 70 tasks divided into two parts with eight phases, it was not easy to visualize the finishing position, understand the sequence of steps, or move from one step to the next.

After a reorganization and another assessment, we had the opportunity to begin again. This time we set a more attainable goal for the action plan: to address the findings and recommendations of our assessment and to begin progress toward Level 2 with methods that help increase process maturity.

Problem 2: Focus on Current State with No Relationship to the Desired State

In the meantime, while the first action plan was being written, some independent improvement actions were undertaken by one of the senior managers. This manager selected a "top ten" list of areas for improvement and initiated 10 Working Groups, giving them three months to come back with a process. This was an ad hoc Level 1-type approach, with a focus on activities and results but no planning or evaluation. Of those 10 Working Groups, only five completed their task. Success rate: 50%.

This was a great opportunity for comparison to learn what worked and what didn't work. Every Working Group that did not produce a process in three months reported either that the desired practices didn't exist in the organization or that the current practices were so diverse that there was no process to be defined. Sometimes people see no value in documenting the current process as it is being performed. They say, "What good will that do? If there are too many problems with current practice, why bother documenting it? If there are too many variations in the way a certain task is performed and if current practice is really ad hoc, what can be documented? If we don't like the way things are done, why bother documenting the way things are done?"

By comparison, every Working Group that completed its task had all of the following:

- A clear charter or clear idea of what it was supposed to accomplish

- A process template for structuring the text description of the process

- At least one person on the team who was a trained facilitator

- At least one person on the team who understood which elements were necessary to define the process

- At least one person on the team who understood how to describe current practice using those elements

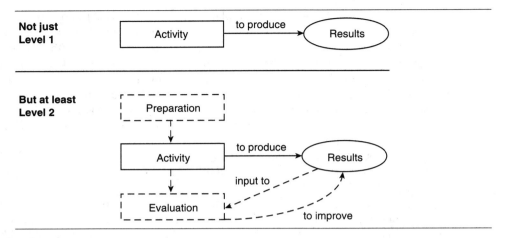

Figure 5.2 Manage software process improvement projects by applying project management principles from Level 2.

Also note that for the Working Groups that completed their task successfully, it was easy for them to visualize the finishing position, understand the sequence of steps, and move from one step to the next.

We learned from this experience, and we built these success factors into the methods that we used for executing the next action plan. Rather than an ad hoc Level 1 approach, we were able to develop a repeatable Level 2 approach to action planning and execution. By applying project management practices to software process improvement projects, and not just focusing on activities and results, we broadened the perspective so that we encompassed preparation, activities and results, and evaluation; a Level 2 approach as shown in Figure 5.2. And when we did this, we had seven of seven Working Groups succeed. Success rate: 100%.

Action Planning Solutions

For envisioning and action planning based on the CMM, use assessment findings to define the starting position, use the Key Process Area goals of the next maturity level to define the finishing position, and then determine the necessary improvement activities and results to put into the action plan (see Figure 5.3). Also remember that you are dealing with real people on real projects, and do what you can with what you have, where you are. Involve the people who must do the work and help them visualize where these efforts will take them. Make it easy for them to understand the sequence of the steps and make it easy for them to move from one step to the next.

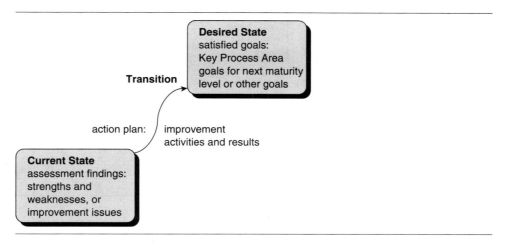

Figure 5.3   Defining the movements to put into the action plan.

Visualizing the Finishing Position

Here is an example of how we made it easier for the people in our organization to visualize the finishing position, providing a focus for the improvement efforts. The assessment revealed a lack of processes and procedures for project management. Specifically, there were no documented processes for the following Key Process Areas:

- Requirements management
- Software project planning
- Software project tracking and oversight
- Software quality assurance

People were having difficulty relating themselves and their work to these Key Process Area concepts. They needed a clearer picture of who would do what. They needed to know what their role would be in satisfying the goals. So we arranged the movements toward Level 2 with an overall process design that related these Key Process Areas to the roles of the people in the organization. This made it clear who should be part of the Working Group to define each process.

The people who worked on defining these processes said that the picture in Figure 5.4 created a focus that made a significant difference. They were able to visualize what had to be done and focus their attention. They could see how their part contributed to the overall effort. Along the way they could see what was done and what remained to be done. People felt that they accomplished something. People could focus on the issues in which they had control without getting stuck on the issues in which they had no control. They were able to raise issues to others who had control.

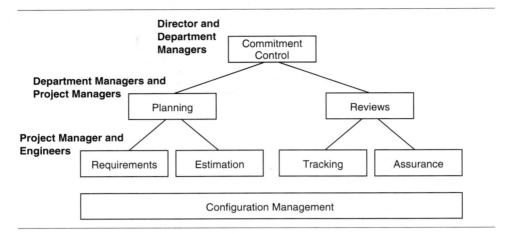

Figure 5.4   Organizing the project management processes by role makes it clear who owns and uses the processes.

The expectation for our action plan was to define and implement seven processes:

- Commitment control process
- Project planning process
- Project management review process
- Requirements management process
- Estimation process
- Project tracking process
- Software quality assurance process

These processes were to be added to our existing processes for configuration management.

This approach helped move the thinking from awareness to understanding—in other words, from "What is it?" to "What does it mean to us?" By determining how the CMM applies to the structure and roles in your own organization, you help people determine their parts in the overall picture so that they can focus on what they need to do.

The Software Process Framework, available from SEI, is another tool that helps you do this kind of mapping to roles. It provides a roles-based perspective at a detailed level; however, the level of detail can be overwhelming, making it difficult to create a focus. But if you use the Software Process Framework to map the roles and then sort the tasks by role, you will take the first step toward a similar process design for your own organization.

Sequence of Steps

Here is an example of how we made it easier for the people in our organization to see the sequence of steps and to see that there was more involved in the effort than simply writing process documents. We are actually moving through the stages of transition, and when we develop the action plan we are preparing during the understanding stage. We plan to take each process through the following stages:

1. **Understanding stage**
   - Objective: Prepare to define the process documents.
   - Activities: Provide training sessions to discuss the Key Process Areas.
2. **Definition stage**
   - Objective: Define the process documents.
   - Activities: Hold Working Groups meetings for each process document.
3. **Installation stage**
   - Objective: Pilot the defined processes.
   - Activities: Deliver all the processes together for pilot use.
4. **Adoption stage**
   - Objective: Approve the processes and put them into practice.
   - Activities: Plan and track the implementation of all the processes.

We used the stages for high-level tracking of progress, and we filled in the details for low-level tracking of task completion.

The training sessions during the understanding stage provide information about the CMM Key Process Areas to the people who are going to participate in process definition. They need enough information about the model to understand how their current practice is related to the model and to understand what improvements might be possible. Some groups are more comfortable with more detail, and other groups are more comfortable with less detail. We have done training as four-hour sessions of complete walkthroughs of the CMM Key Process Areas, using pages from the CMM directly. Some people appreciated that level of detail, but others thought it was too much. We have also done two-hour sessions using the CMM overview presentation in Appendix B; again, some people were more comfortable with that and others wanted more detail. Do what works best for your organization. It took about one month to plan, schedule, and hold these training sessions.

In the definition stage we did not expect to write perfect processes but instead to write processes that would work and get the concepts into practice as soon as possible, knowing that improvements could be made later. We expected to evaluate the process and update it as necessary, perhaps six months later. We created an approach that we called the accelerated process development method, which is described in Chapter 6. Using this method, we were able to complete the definition of seven processes in seven months.

In the installation stage, we wrote an overview that described how these processes were interrelated, and we then provided training on all seven processes to all the project managers, who were the primary process users. We let them choose which processes they wanted to try for three months of trial usage. The issues discovered during that time were addressed before we reached the adoption stage.

In the adoption stage we required all project teams to use the processes, and at this point each team had its own action plan for what needed to be done to put each process into use. The schedule had incremental milestones every two weeks over three months, and the senior managers provided feedback on each manager's progress every two weeks. The feedback was heard, without silent veto. Actually, most of the feedback was positive, so people who were performing the process were encouraged to continue, and those who were hesitant were also encouraged to go forward and adopt the process.

In practice, rather than write an action plan to cover the details of every stage we focused on planning the details of the current step and looking ahead no more than one step. We began with an action plan to cover the details of the understanding and definition stages. Then halfway through the definition stage we planned the details of the installation stage, and halfway through the installation stage we planned the details of the adoption stage. We took it one step at a time, taking into consideration where we were now and where we wanted to go next. We anticipated issues and planned ahead to address them, and we observed the reaction to the current step to determine what was needed for the next step. We were able to adjust our plan to keep it in balance with the needs of the organization.

Something similar occurs in the approach to dance. The dancer memorizes the whole dance, but when she performs she must focus on what she is doing when she is doing it, and she must take the next movement into consideration. If she is performing a gliding step to the side, she will carry her weight differently depending on whether the next step continues in the same direction or whether it turns. The dancer will use her energy to continue the momentum, or she will lift her energy upward to shift her weight and balance to prepare to move in another direction. So looking one step ahead makes a difference in how she uses her energy in the current step. On the other hand, if she is thinking several steps ahead, her mind and body are no longer synchronized, and she tends to rush ahead of the music. By maintaining focus and concentration on the current step, she can be aware of her balance as she finishes the step. If she is off-balance as she completes the current step, she must adjust her balance to self-correct and recover on the next step.

The action plan details would cover the typical project planning questions.

- What are the deliverables?

- How many people do we need to involve, and what are their roles?

- How long do we expect the effort to take?

- What issues need to be resolved?

- What are the risks, the potential issues, that we can do something about before they turn into bigger problems?

A template for a simple action plan is provided in Appendix F and on the CD-ROM.

How do you know which step you are on? You can measure the current status by tracking your progress through the stages of transition for each process improvement. This approach helps you identify where you are today and helps you set realistic expectations for where you expect to be after the next move.

The hypothetical example in Figure 5.5 shows 12 project teams that are working toward adoption of a new technology. Perhaps they are working toward improving their requirements management practices as part of CMM Level 2. One team has moved quickly to document a process and begin using it, two teams are piloting their documented process, and three teams are working on determining and documenting what they will do. Six teams are still working on understanding what requirements management means to their project.

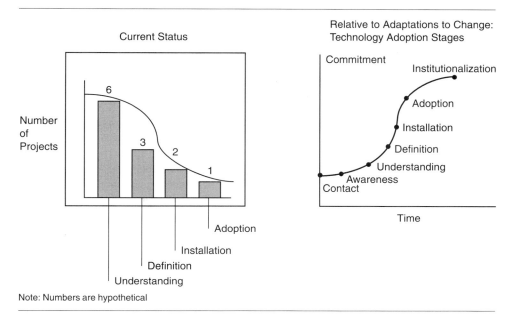

Figure 5.5   Example of the current position of the projects in an organization.

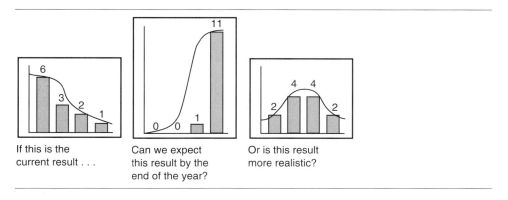

Figure 5.6   Example of realistic and unrealistic expectations for the next step.

If this is the current position, what can we realistically expect by the end of the year? When an organization doesn't understand its current position, the typical goal is to reach the target by the end of the year. The goal of reaching Level 2 by the end of the year can motivate people successfully only if the target is within reach. Otherwise, it causes frustration or gives the impression that people don't really understand what is involved in this change. Rather than expect 11 of 12 project teams to have adopted the new technology by the end of the year, it might be more realistic to expect every team to take one or two more steps in the right direction, as in Figure 5.6.

Moving from One Step to the Next

As several organizations made progress and shared their experiences, we noticed that they made a shift in activity at the beginning of a stage, and if the shift was not smooth it made it difficult to move from one stage to the next. It was at these points that momentum would slow or stop unless this shift was anticipated and addressed. So we added a risk management technique that allowed us to make effective adjustments to the action plan during execution. With this approach, we were able to anticipate what was needed in the next step and build actions into the plan to address these needs. By learning from the experience of others, we knew what to expect and we could prepare for it.

By anticipating what might happen and taking steps to prevent problems, you can make faster progress. You can use foresight to predict the barriers that pose a risk to your progress, and you can identify and take preventive actions as you approach the next stage. These actions will mitigate the risks so that you will have fewer problems to deal with and your efforts will go faster, across the cracks and chasms.

We identified some of the common issues for each stage as well as which actions to take and how to prepare for those actions, and we documented them in the context of a method to use for managing transition. With this transition preparation method, you prepare in advance of each stage by listening to what people are saying and looking at the current process improvement activities to identify the current stage of transition and find out what you can do to improve your focus and progress. The transition preparation method has the same objectives as risk management techniques that help you plan and adjust your plans as you approach and move through each step. This method, developed at Unisys, was presented at several conferences. The materials are included in Appendix G and on the CD-ROM.

Creating a New Focus

Continuing to improve requires that you look at the current business results. By this I mean not only CMM Key Process Areas but also the results of your business and your expectations for future performance. Are the planned actions aligned with the goals and expectations of the organization? If they are not aligned, how do you create the focus that allows you to align them? In our next generation of action plans, we developed a simple technique aimed at ensuring the alignment of our results, needs, and activities.

We aligned the results, needs, and activities in three columns. This helped us identify missing pieces as we developed our improvement action plans. Sometimes we would find a desired result where no associated need or activity had yet been defined, so we had to think about what we needed and what we wanted to do. Sometimes we would find an activity with no connection to a result or need, and we had to think about whether the activity was really necessary. This physical representation of alignment (see Table 5.1) helps you ensure that the activities are defined in relationship to the business results.

Table 5.1   Aligning results, needs, and activities.

Results	Needs	Activities
What current result is not meeting desired expectations?	What must you change to affect this result?	What tasks do you expect to be done to affect the needed change?

Priorities

What about conflicting priorities? It always seems that more work needs to be done than can ever be done. There's not enough time and not enough people to do everything. How do you set priorities so that you don't get swamped with trivia? Not all actions have equal effects, and some actions are better left undefined. When too many actions are defined, people tend to feel overwhelmed, and then nothing gets done. But some actions might have a bonus effect: "If we do this, we get the results we want, and in addition we get another result for free." Looking for the leveraging actions enables you to work smarter and not harder. So it helps to sort things into three categories, as shown in Table 5.2.

One of the difficulties with prioritization is that some priorities fit better than others. The FIU prioritization technique uses the analysis of feasibility, impact, and urgency to rank the priorities of improvement ideas. Typically, a list of improvement ideas will contain a mixture of expected results, needs, and activities, and it becomes difficult to prioritize this mix until it has been sorted. If one item describes an urgent need, it makes sense to rate the characteristic of urgency for this item, but feasibility and impact are not relevant to it. We can consider the feasibility of actions but the feasibility of needs does not make sense. We can consider the impact of changing a result, but the impact of changing a need does not make sense. So if we use the FIU prioritization technique to rate this item, it might be rated with a high priority for urgency and a low priority for feasibility and impact; and then even though this item might be the most important one on the list, it would receive a low overall rating instead of a high rating. If the need were described in relation to a result that we wanted to improve and an activity that could improve that result, then these three items could be prioritized with less confusion. Table 5.3 shows a technique for untangling the priorities.

Using this perspective, the highest priority is given to the most feasible activities related to the most urgent needs related to the results having the greatest impact. On the other

Table 5.2   Look for leveraging actions.

When . . .	Then . . .
The results will not change by themselves and actions must be taken to get improvement	Define actions.
Changing this result doesn't matter much	Let it go for now and check again later.
This result will be positively affected by another result	Let it go for now, and let the side effects of another action take care of this result.

Table 5.3   Prioritize results by impact, needs by urgency, and activities by feasibility.

Results	Needs	Activities
What current result is not meeting desired expectations?	What do you need to change to affect this result?	What tasks do you expect to be done to affect the needed change?
Can this result be improved?	How soon do you need this result to improve?	Can this be done on time, with the desired results?
Prioritize by impact	Prioritize by urgency	Prioritize by feasibility

hand, perhaps more ideas are needed when the priority rating reflects high-impact results and highly urgent needs but none of the related activities are highly feasible. This situation indicates an opportunity to address something important; with a little more thought or a little less perfectionism, a valuable solution might be waiting to be created. The worksheet materials for this technique are included in Appendix H and on the CD-ROM.

Changing the Culture

Moving toward the desired culture requires the following.

- The decision to improve the results.
- The decision to improve the process that produces the results.
- The decision to improve the culture that produces the process that produces the results.

However, if people are not willing to devote their time and energy to taking the actions necessary to reach the desired state, the action plan will not work. If there is no personal motivation for change, there might not be enough momentum for the effort to be successful. We typically assume that people want to participate in improvement efforts, but we seldom verify that assumption, and we rarely do anything about changing the situation if our assumption is false. This is worth discussing because it affects the success or failure of the improvement efforts.

Before you start to improve the process that produces the results, consider these questions for yourself.

- Why do you want to do this?
- Why do you want to improve this result?
- Is this project worthwhile?
- What's in it for you?

Then help other people to consider these questions for themselves. When you're deciding whether this project is worthwhile, make the decision by evaluating its positive and negative aspects from the personal perspective: "What's in it for me?" One way is to use a set of ten questions that are based on the five factors shown in Figure 5.7.

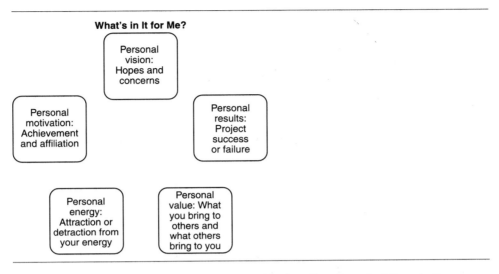

Figure 5.7   Factors to consider from a personal perspective when deciding whether a project is worthwhile.

Personal Expectations: Is this Project Worthwhile?

Following is a set of ten questions that helps people focus on their personal involvement and motivation for working on a process improvement project. These questions apply to any project. Some people tend to focus exclusively on one end of the spectrum and ignore the other end, but to make a balanced decision you need to consider both sides. These questions consider all angles of your relationship to the project. The questions are built from five aspects of the question, "What's in it for me?"

1. What do you hope to achieve by doing this project?

2. What do you hope to gain personally?

3. What do you offer to others?

4. What do others offer to you?

5. What does success look like on this project?

6. What concerns you about the success or failure of this project?

7. What attracts you to this project?

8. In what ways might this project detract from your energies?

9. In what ways might this project be of benefit to another current or future project?

10. Is this project worthwhile?

A worksheet questionnaire with these questions is included in Appendix I and on the CD-ROM.

You might find that some projects are not worthwhile, and it would be better to stop such a project before it starts and before you lose time, energy, and money on it. Or you might find that some projects are worthwhile only if certain changes are made in the project to affect some of your answers more positively. If you make those changes, the project will be more likely to succeed or to benefit another project, letting you leverage the investment of time and energy.

Answering these questions before starting a project helps you set personal expectations that will affect the decisions that you make as the project progresses. If a project has begun but seems to be floundering because of a lack of direction, answering these questions can help clarify or create new expectations. The people on the project become re-energized as they become involved in creating a renewed vision for the project. After the completion of the project, these answers can be reviewed to compare the results of the project against the original expectations.

Making Progress Being Practical

When you are starting a long-term endeavor, the goal is not to finish. Rather, the goal is to start. Once you have started, the goal is to keep going, and if you get stuck, the goal is to start again. How do you start? Begin by understanding the relationship between the current state and the desired state. Three questions bring this relationship into focus.

- What are we doing now?
- What can we change now?
- What can't we change yet?

What are we doing now (in the current state) that meets the requirements of what we need to do (in the desired state)? What can we change now that will bring us closer to the desired state? And to account for the realities of what is feasible today (in the current state), what can't we change yet? Perhaps a few more issues must be resolved before we can make progress with these issues. Perhaps other changes must occur before this change can be made. Do what you can, with what you have, where you are.

I have seen Working Groups take on responsibility for resolving all the issues for a given area, and they struggle for months trying to work on a list of issues that can't be easily resolved. In the meantime, the things that they can change are not implemented. They put the feasible changes on hold for months while they try to resolve the issues with other changes that are not feasible. Then their efforts lose momentum. Once the momentum is gone, it's hard to get the people in the organization to move.

Continuous optimization calls for sustaining the momentum for change and not necessarily for changing everything at once. You make progress by taking one step at a time, and that means acknowledging and accepting that there are some things that we can't change at this time, but we might be able to change later. Then we concentrate on the things we can change now. Even though we can't change everything at once, consider how much we can do in one month. Lay a foundation and come back in six months to make more improvements. Don't wait for perfection, or you might end up writing nothing or writing shelfware. Build momentum by achieving small, successful steps that add up to greater progress. Understand the direction you are heading, and start moving in that direction.

6

Process Documents: Collaborating to Define the Steps

"When love and skill work together, expect a masterpiece."

—John Ruskin

Collaboration

Choreographers can envision movements that look terrific in their imagination but do not work in practice. If the dancer can't perform the step, whether it is too difficult for her or it can't be done by anyone, that step will not be well executed in the performance. The choreographer must work with the practicalities of *this* dancer in *this* place at *this* time. The choreographer and the dancer work together to define the steps. Sometimes a step may be difficult for the dancer initially, but with rehearsal and practice she might learn to do the step with ease. On the other hand, as performance time comes closer, if the dancer is still having trouble with the step and it doesn't look as if she will be able to perform it well, the choreographer works with her to change the step, to define a similar step that still achieves the desired effect in performance.

The same kind of collaboration is needed for processes that people perform. A process developed in someone's imagination might look terrific, but it might not work in practice. It needs to fit those who must perform it. But collaboration is difficult, because those who must perform the process are not identical people with identical needs but rather are individuals with individual needs. As a group they have some common needs, but it takes work to discover what all of them can agree to do. It takes negotiation and collaboration; it is not always clear what the outcome will be, and it is almost guaranteed that the outcome will not match any one person's preconceived notion. When those who perform the process participate in defining the steps, when they are actively involved in collaboration, it makes a difference in the performance.

In this chapter I will share some of my experiences with the process of writing processes. It is about how to work on encoding the process and making decisions for enacting. Writing processes is not simply writing down steps but involving people in making decisions about what they want to do, deciding which steps to do before they begin performing. The best approach to use depends on where you are starting. If you are starting from scratch, you will be defining a new process that has not been documented before. If you are starting with baggage, you will be defining a process that has been documented by groups that have defined their own way to do similar steps and are now joined through reorganizations or mergers.

Coding begins amidst uncertainty and unfocused thinking. When you're starting from scratch, the uncertainty is centered on deciding where to begin. With unfocused thinking, people don't know which steps are important and which steps are unimportant. All the steps are mixed together, and it's difficult to separate them and focus on specific problems and opportunities. When you're starting with baggage, the uncertainty is centered on deciding where to begin again. With unfocused thinking, people want to hold on to what worked in the past and fail to look toward the future. They don't want to lose the benefits of what worked for them before, and they push for doing it their way. But after a reorganization or merger, no one's way is better than anyone else's; the situation is new, and you're working with a new set of process users. No one knows for certain what will be best for the performance this time. The steps will be discovered through a collaborative process, and the approach we use will either help or hinder it.

Starting from Scratch

We typically select a small group of process users to form a Working Group to define a process, and then we involve all the process users in learning and performing the process. It is like dance. When many dancers are involved in a ballet, a choreographer might work with a few of them to ensure that the steps can be done and then involve all the dancers in learning the steps. Most of the time, all the dancers can do the steps, but sometimes the steps that looked good for a few dancers do not work well for the whole group. Sometimes the steps are too intricate or too difficult to synchronize, so they might be simplified. Were the initial, intricate steps better, and were the steps compromised? No. Those steps were just not the right ones for this performance. Through collaboration, the right steps are discovered.

We used to give Working Groups the expectation that they should not stop until they had resolved every issue and created a perfect process document. With those expectations, I have seen Working Groups drag on for 12–18 months. Business went on without improvement, because these Working Groups took too long and tried too hard to do too much. Then when they finally delivered the "perfect" process document, it didn't stay perfect for very long. Senior management began to think that Working Groups took too much time and too many resources. Then senior management didn't want to sponsor any more Working Groups.

So we took a more pragmatic approach and changed the expectations. Because we never have unlimited time and resources to devote to process definition, we set a reasonable time limit and expected Working Groups to do what they could within the given time. This required a change to a shared basic assumption: that "anything worth doing is worth doing right, so do it right the first time." We challenged that assumption by asking the question, "Is this process improvement project worthwhile if we don't come up with a perfect solution?" Although we had once thought it wasn't, we were now thinking differently. We questioned whether this process improvement project would be worthwhile if we let it drag on to the point where everyone would manage to work around his or her individual problems with no process defined, making it increasingly difficult to leverage an improvement from one person to the next or from one project to the next. When you're starting from scratch, what makes the improvement process worthwhile is to make practical changes that help to improve the current situation while providing a foundation for introducing future improvements. What can we do in a month? Lay a foundation and come back to make improvements in six months.

Accelerated Process Development Method

Setting the expectations for practicality instead of perfection, our SEPG developed an accelerated process development method that allowed us to estimate resources and plan the effort for process definition. This method minimized the resources to a level that was acceptable to senior management. An SEPG member facilitated the Working Group, and the team was expected to complete its task in no more than four meetings. The task was to collaborate to create a process draft and an issues list. Selecting representative process users for the Working Group ensures that the people who must do the work also participate in defining the process. Involvement is critical, but the collaboration must be well managed to drive toward a visible end result. Then all other process users are given the opportunity to review and comment so that everyone is involved before performing the process. Figure 6.1 shows the process flow for this method.

At the first meeting, the Working Group reviews the CMM Key Process Area goals and key practices that are applicable to the process being defined. They also look at the process design to understand how this process relates to other processes so that they can determine which issues belong to them and which issues do not belong to them. In this case, the process design was the project management processes organized by roles, as shown in Chapter 5, Figure 5.4. Then they discuss their current situation in a brainstorming exercise and write down their conclusions in three columns, as shown in Table 6.1. The benefit of having all three columns visible during the discussion is that items can be moved from one column to another as the group talks about whether something can or cannot be done. Sometimes one person will express an idea about something that can't be changed, and another person will come up with an idea of how it can be changed now. Similarly, one person might decide that something can be changed now, and another person might identify an issue standing in the way of that change.

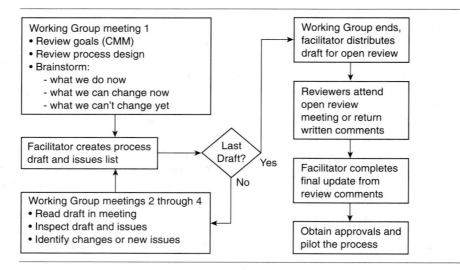

Figure 6.1   Process definition in four Working Group meetings, and review and approval.

Table 6.1   Discussing the current situation in relationship to the CMM Key Process Area goals and key practices.

What we do now (that currently meets the goals of the CMM)	**What we can change now** (to come closer to meeting the goals of the CMM)	**What we can't change yet** (even if it would bring us closer to the goals, let's be practical and concentrate on what we can do now)
1 . . .	1 . . .	1 . . .
2 . . .	2 . . .	2 . . .
3 . . .	3 . . .	3 . . .
etc.	etc.	etc.

The facilitator uses this input to create a process draft and an issues list. The process draft translates what we do now and what we can change now into a process format to be reviewed at Working Group meetings. Sometimes people get stuck when they focus too much attention on what we can't change now. By using these columns, they can put more focus on thinking about what we can change now, and that encourages them to move forward. Before the process is even documented, the seeds are planted and people get an idea of why they would want to follow the process, setting the stage for adoption. The issues list captures what we can't change yet as well as any other issues that need to be addressed either in or outside the Working Group meetings. So at the next meeting, the Working Group reads the process draft and then discusses comments and concerns. People like reading the document at the meeting, because it means that they focus on the topic only once a week during the meeting. This limits the time they must commit, and no outside effort is required for anyone except the facilitator. The Working Group members inspect the draft and issues and identify any changes or new issues for the facilitator to incorporate over the next week.

After the Working Group disbands, the facilitator prepares the process draft for an open review by the rest of the process users who were not on the Working Group. To accommodate those who hate meetings and those who hate writing, the reviewers are given the choice of returning written comments or attending an open review meeting where they can discuss their comments and concerns for the facilitator to capture and incorporate into the final draft. The facilitator then completes the final update of the process based on the review comments and obtains approval to pilot the process.

As a facilitator writing down the process for the first time, I discovered that the first draft is always wrong. Even when I thought I did a terrific job of capturing people's ideas, the Working Group always had major disagreements with the first draft. At first I thought this was a shortcoming on my part, but now I understand that it is part of the process. In a discussion, what you hear may not be what people meant. What people say may not be what they really think. When they see the words in the process draft, they can reflect and think about what they said. They can reconsider it in a new and different light. Further reflection may lead them to change their minds, so be prepared to be flexible and capture what they really want in the process: not the initial ideas but rather the ideas that they will be able to perform. By working through this process and setting the expectations for practicality, I discovered that even though the first draft is always wrong, the fourth draft is almost always acceptable to everyone.

The purpose of the issues list is also to capture what people have said so that they can reflect and think about whether an issue is really a limitation. People can get bogged down debating issues that can't be resolved. The items on the list are classified as open, closed, or deferred depending on the current status of the issue. As the issues are worked out, you can see how much work remains to resolve the issues before completing process definition.

- **Open issues.** These issues must be worked out with the people involved. The people who need to address an issue might not be members of the Working Group. The facilitator contacts those involved and works out the issue with them. In this way, the right people work on the issues that belong to them so that the people in the Working Group don't waste time trying to resolve issues that don't belong to them.

- **Deferred issues.** The Working Group agrees not to do anything to address these issues at this time. A deferred issue might be resolved without direct action, it might be resolved as other issues are resolved, or we might be in a better position to resolve it later.

- **Closed issues.** These issues have been resolved. The issue and the resolution are recorded here so that the Working Group members can review the resolution to ensure that they agree with it, or they can reopen the issue and find a better resolution if they do not agree.

Issues List for: <Process Name>
Date of last update: <Date>

OPEN ISSUES

#	Issue Description and Status	Who is involved (who raised it or is working on it)
1		
2		
3		
4		

DEFERRED ISSUES

#	Issue Description and Status	Who is involved (who raised it or is working on it)
1		
2		
3		
4		

CLOSED ISSUES

#	Issue Description and Status	Who is involved (who raised it or worked on it)
1		
2		
3		
4		

Figure 6.2   Issues list template.

The work on the issues list is considered complete when there are no more open issues; all issues are either deferred or closed. Figure 6.2 is an example of the issues list template.

The Working Group also identifies the people who should be involved in addressing the issue, and this list might include people who are not on the Working Group. Just because an issue is identified doesn't mean that it must be resolved by the people who identified it. (The assumption "You found it; you fix it" is another interesting assumption to be challenged.) With this method, if the issue is beyond the scope of the Working Group, it is taken to the Steering Committee, to another Working Group, or to another person who can address it. And if the issue cannot be resolved within the time allowed, it is deferred.

Some people have trouble with the idea of deferring an issue. They assume that every issue should be tracked to closure. But in practice, of all the issues that were deferred when

Table 6.2 Planning details for estimation.

Roles	Responsibilities	Deliverables	Resources
Working Group facilitator	Writes deliverables Leads meetings Facilitates issues	1. Process document 2. Issues list	One at 50–75% over 6–8 weeks
Working Group members (process users)	Provide input and review of all drafts and issues	Review comments	4–5 for 8 hours each over 4–6 weeks (4 weekly meetings of 2 hours each or 3 every other week of 2.5 hours each)
Reviewers (process users)	Provide review of final draft	Review comments	2 hours each over 2 weeks*

*Number of reviewers depends on process scope

our seven Working Groups completed, none was identified as a problem six months later. Many issues worked themselves out as other Working Groups defined the related processes. Other issues were about how to handle unlikely exceptions; we didn't have enough information to resolve them, and we knew that it would probably take six months to get enough information for us to feel confident about the resolution. If we had enough information to resolve an issue, we would resolve it, but if we didn't, it made more sense to defer it. If an issue became a problem six months later, we would be able to address it using less time and energy than if we let it drag on and drain our energy. We had better things to do with our time.

It can be difficult to convince ourselves and others to let go of what doesn't work. We try to keep the intricate steps, hoping everyone will eventually catch on and learn how to do them, but if they don't work for this performance, it is better to let them go for now. If the steps are more feasible six months later, if they fit the situation at that time, they can be part of the next improvement, but we should be practical for now. By letting go of something that isn't working, we have more opportunity for changes that will enable these steps to be more effective at another time. If it doesn't work it will have a negative effect on performance. The goal of process improvement is not to create perfect processes but rather to create processes that enable us to improve performance.

What senior management liked about this method was that the resource expenditure was contained. The SEPG was able to give them a fixed estimate of the time and effort involved with clearer expectations of the outcome, eliminating the uncertainty of Working Groups that dragged on for an unpredictable amount of time with unpredictable results. This method was created to address our need to document processes more quickly than we had done in the past, using a minimum of resources. Table 6.2 shows the planning details for estimating resources using this method.

This method resulted in a reduction in schedule of 75% or more. With two facilitators working on just one or two processes at a time, in seven months we had definitions for all the processes required to meet CMM Level 2 ready for installation. Once this method was demonstrated to work, it began to be adopted successfully by other groups throughout Unisys. Some modifications have also been demonstrated to work, so the method can be adapted easily. For example, when there was difficulty getting the right people together for four meetings, the facilitator conducted individual interviews to gather the same information and incorporated it into the first two or three drafts. Then the Working Group was able to reach agreement in only one or two meetings.

When the Working Group is seriously working toward consensus, the members seem to agree by the fourth draft. We've tried to cut the schedule by planning to stop at the third draft, but the process users invariably find something wrong with it that they can't live with, so we write the fourth draft, and then they agree. This is a consistent observation. A lot of things in dance are that way, too. Trying to cut a movement short instead of following through all the way results in a step that invariably has something wrong with it. The teacher can't explain why it works this way, but it's a consistent observation.

Experiences

Some of my experiences facilitating these Working Groups illustrate what I have said about using the CMM, the process design, the process draft, and the issues list to help the Working Group to focus. For example, when the senior managers were defining the commitment control process, one of the objections was, "We can't define this process until we determine the contents of the project plan." I showed them the process design and said, "Let the Project Planning Working Group handle that issue. Assume that the project plan contains everything you need to make a decision. Now how are you going to perform the commitment control process?" Then they were able to focus. I recorded the issue, "Determine the contents of the project plan" for the Project Planning Working Group and moved it to the deferred section, because that Working Group was scheduled to begin later.

They also had an issue with the first draft. "There is too much paperwork involved to change a commitment." So we simplified the paperwork and focused on decision making and tracking the decisions. But the underlying issue was balancing between making it too difficult to change a commitment and making it too easy to change a commitment. The opposing perspectives were as follows.

- Too difficult: I see that if the commitment change is just a reflection of a decision that has already been made, the paperwork gets in the way of the process.

- Too easy: I see that too many commitments are changing out from under us without consideration of the impact on other commitments, and not enough information is being considered in the process.

Resolving this issue is a matter of striking the right balance.

When I was facilitating the Requirements Management Working Group, someone caught me in the hallway after a meeting and said that the people in the meeting were not giving her a chance to speak up and give her opinion. She asked me to facilitate the meeting better so that everyone would get a chance to speak. I thought I was giving everyone an equal chance to speak, but, as I discovered, some people don't feel comfortable voicing their opinions until they are invited to speak.

There are two communication styles, and I refer to the people who exhibit them as extroverts and introverts. The extroverts tend to think out loud in a group discussion. They speak up first and express their opinions without hesitation. Once they have heard their own words, they can reflect on what they have said. The introverts, on the other hand, can't think of anything to say immediately, but as they listen to discussion they draw conclusions and put the ideas together as they reflect on what others have said. They won't speak up until later, and only if they are given the chance. Sometimes the extroverts take up all the meeting time, and there is no time left to hear from the introverts.

In a brainstorming technique called nominal group technique, people are given a few minutes of silence to come up with ideas on a topic individually; then everyone is given a chance to share ideas one at a time, and then anyone can add ideas that have been stimulated by the discussion. Unfortunately, although this technique gives the introverts a chance to be heard, it doesn't give the extroverts a chance to think out loud. As a further complication, during the few minutes of silence the introverts often can't think of anything to say. They get a chance to be heard, but they have nothing to say.

To facilitate a result that works well for everyone, I start with a group discussion, in which typically the extroverts do almost all the talking. Then I ask people to take a few minutes to write down the most significant ideas, and then everyone is given a chance to share ideas, one at a time, and the ideas are captured in writing so that everyone can see them.

The first time I did this, the result was very interesting. I had a group of three extroverts and five introverts. The three extroverts began the discussion, and the introverts sat back and said nothing. As the extroverts finished their discussion, they thought we were finished with the topic and were ready to go on to the next topic. But I said, "We're not done— we're just getting started. Now we need to hear from everybody." The extroverts got the opportunity to focus on what was most important to them, and the introverts got the opportunity to hear ideas, draw conclusions, and then express their opinions. Some of the best ideas came from the introverts as they put the ideas together and came up with some great conclusions. And some of the best ideas came from the extroverts after they heard ideas from the introverts. The extroverts realized that even they themselves were not yet finished with this topic. Everyone was involved, and by working together they multiplied their creative energy. What's more, the appreciation for each person in the group grew, as did the respect for what each person had to contribute. The best ideas were the result of their collaboration.

Process Samples

The seven processes that we initially defined are provided in Appendix J and on the CD-ROM. This also includes the Project Management Policy and Project Management Processes Overview documents, which integrate these processes. Since the time these documents were written, these processes have been modified or superseded. The originating group has experienced several reorganizations and other changes in the way it does business, and these changes have led to other adaptations and improvements. The documents themselves are not the solution to implementing the CMM. They are steps to a dance we did once. We are doing other dances now.

Remember that processes developed in another time, in another place, for other people, will not be what you need today, in your company, for your people. In fact, these processes are not what the originating group needs today. They are provided as an example of what we did to get started. They are not intended to be examples of perfect processes or best practices but rather serve as practical examples of what one group did to get a process improvement system up and running. These processes are provided as tools to help you create your own solution and not as solutions to your problems.

Starting with Baggage

In our history of process documentation, at first there were only a few processes and then there were so many of them that people didn't know what to follow. And then when several groups were merged in a reorganization, there was more than one process for doing the same thing. How did we get so much baggage? At first, people gave us the impression that they thought, "If the document is incomplete or imperfect, I don't have to follow it." We worked diligently to write process documents that were complete and perfect. We developed monolithic process documents in exhaustive detail. Then people gave us the very vocal impression that they thought, "This has too many pages, and we don't have time to read it. We also don't have time for process assurance to ensure we are following it." From one extreme to the other, we need to strike the right balance between too much detail and not enough detail.

Opinions differ about how much is too much. For example, soon after we began to use these seven processes, there was a reorganization. The SEPG manager, who came from another group, thought that these seven documents were not detailed enough. Other managers thought they had too much detail; they thought that a process document should fit on one page and that anything longer was too detailed. But is there a difference between one 200-page document and 200 one-page documents? The major issue is how best to organize the needed information and how to decide what information is important.

How long should a process document be? Some people treat this question almost as a religious matter. Without intending to offend anyone, I take a practical approach and look to dance for the analogy. How long should a dance be? It depends on the performance arena and the attention span of the audience. If the audience has come to the theater for an evening of entertainment to be seated with their full attention directed toward the stage, they might expect a performance of about two hours' time. But if it is a performance in the park during a festival with other events and attractions competing for attention, they might expect to watch no more than 15 minutes before turning their attention to other things. If someone tried to give a two-hour performance in the park, some people would stay and watch but most of them would wander away after 15 minutes. And if someone tried to give a 15-minute theater performance, the patrons would probably want their money back. Your organization's circumstances and culture will set the expectations for how much time should be devoted to interpreting process documentation. We need to pay attention to those expectations if we want to meet the needs successfully.

When we tried to give project managers detailed process documents, they had other events and attractions competing for their attention and most of them wandered away. The SEPG had to work with them personally to cut through the detail and help them find the value of the process. Very few of the project managers found the value by reading the documents on their own. The culture didn't support taking two hours to read a process document. Reading took more time than their schedule allowed, so people ignored the documents for as long as they could. When the culture expects the delivery of maximum information in minimum time, people want sound bytes—the essence of the information in a few words. But to communicate in only a few words, people must collaborate to come to a shared understanding of what the words really mean; otherwise, the words in the document are meaningless.

So perhaps we misinterpreted this statement: "If the document is incomplete or imperfect, I don't have to follow it." People are really thinking, "If the document doesn't make any sense to me and doesn't mean anything to me, I don't have to follow it." When a reorganization merged three groups, we needed to redefine the project management processes. The approach we took was intended to address making the document complete and perfect, but it did not help people develop shared understanding and meaning. The approach was to take the existing documents from one group and add best practices from the other groups to create a combined process. Some people thought this approach would save time by making the document complete in a shorter period of time. Instead of developing a shared understanding of what the new group wanted to do, the old groups divided into separate camps. The people from one group thought that they didn't have to change; the people from the other groups thought that the process was being imposed on them and that it didn't matter what they said, so they didn't think it was worthwhile to contribute. Actually, all the groups needed to change and form a single group. All of them needed to participate in the change, but this situation did not help them work together. Their willingness to change was not very high, so these process improvements seemed to go slower instead of faster. This method did not save time; instead, it took six months to develop the documents and another six months to put them into practice across the organization.

After another reorganization, we were having problems with our requirements management process. Issues arose in the interaction between Marketing and Engineering, so the requirements management process needed to be updated to handle these intergroup issues. Here again was a situation in which we were starting with baggage. This time we focused on collaboration, and a team of 13 people was formed, representing all the involved groups and one SEPG facilitator. The approach was to do as much as possible by e-mail and then meet to discuss any diverging opinions. Our plan was to do as much as we could within one month.

We started by having the facilitator write a draft of the current process with some suggested changes to address the issues. A couple of people on the team suggested that we have a central database of all the requirements and their status, and this suggestion was incorporated into the next draft. Suddenly the e-mail discussion got very active, and the team appeared to be dividing into two camps over whether there should be a central database. The third draft removed the suggested database and addressed a few of the other comments. As it became obvious that e-mail discussion was not leading to resolution, I called a meeting of the entire team to work through the conflicting opinions. There were a few heated debates, but we didn't get stuck. In just two meetings, the entire team reached agreement and the process was completed within the time allowed. The meeting agenda helped people collaborate by focusing on what was most important to them and helping them decide what would work for the group.

Meeting Agenda for Process Improvement

The meeting agenda in Figure 6.3 helps people focus on what is most important to them. When you're handling conflicting opinions, sometimes it gets worse before it gets better. It helps to remember that opinions are formed by good and bad experiences, so look beyond the opinions to the experiences behind them. Then consider how common an experience is today and how common it will be tomorrow. If it is common today, it is likely to indicate an issue that is shared by the group. If it is not common, it might be an isolated incident that the group does not need to be concerned about. If an isolated incident is only the first occurrence of many, however, the group needs to be concerned about it. The key is to allow people to say what they think and to be willing to accept it. People have a right to their own opinions. Then let them consider the factors that led them to form the opinion and determine whether those factors affect the project or the process. This meeting agenda gives everyone the opportunity to express what is most important to him or her individually and then to discuss what is most necessary to the group.

Meeting Agenda:
1. Individual voices, once around the room:
    The process must include:
    The process should not include:
Write summarized answers where everyone can see (in separate columns):

Must include	Should not include
1.	1.
2.	2.
3.	3.
4.	4.

2. Work through the list item by item:
    "What does this item mean?"
    (clarify and edit as the group agrees)
    "Can everyone live with this item?"
        Yes—Adopt it and go on to the next item.
        No—"What are the objections?"
    "Can we modify this item to something everyone can live with?"
        Yes—Adopt it and go on.
        No—Drop the item.

Figure 6.3   Meeting agenda for process improvement.

Some of the items that were deferred for this process were raised to senior management as issues to be addressed by other processes. All the accepted items were incorporated in the process draft. People felt that by working together they had resolved the issues in the areas where they had some control. They had also uncovered issues beyond their control, but they did not let those issues get in the way of taking this step toward process improvement. They made progress and resolved some long-standing intergroup issues. Members of the group were able to contribute knowledge and experience and to make sense of what they would need to change to make the improved process work for them. Some people had to change more than others, but they did not feel that the process was being imposed. They felt that they were involved in deciding what was most important. They participated, and they knew their voices would be heard. And even though people started with opposing perspectives in many cases, they listened to one another and understood the perspectives of others in the group. They discovered what made sense to do at this time.

Process Definition Pitfalls: Shoulds and Passive Voices

Some of the first process documents we wrote were more like training materials than process descriptions. Dance notation captures a description of the dance steps, but it does not teach you how to dance. Writing about how to dance would include many sentences describing what should be done. Guess what many of our early process documents contained? Many sentences about what should be done. When we read these documents later, it wasn't clear who was supposed to do what steps, and sometimes it wasn't clear what steps we decided to do versus what steps we hoped to learn to do someday. Sentences in passive voice would often describe an activity that "is done" but did not identify who was expected to do it. So as we started with baggage from our early process documents, some of the baggage included a lack of clarity about who did what.

A typical process outline would contain the following sections:

- Introduction (sometimes divided into purpose, scope, objectives, and definitions)
- Customers and suppliers
- Needs and expectations
- Activities (sometimes divided into input, activity, output, and exit criteria)
- Flowcharts
- Interdependencies
- Metrics
- Recommendations

This outline helped us organize and cover the important information for a process. It allowed for flexibility and free form, but it also allowed a lack of clarity and lack of precision to creep into the documents. It was not always clear who did what and why. To solve this problem, we improved the way we captured the activities by organizing the information in a new format. This made it easier to find information in the process, to make changes to the process, and to audit process usage.

Examples

The following examples show how the use of tables helped us improve the clarity and organization of the activities in our process descriptions. Figure 6.4 shows a Process Flow document for an inspection process. In an earlier version of the process document, the list of activities appeared as in Figure 6.5. In a later version, the revised description used a table format; as we converted the existing text into this format, the deficiencies in the process description became apparent, as shown in Figure 6.6. Using this format, we were able to clarify the process and improve the process description, as shown in Figure 6.7.

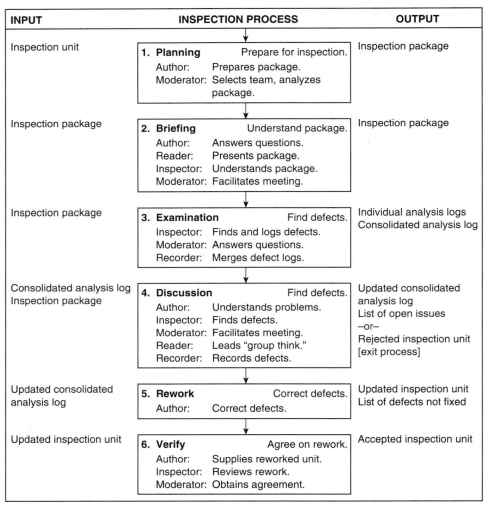

Figure 6.4 Example of inspection process flow.

Activities
1. The author and moderator plan the inspection, including schedule and participants.
2. The author and moderator select the members of the inspection team, and the moderator confirms their availability.
3. The author prepares the inspection package, the target materials, and other supporting materials, including upstream definitions, and submits them to the moderator for approval.
4. The moderator distributes the approved inspection package to the inspectors.
5. The inspection package is reviewed at the briefing meeting, which is usually led by the author.
6. Each inspector individually examines the target for the designated purpose of detecting defects, including accurate implementation of upstream definitions.
7. Each inspector records any defects, any related issues, and examination hours invested.
8. The recorder collates the defects and issues discovered during the examination.
9. The discussion meeting is conducted by the moderator. At this meeting, the collated examination discovered defects are distributed to all, and the meeting focuses on discovering additional defects through various techniques—for example, "hot areas" (those with the most defects found), and so on. Also ensure that all issues and defects are properly classified.
10. All defects, issues, and effort hours are summarized for the inspection and recorded by the recorder.
11. The number of rework hours to repair defects is captured.
12. To verify, the team evaluates the need for a reinspection.
13. Open issues are reviewed by the team/project.

Figure 6.5   Earlier description of the inspection process activities.

From Whom	Activity/Document	To Whom for What
Author and moderator	Plan the inspection, including schedule and participants.	?
Author and moderator	Select the members of the inspection team.	Moderator to confirm availability?
Author	Prepares the inspection package.	Moderator for approval.
Moderator	Distributes the approved inspection package.	Inspectors
?	The inspection package is reviewed at the briefing meeting, which is usually led by the author.	?
Each inspector	Individually examines the target for detecting defects, including accurate implementation of upstream definitions.	?
Each inspector	Records any defects, any related issues, and examination hours invested.	?
Recorder	Collates the defects and issues discovered during the examination.	?
Moderator ?	Conducts the discussion meeting, distributes the collated examination discovered defects to all, and the meeting focuses on discovering additional defects.	? Also ensure that all issues and defects are properly classified.
Recorder	Summarizes and records all defects, issues, and effort hours for the inspection.	?
?	Captures the number of rework hours to repair defects.	?
Team	Evaluates the need for a reinspection.	? To verify?
Team/ Project	Reviews open issues.	?

Figure 6.6   When you reformat the information, you can see the holes in the description.

From Whom	Activity/Document	To Whom for What
Author and moderator	Select members of the inspection team, confirm availability, schedule the meetings.	Inspection team to confirm availability.
Author	Prepares the inspection package.	Moderator for distribution to inspection team.
Moderator	Checks inspection package and distributes.	Inspection team for inspection.
Author	Leads briefing meeting for inspectors.	Inspection team for inspection.
Inspectors	Individually examine the target materials for detecting defects and ensuring accurate implementation of upstream definitions and materials, and record the defects, issues, and examination hours.	Recorder for discussion meeting preparation.
Recorder	Collates the defects and issues discovered during examination.	Inspection team for discussion meeting.
Moderator and reader	Conduct the discussion meeting, focus the inspectors on discovering additional defects, and ensure that all issues and defects are properly classified. Identify verifier if necessary.	Inspection team at discussion meeting.
Recorder	Records all defects, issues, and discussion meeting hours.	Defects and issues to author for rework.
Author	Performs rework and records data and rework hours.	Verifier for verification of repairs.
Verifier	Performs verification of the repaired artifacts.	Author, moderator for results of verification.
Moderator	Identifies rework for acceptance or reinspection according to the team's disposition.	Author for information.
Moderator	Ensures issues are raised to project team and required data is recorded for the data repository.	Project team for issue resolution, and data repository for future data analysis.

Figure 6.7   Revised version of the inspection process description.

With this format, the columns make it easier for someone who is performing a certain role to find the information that pertains to that role and to see how the work relates to the work of others within the context of the process. This format relates an individual's activity to the expectations of the "process customers" of that activity. You can see the person you are doing this activity for and see what that person expects to do with your results, and this information can affect how you perform the activity. As you compare these tables, you will see that in the revised version, some of the steps are almost identical to the original, other steps have been combined, and still other steps have been split apart.

Single-page Summary

Process Objective:	Key Milestones:

People Involved:
   Primary:
   Secondary:
	Data Records Required:
	   Tools or Databases:
	   Forms or Deliverables:

When to Perform These Activities: 1. 2. 3.	Input Data: 1. 2. 3.
Communication Activities: 1. 2. 3.	Recording Activities: 1. 2. 3.
Results (Closure Agreements or Decisions): 1. 2. 3.	Results (Output Data): 1. 2. 3.

Figure 6.8   Blank template for a single-page summary. People and communication are on the left side, and data and information are on the right side.

People and Communication, Data and Information (PCDI)

The underlying purpose of a process is to relate people to their work environment, the way they interact with other people, and the way they interact with information. In the industry we tend to define these interactions as rules. For example, the ETVX method identifies the entry criteria (E), tasks (T), verification activities (V), and exit criteria (X) for each process or process step. But not everyone relates to these interactions as a set of rules and regulations.

Another perspective is to put a greater emphasis on collaboration: how we work together (people and communication) and what we have to work with (data and information). This method, called PCDI (people and communication, data and information), uses a single-page summary of a process. The left-hand side focuses on people and communication, and the right-hand side focuses on data and information. Figure 6.8 shows the template, and Figures 6.9 and 6.10 are examples.

Is this Detail Worthwhile?

Depending on the expectations of the culture, these summaries might be all that is needed in a one-page process, or they might be backed up with more details. It might be necessary to provide more detail to help people feel comfortable with capturing the descriptive information. Evaluate how much detail is necessary and worthwhile. At some point, it will become more worthwhile to work on another process improvement instead of continuing to add details to the existing description. At some point, embellishing the description improves only the description and not the process.

Single-page Summary

Process Objective: • To ensure the submitters and developers have a common understanding of the requirements. • To maintain agreement on the requirements during the life of the project. To ensure changes are negotiated and understood. • To ensure that the product and other deliverables reflect those requirements.	*Key Milestones:* 1. Requirements submitted and analyzed and responses determined. 2. Any changes to requirements negotiated. 3. Finished product verified to meet requirements.
People Involved: • Primary: Marketing, Program Owners, Senior Management Team • Secondary: Engineers	*Data Records Required:* 1. Documented Requirements and Engineering Response (documents or database). 2. Status Records (project plan or database).
When to Perform These Activities: 1. **Review new market demands:** quarterly. 2. **Clarify the requirements and determine the response:** when new requirements are submitted and reviewed. 3. **Negotiate changes:** when changes are proposed in strategy, requirements, or delivery targets.	*Input Data:* 1. Problem statements and objectives that resulted from strategic business planning.
Communication Activities: 1. **Review new market demands:** to prioritize and determine which Op Plan line items are affected. 2. **Clarify the requirements and determine the response:** to ensure common understanding between Marketing and Engineering. 3. **Negotiate changes** to consider and address impact of changes to requirements or delivery targets.	*Recording Activities:* 1. **Document the requirements and responses.** 2. **Track status** of the implementation of the features that satisfy the requirements.
Results (Closure Agreements/Decisions): 1. Determine which Op Plan line item will address the requirement. 2. Assurance that requirements are understood. 3. Determine the delivery target for features that satisfy the requirements. 4. Assurance that products meet their requirements (i.e., testing has validated that the features in the product satisfy the requirements).	*Results (Output Data):* 1. Documented Requirements and Engineering Response (documents or database). 2. Status records (project plan or database).

Figure 6.9   Example from a requirements management process.

Single-page Summary

Process Objective: To provide visibility to project status and issues so that we can ensure that we meet our commitments.	*Key Milestones:* Review Forms Update: 　First Friday of the month Project Review Meeting: 　Second Friday of the month
People Involved: 　Primary: 　　Project managers, 　　software component managers, 　　development manager 　Secondary: 　　Project teams and interdependencies	*Data Records Required:* 1. Project review forms 2. Component review forms If applicable, attribute sheets and roadmaps
When to Perform These Activities: 1. Weekly: Report issues that require immediate attention in the weekly status. 2. Monthly: Update the review forms. 3. Monthly: Project review meeting for any projects/components that indicate significant factors need to be discussed and addressed by the primary people involved.	*Input Data:* 1. Project plans 2. Product strategy 3. Attribute sheets 4. Product roadmaps 5. Status or issues reported from project team or interdependencies
Communication Activities: 1. All managers send weekly status reports by e-mail. 2. Selected software component managers and project managers present information at project review meetings with the development manager. Secondary people involved may be invited as needed.	*Recording Activities:* 1. Project managers prepare the project review forms. 2. Software component managers prepare the component review forms. 3. Development manager reviews the project review forms and the component review forms and selects projects/components to schedule for the project review meeting.
Results (Closure Agreements or Decisions): 1. Decision to continue with current plan or to make adjustments to project plans or product strategy.	*Results (Output Data):* 1. Action items from project review meeting. 2. Evaluation of effectiveness of project review process.

Figure 6.10   Example from a project review process.

Remember that the goal of process definition is not perfection but collaboration. Processes are dependent on people, and people are human, and humans are not perfect. People tend to disagree with one another more often than not, so if the process involves more than one person you will never make it perfect for everyone. Just make it workable for everyone. Even though some people might not like the process, if they are involved in the decisions they will be more likely to understand and go along with the decisions. They will be more prepared to perform the process and to perform it well. They will be more likely to work together to succeed.

7

Process Implementation: Lifting the Spirits of the Performers

"What a beautiful step! I shall never be able to dance it!"

— *Dame Margot Fonteyn*

In her autobiography, the great ballerina Dame Margot Fonteyn tells of many experiences when a choreographer would demonstrate a beautiful step. Her frequent reaction was to say, "What a beautiful step! I shall never be able to dance it!" But after several attempts in rehearsal, she performed those beautiful steps beautifully. Those of us who are asked to try something new and different often have the same reaction, but we feel pressure to perform all the time with little or no allowance for rehearsal. We might think we should display confidence all the time, but when we are trying something new and different we might not feel very confident about our performance. Even if we have done similar things successfully in the past and even if other people have confidence that we can succeed again, we might still need rehearsal and practice to build our own confidence.

When dancers are being taught a new step, if you watch them carefully you will notice some differences in what they do to learn the steps. Some of them get up near the front of the room, close to the teacher, and eagerly try the movements using their full energy, experimenting with the shifts in weight and balance. Others are a little more cautious, watching the steps from the middle of the room and learning the steps mentally. They mark the movements but do not try to do them with full energy until they feel more confident. Still others are even more cautious, standing at the back of the room, not paying much attention at first in case the steps change. These dancers let others do the experimenting, saving all their energy and expecting to be able to catch on quickly by watching others do the steps. You can almost predict a dancer's attitude toward learning new steps by where she is standing in the room.

This kind of assessment is a little more difficult with managers and engineers, but after observing them experience a process improvement or two, you can almost predict those who will move first, those who will be more cautious, and those who will drag their feet. Everyone can learn to perform the steps beautifully, but some are more eager and others are more cautious. Some people will give you their full energy, and others won't. The difference is in their attitude and not their capability. Perhaps those who are more cautious are not confident in the steps, or perhaps they are not confident in their ability to perform the steps. Even though they are perfectly capable of performing the steps, they might be thinking, as Fonteyn did, "I shall never be able to dance it!" They need a little more confidence. When they see others do the movements and see that the steps are not impossible and when they have a chance to try the steps themselves, it helps to convince them that they can do it, too.

In the context of the three basic steps of envisioning, encoding, and enacting, the enacting step is the active performance of the process. It is in this step that you put into practice what you envisioned in the action plan and encoded in the process document.

The adoption of new practices by a group means the adoption of new practices by individuals within a group, and those individuals bring their own attitudes toward learning something new. Some people are more willing to try a process improvement, whereas others are thinking, "If it ain't broke, don't fix it." People become attached to their work habits. If the process was successful in the past, there won't be much motivation to change it. This hesitation is not a problem if the organization and the business environment are stable. A process that has worked successfully will continue to work successfully. But people develop the process in response to two parameters: the needs of the organization and the needs of the business environment. The process might need to change, not because it's broken or wrong but because the parameters have changed. Process improvement is a response to the new parameters. Problems occur when the parameters change but everyone is too busy with day-to-day business to notice that the process is no longer aligned with the needs.

As the organization strives to meet the demands of its customers, there is a rhythm and timing for organizational change. But the organization is made up of individuals who have their own rhythms and their own favorite tempo. It helps to understand these rhythms when you try to get people to dance together. This is the work of aligning the practices, individually and collectively, to produce the results you want.

Some people have a visionary attitude and are open to change as they consider future opportunities. They think, "Even if we've always done it this way, we need to find a better way to do it, because it won't be long before it doesn't work for us anymore." Such people tend to move faster than most others. A second group of people have a pragmatic attitude and are open to change if the change is practical. They think, "We've always done it this way, but if you've got a better way to do it, we could be persuaded, if it works for us." Still other people have a conservative attitude, thinking, "We've always done it this way. It works for us, so we will continue to do it this way." People in this group tend to move more slowly than most other people.

These basic attitudes toward behavioral change (see Table 7.1) are the filters that characterize people's initial reaction to process improvement ideas.

Table 7.1   Basic attitudes toward change.

Filter	Initial Reaction to Process Improvement Ideas
Visionaries	"I want it to get better than it is. What do I have to gain?"
Pragmatists	"If it is useful, it might help me. What do I have to gain?"
Conservatives	"I don't want it to get any worse. What do I have to lose?"

I tend to have a visionary attitude toward process improvement, but the attitudes of the people I work for are mostly pragmatic and conservative. Something that convinces me that process improvement is important will not convince them. If I were to talk to them about what they had to gain and how this process was going to make it better, while they were thinking about what they had to lose and how this process might make it worse, we would not be communicating very well. I must look at it from their perspective. I must tell them how process improvement will be useful, how it will help them, and how it won't destroy what worked in the past; instead it will build on what works today and will be better suited to the changes in the business environment.

These attitudes are not unchangeable labels. I have seen the attitudes change when people are under time pressure. Someone who normally has an enthusiastic, visionary attitude might suddenly take on a conservative attitude when pressed for time. If an entire organization is constantly under time pressure, it tends to become conservative. Everyone begins thinking, "What do I have to lose? Time. I don't have time to learn something new." As this kind of thinking becomes a shared basic assumption, the result is a conservative culture. When the culture is conservative but the business environment indicates the need for change, people might not want to change. Even if the process was successful in the past, it might need to change to be successful in the future. If we want the process to be "right" all the time, we must be prepared to change it continuously. If the environment changes but the process doesn't change, what once was right could go wrong as people get too busy to notice what is happening around them.

An SEPG needs to be sensitive to the timing and rhythm of the organization and the individuals within it. Fighting against the rhythm only spoils the choreography. The SEPG needs to be responsive to individuals to give them the support they need and to build their confidence to move when the timing is right, just as in dance. Eventually, the dancers' movements look natural, but they must first learn the steps. The steps might look natural at performance time, but they are not natural; rather, they are trained, practiced, and rehearsed. And when the dancers have confidence, the steps are performed beautifully.

Different Strokes for Different Folks

The Technology Adoption Curve, from Everett Rogers's *Diffusion of Innovation,* is a bell curve representing the distribution of people who buy or adopt high-tech products. The number of buyers starts small, grows to a majority, and then tapers off. In the middle is the

Wants to be the first to adopt the new stuff. Enjoys "the latest and greatest," pushing the envelope.	Highly motivated and driven by a "dream." Seeks quantum breakthroughs, not just improvement. Willing to take risks to achieve goals.	Does not want to be a pioneer—too much risk. Seeks to gain a percentage improvement. Values the opinions of others like them.	Believes more in tradition than in progress. Not looking for improvement but doesn't want to be left behind to get stung. Prefers "whole solutions."	Tends to see through the marketing hype. Continually points out flaws and costs and doesn't see the benefits as justified.
Innovators	**Early Adopters**	**Early Majority**	**Late Majority**	**Laggards**
Technology Enthusiasts	*Visionaries*	*Pragmatists*	*Conservatives*	*Skeptics*

Figure 7.1   Technology adoption life cycle curve, a profile blending psychology and demographics.
Adapted from *Crossing the Chasm* by Geoffrey A. Moore, HarperBusiness, 1991

majority of buyers, divided into categories labeled Early Majority and Late Majority. Before them, there are some early adopters, and at the two ends of the curve are a few innovators at the start and a few laggards at the end.

This curve is correlated to psychological factors in Geoffrey Moore's *Crossing the Chasm.* The timing of the purchase of a new technology or technology product depends on psychology, as shown in Figure 7.1. This curve was originally intended for use in marketing high-technology products, but the same principle applies to "marketing" process improvement and culture change. The marketing strategy needs to match the psychology of the type of people you are dealing with, and you will have problems if you use the wrong strategy. Although people often have varying motivations or attitudes toward process adoption, they generally fall into these five categories. Fortunately, you need to concentrate only on the middle three categories. The technology enthusiasts will adopt it no matter what you do, and the skeptics will not adopt it no matter what you do.

Moore revised this model when he observed that in reality the transition between these groups is not continuous but discontinuous. He called the discontinuities cracks in the bell curve and then noted that the crack between the early adopters and early majority is so difficult to get across that it should be called a chasm (see Figure 7.2). If you do not know about the chasm, you fall in and wonder why you cannot make progress anymore. It is difficult to cross the chasm, because these two groups have different attitudes. When you try to convince the pragmatists by using the message that works for the visionaries, it has the opposite effect.

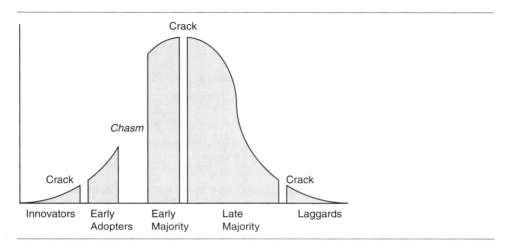

Figure 7.2   Discontinuities in the adoption curve.
Adapted from *Crossing the Chasm* by Geoffrey A. Moore, HarperBusiness, 1991

- **Visionaries.** Visionaries prefer to see their vision become reality. They are most likely to adopt the process when you show them the big picture of the improved results of using the new process and then give them all the tools they need to make it happen. It also helps if you give them a way to visualize and track their own progress.

- **Pragmatists.** Pragmatists prefer what is practical. They are most likely to adopt the process when it makes sense, helps them do their job, and meets their needs. They might not be able to visualize what it will be like when they adopt the new process, so it helps to give them a demonstration, assist them in setting up and starting to do the process, and then turn it over to them when they get the idea. As their peers begin to adopt the process, they become examples who demonstrate that the process works and will meet their needs. It helps to set up a peer group so that those who are working toward adopting new processes can share successes and issues to work through together.

- **Conservatives.** Because conservatives prefer tradition, they might not want to adopt the process until it becomes the new tradition. They need to be convinced that this new process is the new tradition. Depending on the culture, this might include strong backing from management or from the opinion leaders or evidence that the majority of the group has already moved to adopt the process and that the conservatives should also adopt it if they don't want to be left behind. It helps if they see evidence that the change is real and not just an experiment. They don't want to waste their time and energy.

I've seen the difficulties of using a divide and conquer approach for moving an organization toward process adoption. This approach begins by working with the visionaries (early adopters), then with the pragmatists (early majority), and then the conservatives (late majority). The greatest difficulty occurs after the visionaries are sold; the pragmatists have such a different attitude that you can't use the same sales pitch with them, and if they don't accept it the change falls into the chasm.

My observation is that an exclusionary focus on the early adopters might actually create the chasm. When you isolate the early adopters, you make them a special project and basically give everyone else permission to ignore the change. They think, "Let the early adopters work out the details, and we'll see if we're interested later." People who are not involved in that special project will seldom be interested later. The people who are not involved when the steps are developed will have less confidence in their ability to perform the steps, and they will drag their feet.

Although the divide and conquer approach might be an effective approach for complex problem solving (to divide tasks into subtasks), it's not very effective with people. People don't want to be divided, and they certainly don't want to be conquered. On the contrary, we want people to work together in teams, and we want them to develop their capabilities to do their best work. So we should be using a "join and grow" approach to give people the support they need to work together and be most effective.

If you want people to learn the steps, build their confidence in their ability to learn to do the steps well. Rather than create a chasm, involve everyone in learning to do the steps together. As their natural tendencies exhibit themselves in an even distribution, the visionaries will start moving first, the pragmatists next, and the conservatives last. Some people will start moving sooner than others, but all of them will know that they are expected to be moving. Respect the natural tendencies, but reinforce the expectation that everyone needs to perform the process. Especially if projects are interdependent, people need to learn, change, and grow together. If one project team changes and another one does not, it is likely that both of them will have difficulty. It's hard to practice dancing when the other performers don't show up. There is only so much you can do on your own.

It is the pragmatists who tip the scales, determining whether the process will be adopted or will fall into the chasm. At first they sit on the fence, as noncommittal as possible, and then they either move forward with the visionaries to adopt the change or fall back with the conservatives. Reinforcing the expectation that everyone needs to perform the process helps move the pragmatists forward, whereas without reinforcement they will tend to stick with the conservatives and the change will fall into the chasm. But no matter what attitude you find in each person, work on lifting people's spirits and building their confidence. Give them the support they need, and provide opportunities for others to give support.

- To give visionaries more confidence, help them to envision the effects of the improvement and give them opportunities for experimentation as they try to do the steps themselves.

- To give pragmatists more confidence, help them to see that the improvement is useful, that it might help them, and that the effects of the improvement are beneficial.

- To give conservatives more confidence, help them see that the improvement works for most people, that they have the support of managers, the SEPG, and peers, and that the change is becoming the new tradition.

Merely telling pragmatists and conservatives about the vision won't be convincing enough for them. They want to know whether the change will be useful and practical and whether they will get full support. They won't be willing to change if they think it is just smoke and mirrors. Because their attitudes are so different, it helps to include visionaries, pragmatists, and conservatives in the Working Groups who define the processes. Each person can provide unique insights about potential reactions to the change. Then the process and the plan for introducing the process can take this information into consideration to make it easier for each of these types to adopt the change.

Measuring Overall Progress

When we first started using the CMM, our initial expectation about climbing the maturity ladder was to set up annual milestones and complete the work required for each level in 12–24 months. As we understood more about what was required for Level 2, we would revise our estimates and add another year to the schedule. The goal always seemed to be "Level 2 by the end of the year." It always seemed to take longer than we thought, and we were tired of the disappointment of not reaching our goal year after year. As a result, we created an alternative method for setting milestones that would provide more-realistic expectations of progress. This method is based on the stages of technology transition.

Population Distribution

Being mindful of the varying attitudes people have, we stopped expecting a lockstep migration as the organization moved through the stages of transition. Rather, we expected that some groups in the corporation would adopt the changes faster than others. We looked at the population overall and saw the migration over time. The following series of charts shows three snapshots in time.

At the start of the transition the innovators and early adopters are at the leading edge, but the majority of the groups are still at the awareness and understanding stages. At one point we counted the number of groups at each stage and created a bar graph; the shape of the curve was an early skew curve (see Figure 7.3). We predicted that in a year the curve would show a normal distribution.

Figure 7.4 shows the midpoint of the transition, with some groups complete, other groups just starting, and a majority of the groups defining and installing their processes. When we counted the groups after six months of progress, we found that our prediction was accurate. The shape of the curve was a normal distribution.

Figure 7.5 shows the completion of the transition, when the change can be considered institutionalized. When the majority of the groups complete the transition, we expect that

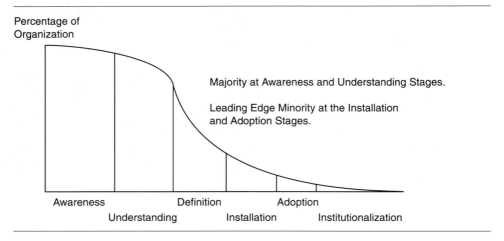

Figure 7.3   Population distribution: early skew. Unfreezing the current state, early transition.

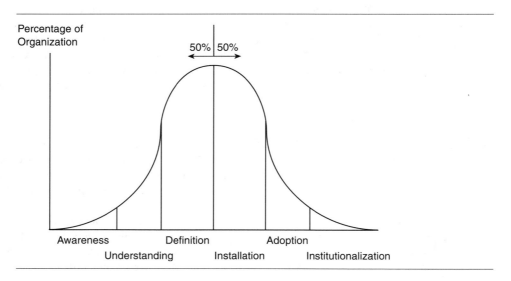

Figure 7.4   Population distribution: normal bell-shaped curve. Midpoint of transition.

there will still be some groups trailing. Because the normal way of doing business has changed at this point, the change can be considered institutionalized even though there may be some people who never accept the change. If we were looking for perfection, we might expect 100% of the groups to reach the institutionalization stage, but it would be more realistic to expect a late skew curve as the end result. When our measurements for most

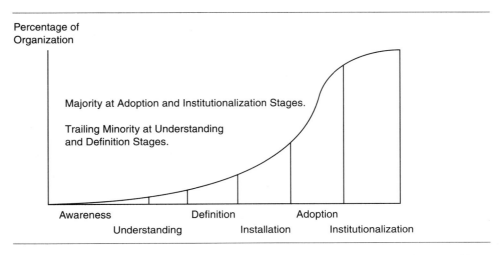

Percentage of
Organization

Majority at Adoption and Institutionalization Stages.

Trailing Minority at Understanding
and Definition Stages.

Awareness   Definition   Adoption
    Understanding   Installation   Institutionalization

Figure 7.5   Population distribution: late skew. Refreezing the desired state, late transition.

of the Level 2 Key Process Areas were close to this late skew curve, our measurements for the Level 3 Key Process Areas were close to the early skew curve. Although reorganizations made it difficult to compare the measurements taken at six-month intervals, we were able to see the progress of the transition.

This concept of population distribution applies not only at a corporate and group level but also to individual project teams or project managers within a group. When compared to other groups in the corporation, the group I worked for could be categorized as a pragmatist group. However, of the seven project managers within the group, two adopted the new processes more readily than the others, three waited to see some results before they were inclined to adopt the new processes, and the last two waited as long as they could. Of the seven project managers, two were visionaries, three were pragmatists, and two others were conservatives. As the visionaries adopted the new processes and talked about how the change was helping them, the pragmatists gained enough confidence to move forward to adopt the processes. When the conservatives were the only ones who were not following the processes that senior management supported, they finally adopted the new processes, too.

Rehearsal and Performance

In software process improvement, we prepare and then we perform a new or improved process. In dance, we rehearse and then we perform new or improved choreography. The dance may be rehearsed many times in a rehearsal studio before it is rehearsed on stage. The last rehearsal before the performance is the dress rehearsal, when all the elements come together on stage, usually for the first time: the lights, the costumes, the music, and the dancing. This is when we find out whether it all works together or whether we must change something. Then rehearsal is over and it's time to perform. Stage fright. Adrenaline rush.

The dancers are thinking, "I want to do everything perfectly, and I don't want to disappoint the audience." Have the dancers been encouraged enough? Will they be mentally strong enough to get out on stage and perform? With all the excitement and the pressure of opening night, they hear the music and they perform.

For the software process, the activities to create the process document are a rehearsal of the steps in the minds of the process users. Pilot use is when all the elements come together and we find out whether it all works or whether we need to change something. And then it's time to perform the process. Have the managers and engineers been encouraged enough to join in the dance? With all the excitement and the pressure, can they hear the music? If so, they will be ready to perform. Just before the performance begins, that's when you see the real excitement. Sparks fly. Nerves are on edge. Some people get angry, other people want help, and still other people act as if nothing is bothering them, as if nothing is going to change even though everything around them is changing. The energy level rises to prepare for the performance. People want to do their best, and they don't want to disappoint the people who depend on them.

Adoption Techniques

After observing several organizations as they moved through the adoption stage—some struggling and others succeeding easily—we were able to anticipate the barriers we might face and know what we could do to prevent problems so that we could increase the likelihood of success. In the adoption stage, our goal was to achieve active use of the processes for all projects in the organization. We anticipated barriers such as

- Management not creating the need for change
- Lack of sustained communication of progress
- Lack of monitoring

We learned from what had worked for other groups such as

- Sharing success stories
- Sharing approaches
- Taking progress measurements

Although your organization might be categorized overall as visionary, pragmatist, or conservative, most likely you have people in each category, so use multiple approaches to cover all the needs. Have people track their own progress. Provide assistance from the SEPG and from peers in a peer group meeting, and have senior management visibly demonstrate support. For CMM-based process improvement, the SEPG learns first, followed by the managers and then the engineers. As the managers learn the steps, have them demonstrate leadership by involving the project teams in identifying and executing more improvements for their projects and for the entire organization. The following sections provide techniques used in one organization, will give you ideas to adapt to your own organization's needs. We'll look at the following techniques.

- Progress measurements
- Project action plans
- Management feedback
- Peer networking
- CMM action planning workshops

Progress Measurements

Process adoption is not an overnight event but rather occurs over a period of time. To acknowledge this, when our projects were expected to adopt new project management processes toward Level 2 capability maturity, we gave the project teams three months to integrate the new processes into their work. We set measurement objectives and selected a measurement method for determining progress against objectives from the beginning of the adoption stage.

At first we used the CMM Maturity Questionnaire that is used for software process assessments, but because of the unfamiliar terminology we translated the questions to more familiar terminology for the project managers. This questionnaire is provided as an example in Appendix C. You can use this questionnaire as a starting point for creating your own. Project managers answered the questionnaire monthly, with an initial goal that all project teams would respond "Yes" to at least 80% of the questions within three months. This goal was arbitrary, but the intent was to observe the trend increase as each project put the processes in place. The baseline measure at the start of the first month had some teams exceeding the 80% goal and some less than the goal. By the second month, all teams scored greater than the 80% goal, and by the third month all teams scored more than 90%, with an average score of 97%. A sample chart is shown with the spreadsheet in Appendix C.

Several factors affected the change in the scores from the first month to the second month. The scores were distributed as a bar chart graphing the scores of all projects side-by-side so that the project managers could see where they stood relative to the other teams, creating some peer pressure. The director met with all the project managers to assure them that senior management was serious about this. So those who were dragging behind and not paying attention decided it was time to start paying attention and learn the steps. Because the CMM was the foundation of the processes, when the project managers actually used the processes they could answer "Yes" to the questions. It was not hard to meet the target score, because we had created the foundation and support from the beginning as the processes were defined.

Another key factor in administering the questionnaire was that it was made clear that the score was not as important as knowing which questions were being answered "No."

An answer of "No" meant that there were still actions to be taken and work to be done. It was an indication of progress and not "goodness"—an indication of where the issues were—so people could be honest about their data without fear of repercussions regarding their scores. Surprisingly, some scores actually decreased by a question or two as the project managers found other actions they felt were necessary.

Project Action Plans

For each project, we created project notebooks containing sections for each process and for each working document called for by that process. The project manager could either keep the working document in the notebook or have a pointer referencing the file location of the working document.

Each project manager had a project action plan, which had a schedule of milestones of two processes every two weeks. Every two weeks, the SEPG would check that the initial working documents for these two processes were in the project notebook. This pace kept the momentum going. The project action plans also included the actions and expected dates for meeting the measurement objectives. Using the questionnaire, each project manager tracked the questions that had been answered "No," and they were required to determine action items to address those issues. The plans became process improvement action plans at the project level.

We anticipated how the project managers might react, and we anticipated that the change to the new processes might be seen as an unmanageable disruption. Project managers might say that they did not have time to do this. So the SEPG members acted as extra resources, another pair of hands, to help support the project managers during the transition. For example, rather than let a project manager struggle with creating an initial working document, the SEPG would gather the necessary information from the project manager and create the initial working document. In this way the managers learned faster—by example—and felt supported rather than left to struggle on their own. This approach made adoption of the processes easier for them.

An important aspect of the project notebooks was the way they physically reflected the progress being made. The notebook contents were fairly thin at the start, but each week we saw the notebooks grow thicker and thicker. Some project managers had to split the contents into two notebooks. They found it much easier to get their hands on information when they needed it. Anyone who had a question about the project knew right where to look. Because the information was organized, it saved time and frustration.

At first, many project managers were skeptical about having to maintain the project notebooks, which were perceived as paperwork and overhead. But with use the project notebooks became a valuable supporting tool. In fact, after a reorganization, one project manager suggested discontinuing the project notebooks, but the other project managers convinced him of their value. They relied on the notebooks to manage their project data and could not imagine running their current projects without them. The project managers also relied on the project notebooks as a guide for gathering and creating information necessary for starting a new project.

Management Feedback

The senior managers on the Steering Committee provided visible support of the processes by giving feedback to the project managers during the adoption stage. The Steering Committee had monthly meetings at which the senior managers reviewed the working documents that were scheduled to be in project notebooks since the previous meeting. Feedback notes from the review discussion were given to the project managers. This written feedback included comments on all projects for all project managers to see. Because positive feedback was given to those leading the way, it reinforced that they were doing what their managers wanted. It sent a clear message that those who were doing it right should continue and that those who were stalling should move forward.

As a side benefit, these reviews turned out to be good vehicles for communication. In reviewing the working documents, the senior managers found some discrepancies in the information. There were things that the senior managers thought the project managers knew about, but they discovered some instances of miscommunication that they otherwise would not have known. These reviews provided the senior managers with the opportunity to correct the issues that surfaced.

Peer Networking

The project managers had the opportunity to support one another as peers at a peer networking meeting facilitated by an SEPG member. During this meeting, the project managers filled out the questionnaire, looked at their progress measurements, and then shared their problems and success stories. As peers facing the same problems, they were able to discuss problems out in the open, work on them together, ask each other questions, and leverage solutions from one another. They also raised issues that senior management needed to address. Throughout the adoption stage, the project managers who had to make the changes were constantly supported by the SEPG, by senior management, and by one another.

CMM Action Planning Workshops

After the project managers met their target milestone to adopt the processes in three months, we expanded the participation in the CMM Level 2 processes by involving the project teams. To educate the project teams about what was being done and to involve them in the practice and improvement of these processes for CMM Level 2, we held CMM action planning workshops for each project team.

These workshops helped project teams relate their experience to the goals of the CMM Key Process Areas and involved them not only in issue identification but also in action planning. These workshops also helped facilitate communication and teamwork among the project team members. The presentation materials are included in Appendix M and on the CD-ROM.

The workshops are a series of four meetings of one hour each. The meetings begin with a warm-up exercise to lighten up the team (you could substitute a different warm-up exercise). Then the facilitator presents a summary of the Key Process Area for the meeting discussion, followed by a summary of the organization's processes that address this Key Process Area. Then the project team divides into small groups of two or three people to develop a list of the issues they see on their project relative to this Key Process Area. They also produce a list of recommended actions to address those issues.

The worksheet has the following questions.

- What issues are specific to this project? What issues need to be addressed for this project to make progress?

- What actions are we going to take to address those issues? What actions are required for us to get from the current state to the desired state?

The ideas are then shared with the entire project team, and additional recommendations are solicited from the group.

When all four meetings are complete, the issues and actions are consolidated on a worksheet and are given to the project manager to work with the project team to prioritize, assign, and complete the actions.

More Rehearsals and Performances

Sometimes the dance is performed only once, but usually there is a longer run of many performances over the season. When there is more than one performance, there is usually a pick-up rehearsal between performances. If something didn't go well in the previous performance, you can be sure to find the dancers in the studio the next day, rehearsing the steps and improving their work so that the next performance goes well.

The dancers consider what worked and what didn't work in the previous performance and what they need to do in the next one. At the pick-up rehearsal, they make a connection between the past and future performances; they make decisions about what to change, and then they rehearse the changes. They might experiment with new steps, or they might simply clean up their technique.

With software process improvement, after a process is adopted and performed the managers and engineers consider what worked and what didn't work in their previous performance and what they need to do in their next performance. They conduct evaluations and analyze improvements using postmortem and risk analysis methods.

What happens if there is no pick-up rehearsal? Bad habits creep into the performance. The dancers' technique is not as sharp, and dancers who have poor memories might even forget the steps. The purpose of the pick-up rehearsal is not only improvement but also prevention: prevention of poor performance overall as well as prevention of injury to the dancers.

By using a combination of postmortem and risk analysis methods, we can keep our performance technique sharp and ensure that people don't forget the steps. This is the work of institutionalizing and internalizing the process.

From Adoption to Institutionalization

Eventually, when enough people are following the process it becomes the new tradition, and people forget that things were ever done a different way. They start to think, "We've always done things this way around here." The process becomes institutionalized and eventually becomes internalized. Institutionalization is easier if you involve people before the process is developed and identify what will help them to absorb and internalize the process. So you are preparing for these final stages from the beginning.

During the planning and as you gain the initial agreement from senior management to pursue the process improvement, think about the benefits: the potential gains that will come as a result of making the process improvement. The benefits are expressed at different levels:

- Benefit to the organization
- Benefit to the project teams
- Benefit to the individuals who perform the process

Then the results of the actual practice of the process can be compared with the expectations of these benefits. If the expectations are not being met, changes can be made to make the process more effective. Be sure to consider personal motivation, because in the end you sell the process to the organization one person at a time. The individuals put the process into practice, because they are the ones who perform it. A process is not institutionalized by proclamation; rather it is institutionalized by practice.

After the Performance

Postmortem evaluation methods examine the past project, looking for what worked well and what did not work well. The postmortem results typically provide an exhaustive list of recommendations for improvement. However, as the urgency of the next project takes priority, fewer resources are available to initiate improvements. The unfortunate result is that recommendations are ignored and the same mistakes are repeated. It is as if we know what is wrong, but we don't take the time to do anything about it. If we don't take time to rehearse, we risk poor performance and individual injury.

If a problem has occurred in the past and if there is no change to the process, the problem is likely to recur in the future. In other words, doing the same thing in the same way is not likely to produce a different result. If a problem has occurred in the past but the situation will be different in the future, the problem might not be as likely to recur, or perhaps the impact might not be very severe. Even though the original problem might indicate the need for a major process change, future circumstances might render the change unnecessary.

Risk analysis methods examine the new project, looking for what could go wrong, and assess the probability and impact of the risks. The risk analysis results provide a prioritized list of risks. These results are addressed through mitigation actions or recommendations for improvement. Identifying risks involves conjecture and prediction. We should be able to use past experience to estimate risks just as we use past experience to predict or estimate future performance for cost and schedule factors.

This is what ties the postmortem process to the risk analysis process.

- Postmortem methods provide the input from past experience.

- Risk analysis methods provide a filter for viewing the past problems in light of future circumstances.

- Future circumstances are the selection criteria for recommendations with respect to initiating change.

In dance, both concepts are applied during the pick-up rehearsal, but in software development I've seen a lack of connection between the postmortem and risk analysis. I've seen postmortems treated as an activity that captures the past but doesn't connect to the future, looking backward but not forward. The exhaustive list of recommendations is ignored. I've seen risk analysis treated as an activity that doesn't connect to the past, because everyone thinks, "This is a new project, and it's going to be different this time." In this case, looking forward but not backward, some of the most critical risks could be missed. Once the connection is made, you can make the right improvements with the right timing.

Postmortem and Risk Analysis Techniques

A simple method for connecting postmortem and risk analysis techniques is to rephrase each issue from the postmortem results as something that might occur in the future. This method converts a past problem into a potential problem, a risk to be analyzed. Reviewing these risks can also stimulate the discovery of new risks that were not considered before. Table 7.2 shows examples of converting the description of a past problem into a risk statement.

Some formalized methods for risk management are available in the *Continuous Risk Management Guidebook* from SEI. However, at Unisys our organization's culture is not so formal, so we developed some simple, less formal methods that seem to better fit how we do business.

In actual use, depending on the project scope and the needs of the project team members, we select from among the following postmortem methods. We choose the method that best suits our needs at the time. Some of the factors we consider when selecting a technique are shown in Table 7.3. When considered as a series, these methods illustrate the development of increasing repeatability and discipline, leading to a foundation for continuous optimization.

Here are the postmortem and risk analysis techniques:

- Simple postmortem method
- Structured meeting postmortem method
- Software process assessment postmortem method
- Risk analysis method using postmortem findings

Table 7.2   Converting postmortem issues into risk analysis risk statements.

Postmortem Issue	Restated as Risk Analysis Issue
Feature implementation took longer than the available time.	Feature implementation might take longer than the available time, and that might cause a schedule delay.
Interdependency commitments were assumed or changed without everyone being informed.	Interdependency commitments might be assumed or might change without everyone being informed, and that might result in interface defects.
Early prototype exposure for graphical user interfaces was canceled because of lack of time.	Early prototype exposure for graphical user interfaces (which could uncover problems earlier) might be canceled because of lack of time, and that might adversely affect the effectiveness of the user interface.

Table 7.3   Selecting a technique.

Factor	Questions	Options
How	How will the information be collected and disseminated?	• Surveys • Meetings • Interviews
When	How much time do you have?	• 15 minutes to an hour by survey • 1–2 hours in a meeting • 1 hour per participant by interview
	How much preparation and follow-up activity is involved?	• Up to 8 hours preparing to collect information and consolidating a report of the results

Simple Postmortem Method

This method (see Table 7.4) is the most flexible and least structured. It does not require very much effort or lengthy instructions. It is a simple survey of the participants to collect their opinions:

*   What are your issues relative to the project?
*   What are your recommendations of what should be done to address the issues?

Table 7.4   Simple postmortem method.

Factor	Need	Selections for This Technique
How	Confidentiality Flexibility Minimal interaction	• Survey
When	Participation at different times Minimal time	• 15 minutes to an hour by survey • Up to 8 hours preparing to collect information and consolidating a report of the results

The steps are as follows.

1. Collect the issues.

2. Categorize and clarify the issues.

3. Collect the recommendations.

4. Report the results.

Typically, one person acts as the facilitator, who solicits, collects, and reports the issues and recommendations of all involved parties. The facilitator solicits issues, collects the input, and categorizes the issues in a preliminary report. The facilitator then sends the report to all involved parties for clarification, perhaps also holding a discussion meeting. Once the issues have been clarified, the facilitator requests recommendations and collects the input. The facilitator consolidates the issues and recommendations in a final report of the postmortem results.

Structured Meeting Postmortem Method

This method (see Table 7.5) provides a standard meeting agenda and a standard report format, leading to a consistent and repeatable postmortem process. It provides a structure that project team members can use to organize their thoughts regarding their experience on the project. The meetings take from one to two hours. It typically takes two meetings to work through the agenda, and the break between meetings gives people time to think about their recommendations. The report is almost a direct capture of the meeting notes, and this minimizes the facilitator's effort.

Here is the postmortem meeting agenda.

1. Timeline chart of major events and activities. The facilitator puts the project start date at the top of the chart and the end date at the bottom, and together the participants discuss the occurrence of major events and activities to add to the chart. This chart provides a common frame of reference for the discussion.

2. Discussion areas. Each participant identifies the most important area to discuss.

3. What worked and what did not work. Considering each discussion area one at a time and using the brainstorming discussion technique, participants take turns identifying

Table 7.5   Structured meeting postmortem method.

Factor	Need	Selections for This Technique
How	More structure Maximum interaction	• Meeting
When	All participants at the same time Minimal report effort	• 1–2 hours in a meeting • Up to 8 hours preparing to collect information and consolidating a report of the results

one thing that worked well (positive) and one thing that did not work well (negative) until all the ideas have been expressed.

4. Major strengths and weaknesses. Review each list for the items that stand out by comparison. Identify the major strengths from the lists of what worked well and identify the major weaknesses from the list of what did not work well.

5. Recommendations. Using all the postmortem data, participants develop recommendations.

Instead of waiting until the end to discuss recommendations for all topics, some groups find it easier to combine agenda items 3 and 5, discussing what worked and what did not work and the recommendations in a single topic. Others prefer to cover all topics and look for recurring themes at the end.

The report template is included in Appendix N and on the CD-ROM.

Software Process Postmortem Method

This method (see Table 7.6) involves a series of questions that categorize the areas for process evaluation. The participants answer the questions, and the facilitator analyzes and combines the answers in the postmortem report. The answers can be gathered at a meeting or by individual interviews. My experience has been that the interviews take 30–60 minutes each. This method focuses on the details of the software process. It takes more time than the other methods, but the results are more precise. The facilitator analyzes the responses to the questions and separates the results into activity statements and evaluation statements. This analysis makes the report easy to read and makes it easy to find information when the report is reviewed. The steps are as follows.

1. Distribute the questions and schedule meetings or interviews.

2. Collect the answers to the questions at meetings or interviews.

3. Reorganize the responses according to the format of the postmortem report.

4. Distribute the draft postmortem report to participants for comments and validation.

5. Complete and distribute the final postmortem report.

Table 7.6 Software process postmortem method.

Factor	Need	Selections for This Technique
How	Structured approach, balance of confidentiality and interaction, more precision and analysis of results	• Interviews
When	Participation at different times	• 1 hour per participant by interview • Up to 8 hours for preparing to collect information and consolidating a report of the results

The questions were developed in relationship to the CMM Key Process Areas from a project-level perspective. The questions are shown in Figure 7.6, in Appendix N, and on the CD-ROM, so you can use these questions or change them to meet your needs. The report template is also included in Appendix N and on the CD-ROM.

Risk Analysis Method using Postmortem Findings

The postmortem evaluation results will be useful when analyzed from the perspective of future risks to current and future projects. This method connects the postmortem results to risk analysis and includes data gathering and analysis for each risk. The steps are as follows.

1. Collect issue statements (use any postmortem technique).
2. Convert the issue statements to risk statements for a Risk Analysis Survey form.
3. Collect ratings of the probability and impact of each risk.
4. Analyze the data to identify the priority risk ranking.
5. Select the top-priority risks, make recommendations for improvement, and assign mitigation actions.

Figure 7.7 provides an example of the format for the Risk Analysis Survey with three risk statements that were derived from postmortem issues.

The priority ratings for the probability and impact of each risk can follow whatever priority scheme makes sense for the group. It could be a simple rating of major or minor; high, medium, or low; or a rating from 0 to 10. In one case, we used a 0 to 10 rating with the following instructions:

> Rate from 0 to 10 the probability and severity of the risk occurring, where a rating of 0 means it can't happen or it has no impact, lower numbers indicate low

---

Software Process Postmortem Questions:
Please consider these 14 questions to assess the process used on this project, and, in contrast to prior practices, what was better and/or what was worse?

1. Communication and Information
What was done to ensure communication and definition of the project (internally, with interdependencies, with marketing and clients)?

2. Software Life Cycle
What was the overall sequence of events or milestones for the project?

3. Program Statement and Requirements
How did you know "what was in and what was out" for requirements and features?
If requirements changed, how was this communicated?

Figure 7.6 Software process postmortem questions.

4. Requirements Verification and Release Criteria
How did you determine a requirement was met or a feature was complete?
How did you determine the product was ready?

5. Design and Design Verification
How were product functions designed (prototype? formal designs?)?
How were the designs evaluated (reviews? inspections? approvals?)?
How were design errors identified and removed?

6. Code and Code Verification
How was the software code developed?
How was code evaluated, and how were defects discovered (inspections? unit test?)?
If multiple evaluation methods were used, what selection criteria were used?
How were software defects identified and removed?

7. Integration and Qualification
How was the software integrated and tested?
How was the testing planned?
How were defects handled (tracked to closure? deciding who gets to fix the defect?)?

8. Preparation for Support
How were regression tests developed and maintained?
How were test results reported and to whom?
What information is available to those who will maintain or interface with the product in the future (training materials? designs? documentation?)?

9. Packaging and Delivery
How was user documentation designed and integrated with the product?
How was the product packaged and delivered for release?

10. Project Planning and Tracking
How were the project tasks determined, estimated, communicated, and tracked?
How was status evaluated (such as "schedule on track" or "behind schedule")?
How were impacts of changes accounted for on the project (for example, requirements changes, defect levels, staffing changes)?

11. Configuration Management
How was the code managed and controlled for version control (tracking the "current levels" or current files or patches? patch reviews or approvals?) (source code control tools?)?

12. Project Coordination and Risk Management
How were commitments managed and communicated?
How were risks managed and communicated?
How were corrective actions identified, planned, and tracked?
How were project activities reviewed or verified?
How were the needs for tools or training identified, planned, and tracked?

13. Process Effectiveness
What was most effective about doing the project in this way?
What would you recommend to keep or change about the process based on this?

14. Process Risk
What was most risky about doing the project in this way?
What would you recommend to keep or change about the process based on this?

Figure 7.6   *Continued.*

ID#	Risk Description	Probability	Impact
1	Feature implementation might take longer than the available time, and that might cause a schedule delay.		
2	Interdependency commitments might be assumed or might change without everyone being informed, and that might result in interface defects.		
3	Early prototype exposure for graphical user interfaces (that could uncover problems earlier) might be canceled because of lack of time, and that might adversely affect the effectiveness of the user interface.		

Figure 7.7   Example of a format for a Risk Analysis Survey.

probability or low severity, and higher numbers indicate high probability or high severity. Indicate "DK" if you don't know or don't have enough information.

Then for data analysis, we calculated risk exposure by multiplying the probability and impact numbers. We calculated the averages for the responses to each item to get the overall priority rating by risk exposure. We set up a spreadsheet for data entry and automatic calculation of individual responses and average risk exposure. The final report for the risk analysis provides a prioritized list of each risk ranked by average risk exposure from highest to lowest. This prioritized list serves as the input to risk management activities and associated software process improvements. This approach places the focus on the top-priority risks.

Risk Management Tracking and Control

For on-going risk management tracking and control, the project managers can maintain an active list of risk management data in their project meeting minutes to be reviewed and revised at project team status meetings. This active list of risks includes the information shown in Table 7.7.

At project team meetings, the project manager and the team review the status of the risks and mitigation actions. If the risk is no longer likely to occur, it is closed. If the risk still exists, the team may revise the probability and impact ratings based on current circumstances. If the risk occurs—that is, if it happens to change from a potential problem into a real problem—the risk is moved from the list and an issue is added to an action items list for assignment of actions to address the problem. In addition to tracking the known risks, the team also considers new risks that can be identified and added to the list.

Table 7.7   Example format for risk tracking and control.

Item Identifier	Risk Description	Probability	Impact	Mitigation Action(s)	Assigned To
Track the item by date and number.	Describe risk conditions in terms of the chance that it might happen and the cost incurred if it does. Classify the item as a risk only if you have a choice to influence the outcome.	Rate the probability or likelihood that the event will occur (high, medium, low).	Rate the impact of the loss if the event were to occur (high, medium, low).	Describe what is being done or will be done to reduce the probability and/or impact of the risk.	Track who is involved in the mitigation action.

Begin with the End in Mind

When you're looking ahead to a new project, consider how the project's software process will be evaluated at the end. This approach gives you insight about how to prepare to make the project successful right from the beginning. For example, you can change the perspective from evaluating past performance to determining future performance. The following example (see Figure 7.8) demonstrates this idea using the questions from the software process postmortem method (see Figure 7.6) and converting the questions to help a new project team define how it wants to do its work. These questions are also provided in Appendix N and on the CD-ROM.

New Project Questions:
Please consider these 14 questions to determine the process to use on this project.

1. Communication and Information
What will be done to ensure communication and definition of the project (internally, with interdependencies, with marketing and clients)?

2. Software Life Cycle
What will be the overall sequence of events or milestones for the project?

3. Program Statement and Requirements
How will you know "what is in and what is out" for requirements and features?
If requirements change, how will this be communicated?

4. Requirements Verification and Release Criteria
How will you determine a requirement has been met or a feature has been completed?
How will you determine the product is ready?

5. Design and Design Verification
How will product functions be designed (prototype? formal designs?)?
How will the designs be evaluated (reviews? inspections? approvals?)?
How will design errors be identified and removed?

continues to next page

Figure 7.8   Preparing for a new project.

6. Code and Code Verification

How will the software code be developed?

How will the code be evaluated, and how will defects be discovered (inspections? unit test?)?

If multiple evaluation methods are used, what selection criteria will be used?

How will software defects be identified and removed?

7. Integration and Qualification

How will the software be integrated and tested?

How will the testing be planned?

How will defects be handled (tracked to closure? deciding who gets to fix the defect?)?

8. Preparation for Support

How will regression tests be developed and maintained?

How will test results be reported and to whom?

What information will be available to those who will maintain or interface with the product in the future (training materials? designs? documentation?)?

9. Packaging and Delivery

How will user documentation be designed and integrated with the product?

How will the product be packaged and delivered for release?

10. Project Planning and Tracking

How will the project tasks be determined, estimated, communicated, and tracked?

How will status be evaluated (such as "schedule on track" or "behind schedule")?

How will impacts of changes be accounted for on the project (for example, requirements changes, defect levels, staffing changes)?

11. Configuration Management

How will the code be managed and controlled for version control (tracking the "current levels" or current files or patches? patch reviews or approvals?) (source code control tools?)?

12. Project Coordination and Risk Management

How will commitments be managed and communicated?

How will risks be managed and communicated?

How will corrective actions be identified, planned, and tracked?

How will project activities be reviewed or verified?

How will the needs for tools or training be identified, planned, and tracked?

13. Process Effectiveness

What do you expect to be most effective about doing the project in this way?

14. Process Risk

What do you expect to be most risky about doing the project in this way?

Figure 7.8   *Continued.*

8

Perspectives:
Dancing Together and Creating
a Better Performance

"Treat people as if they were what they ought to be, and you will help them to become what they are capable of being."

—Johann Wolfgang von Goethe

Partnership and Teamwork

Once a dancer learns how to dance with correct technique and musicality, she must learn to dance with a partner. Many of the steps are the same, but some of the techniques are different. Some techniques that are always correct for solo dancing are always incorrect when she is dancing with a partner, because the adjustments for positioning and balance are different. She cannot dance in exactly the same way but must now rely on her partner for support and balance. She must rely on her partner to catch her when he tosses her in the air. When she is supported by a partner, she can balance in a single position longer, turn for more revolutions, leap higher in the air, and perform steps that she could never do alone.

Dancing with a partner takes a high degree of trust, because the risk of injury is greater to both partners if either dancer is not attentive or does not understand how to do the steps. For example, the man is expected to lift the woman with his hands on her waist, just below the rib cage. If instead he lifts her on the rib cage, he could easily crack one of her ribs. (Yes, I am speaking from experience; it's a very painful injury.) Conversely, the woman is expected to carry her own weight and jump, inhaling and holding her breath and holding her muscles, so that she is as light as possible when the man lifts her. The timing of the jump and lift must be synchronized; if her jump is not timed with his lifting, she becomes dead weight and causes muscle strain or injury to his back. Because of the risk of injury to both partners, each one has the responsibility to be attentive and responsive as they rehearse and perform the steps. As they live up to this responsibility, they develop a relationship of rapport and trust.

In a partnership of two dancers, if one partner is off-balance or off timing, the other partner can make adjustments to keep the movements synchronized. With just two dancers, the audience is not likely to notice that anything was off, but the audience is very likely to notice with several dancers dancing together. The corps de ballet typically consists of 16 to 24 women dancing together to create synchronized movements in various formations and patterns. Although there is less risk of personal injury, there is more risk of imperfect results. If one dancer is slightly off-balance, off timing, or even slightly out of line with the other women, the audience notices her errors. Errors in movement are not easy to hide. But the teamwork of an excellent corps de ballet involves the same kind of trust and responsibility as in partnerships. Each dancer adjusts to the other dancers near her so that the entire team appears to be working flawlessly. As they dance, they keep one another in line.

The dancers adjust and respond to one another during the performance. Continuous optimization during the performance is ultimately experienced as teamwork. All the dancers are working together as they rehearsed, although things may not go exactly the same as in rehearsal. It is not unusual for the performance to be even better than in rehearsal, because there is a greater focus of concentration on the moment of performance. And all the dancers work toward a common goal, which started as the vision of the artistic directors and choreographers and became the dancers' own vision during the process of rehearsal and performance.

Partnerships and Teamwork in the Software Process

The partnerships in the software process are often described as customer-supplier relationships. The suppliers support the customers to enhance their performance so that they can do much more than could ever be done alone. A relationship of rapport and trust develops as customers and suppliers assume the responsibility to protect one another from risks and become attentive and responsive to one another's needs. Most of the problems with customer-supplier relationships occur when one partner is not attentive or does not understand how to do the steps. Fortunately, the resolution is to pay more attention and learn the steps. Everyone wants to work with capable partners, and capable partners develop themselves with attentiveness and learning.

In the software process, teamwork is experienced at the project level and the organizational level. Project teams perform the process steps together for their project. If the team members act like individuals performing solos, they are likely to run into one another and step on one another's toes. But if they act like a polished corps de ballet, they respond to one another's needs and keep one another in line. Each project team performs together with other project teams within an organization. If the teams act as if they were individual projects, they probably won't learn anything from one another. However, if each project team were to act as if it were a member of an organizational team, each team could learn from the others by sharing knowledge and information. When the teams learn from one another, the team members can learn and improve their performance, too.

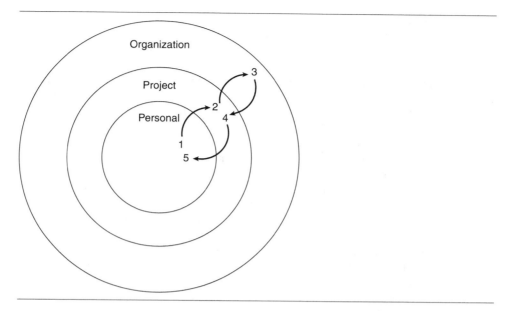

Figure 8.1   The capability maturity levels in relationship to the movement of knowledge and awareness.

Levels of Shared Knowledge and Awareness

Moving up the capability maturity scale involves increasing knowledge and awareness in an outward direction, from the personal level to the project level to the organizational level, and then taking that knowledge back inward to serve the project and the individual (see Figure 8.1). The increasing levels of knowledge and awareness form a pattern of outward movement followed by an inward movement.

- Level 1 to Level 2 moves outward.
- Level 2 to Level 3 moves outward.
- Level 3 to Level 4 moves inward.
- Level 4 to Level 5 moves inward.
- Level 1 to Level 2 moves from personal to project knowledge.
- Level 2 to Level 3 moves from project to organizational knowledge.
- Level 3 to Level 4 moves from organizational to project knowledge.
- Level 4 to Level 5 moves from project to personal knowledge.

The steps begin and end with the personal knowledge of the individual who is ready to learn, experience, and learn from experience.

Notice that Level 1 and Level 5 are figuratively at the same place but at a different point in time, like a dance that begins in one corner of the stage and ends in that same position in that same corner of the stage. Level 1 is ad hoc, and things are constantly changing. Level 5 is continuously optimizing, and things are constantly changing. The difference is in the degree of control, awareness, and knowledge and in the precision of the steps and the responsiveness to the needs of the people and the business environment. To provide that precision and responsiveness, people develop awareness and knowledge at the project and organizational levels and bring that knowledge back into the project and personal levels to be used for decision making and improvement.

Also notice that this model is circular. Because each movement provides a foundation for the next movement and because the system is a closed loop, improvements in one part of the system will enable improvements in other parts. This image provides a different perspective on the use of the CMM.

Typically, people look at the CMM as a linear model and begin by focusing exclusively on the Key Process Areas for Level 2. This means focusing on moving awareness and knowledge from the personal level to the project level. The next step would be to focus exclusively on Level 3, moving from the project level to the organizational level. As many organizations have discovered, the work to achieve Level 3 is very different from the work to achieve Level 2. Some organizations that easily reach Level 2 find it much more difficult to work on Level 3 issues. If the approach for Level 2 allows each project team to do the work independently, there will be more conflicts to resolve for Level 3, which calls for interdependence. If the organization lacks cross-project and cross-functional communication, this work will be much harder, because it requires a culture change. Working independently, individuals can improve only so much; working independently, project teams can improve only so much. The major issues caused by problems with interdependencies, such as miscommunication or lack of communication between projects and functions, cannot be addressed with an independent project approach.

On the other hand, some organizations have approached Level 2 with an organizational perspective and have satisfied most or all of the goals for Level 3. If the approach to software process improvement on the Key Processes for Level 2 calls for people to work together and if it generates more communication between projects and functions—thereby building an organizational foundation for process definition, assessment, and training— then the transition to Level 3 will not be as difficult. The energy is already moving in the right direction.

With the circular nature of this model, the statement in the CMM that each level provides a foundation for the next still holds true. Furthermore, each level in the circular system provides a foundation for every other level, whether higher or lower in the numbering scheme. Higher-level practices provide foundational support for lower-level practices, too.

The Key Process Areas for Level 4 and 5 can be used to bootstrap the entire continuous improvement system. People can gain project knowledge by gathering data for a project and comparing it with data for other projects within the organization. This approach moves awareness and knowledge from the organization level to the project level, as in Level 4. The disciplined approaches for defect prevention, technology change, and process change in Level 5 involve learning and change at the personal level but with more-effective and consistently applied techniques.

Choreographing Steps for More than One Person

When you are choreographing steps for more than one person, your vision is broader. A choreographer can perform the steps that she creates for a solo, but steps for more than one person cannot be performed by one person. If you are choreographing for yourself, you don't have to deal with relationships between you and other people. As the number of people increase, the number of relationships increase, and the relationships become even more complex. It can be difficult to stay focused on the vision and to manage the details of the steps without making them so intricate that the dancers cannot perform them. The steps must work for the dancers or else the choreography will not be performed well.

The same thing applies to choreographing software process improvement. These are the common pitfalls.

- Complexity: If it's too complex, it never gets completed.
- Quantity: If there's too much to do, it never gets completed.
- Diversity: If there are too many opinions, it never gets accepted.
- Usability: If it's not useful, it never gets accepted.

Table 8.1 shows some of the things to keep in mind to help you simplify the choreography and avoid the pitfalls.

Table 8.1   Common pitfalls.

Pitfalls	What to Check	What to Do
Complexity	Relationships	Combine similar issues and look for relationships between them.
	Details	Oversimplify to get started, and add more details later if necessary. Keep the solution as simple as possible.
Quantity	Scope	Reduce the scope. Tackle a subset first and defer the rest for later.
	Trivia	Eliminate the trivial things that take so much effort that too little effort is left for more important things.
Diversity	Perspectives	Find a common, higher-level perspective when opposing opinions are like two sides of the same coin, amounting to the same thing from two different perspectives.
	Relevance	Remember the problem you are trying to solve. Avoid trying to resolve opposing opinions that are valid but not relevant to the goal at hand. Defer these issues.
Usability	Practicality	If it doesn't make sense, change it. If it isn't useful and effective, change it.

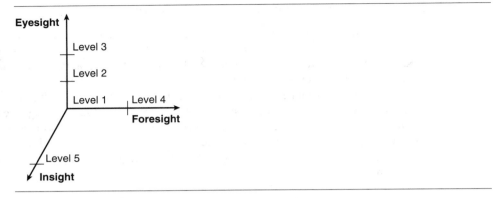

Figure 8.2   Eyesight, foresight, and insight. Capability maturity moves along three dimensions instead of just one.

The choreographer attempts to transform complexity and quantity into simplicity and transform diversity into consensus. When the steps are simple and sensible, it isn't hard for the dancers to learn the steps and perform them well.

The Three-Dimensional Perspective

Moving from lower levels of capability maturity to higher levels can be depicted as a growing awareness of several potential capacities, or several different dimensions. The dance stage allows for movement in a three-dimensional space: up and down, forward and backward, and side to side. Consider aligning the maturity levels along three different dimensions, where each dimension represents progress from the point of origin (representing lack of clarity and lack of precision) toward increasing degrees of clarity and precision. The dimensions can be defined as follows.

- Eyesight: the ability to observe (to identify status and progress).
- Foresight: the ability to aim (to aim or direct to targets or goals).
- Insight: the ability to improve (to take corrective actions, to learn, and to change).

This concept is illustrated in Figure 8.2.

The Relationships between These Dimensions

The lower maturity level key practices focus on improvement along the eyesight axis: improving the ability to observe status and progress. If you can't see what you're doing, you can't improve your results or your ability to predict results. So it seems logical that the first step would be to improve the ability to observe. But that is not enough to reach a continuously optimizing capability; it's necessary but insufficient. In ballet, the first steps that are taught are *plié* and *relevé*: a bend of your knees and a rising on your toes. You can work on these up and down movements until you can perform them perfectly, but that's not all there is to dancing. You must learn how to move in the other dimensions at the same time. A *glissade* is a gliding step. You start by bending your knees, and as your knees straighten, you make a gliding step to the side while at the same time rising. Then you close your feet together into the finishing position bending the knees again and simultaneously bringing your arms forward with your hands in front of your body. It is one step, but the movement uses all three dimensions.

Software process improvement steps also use all three dimensions, and progress toward learning how to continuously improve is hindered when you place attention on one dimension at the exclusion of the others. If you work on improving your eyesight and pay no attention to improving your foresight, you might become very good at seeing how far away you are from hitting your targets. If you work on improving your eyesight and pay no attention to improving your insight, you can become very good at seeing how right you are as you do the wrong things.

And how effective is it to work on improving your eyesight without the aid of optical technologies such as glasses, contact lenses, or laser surgery? How long can you squint before you determine that squinting is not very effective or long-lasting? When you have squinted long enough without seeing any improvement, will you give up and decide that it isn't possible to improve your eyesight? If you don't have any awareness of optical technologies, you might think it impossible. In software process improvement, the technologies of Level 4 and Level 5 are based on foresight and insight, and they can help improve the ability to observe. Perhaps the appropriate prescription to improve eyesight is to bootstrap lower-level maturity improvements by using higher-level maturity techniques.

Can you imagine setting a goal of "20/20 vision by the end of the year" and expecting it to happen without the aid of optical technologies? And yet in our industry, we typically set such goals even when experienced people tell us that such goals do not work. The path to continuous optimization is not a straight-line, step-by-step, "follow the instructions for success" kind of activity. It is not a one-dimensional path of doing one-dimensional activities. But successful techniques can be learned and applied. As with choreography, you need to understand the overall vision, the techniques for good performance, and the people who must perform the steps.

Reconceptualizing the levels in three dimensions can open up the possibilities for many paths to reach continuous optimization. I envision a three-dimensional spiral as the normative path described by the CMM (see Figure 8.3). The path from one capability maturity level to the next level crosses all three planes. The movement from one level to the next level uses the techniques from all of the levels.

Development and Discovery

For many years we have approached software process improvement as a development task. We developed processes to help the organization achieve higher maturity levels. We developed processes just as we developed software, and we thought that by developing the right

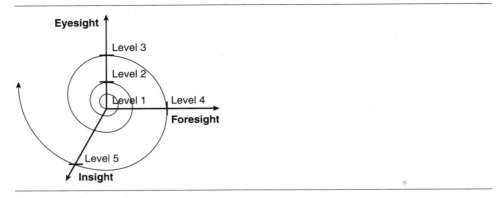

Figure 8.3   Making progress by improving the ability to observe, to aim, and to learn. The improvement path must cut through all three dimensions.

processes, the organization would develop capability maturity. The assumption was that an organization that showed only low-level capabilities lacked higher-level capabilities. But rather than assume that we start from a place of insufficiency, we could assume that we start from a place of potential and promise.

If an organization includes capable people who have some degree of foresight and insight, the organization does not lack these higher-level capabilities. They exist in the people who make up the organization. Perhaps the people in the organization have not yet discovered these capabilities or have not yet determined how best to use them, but the organization does not lack higher-level capabilities. So the approach would not be to develop capabilities that are assumed not to exist but rather to discover these capabilities from a place of potential and promise.

Changing this basic assumption implies that there is another way to approach software process improvement: Help people become what they are capable of being. Rather than operate on the organization as if it were software, we treat the organization as a group of people who are trying to learn how to interact with one another in the most effective way possible. This approach changes the way we perceive the software process.

- Processes are a tool that helps the organization observe its behavior.

- Process development is a method that helps a group discover how it interacts now and how it wants to interact in the future.

- Process development in and of itself does not lead to higher capability maturity. Rather, the organization's increasing self-awareness leads to higher capability maturity.

Because the software industry tends to be oriented toward development, sometimes we tend to downplay the significance of discovery. But progress in software process improvement and capability maturity occurs most effectively with a combination of development and discovery. Working on developing the key practices helps lead us to discoveries about the organization, and these discoveries lead us to developing the key practices.

Metrics and Measures

Metrics and measures are tools that help develop foresight, which in turn helps increase the self-awareness of the organization. But as we use metrics and measures we must also discover the relationship between the people and the data. Metrics and measures give you the information that you need to make informed decisions. However, information gathered for one purpose and used for another purpose is no longer information but misinformation. You cannot make an informed decision without information, but neither can you make an informed decision with misinformation. People do not want decisions to be made based on metrics that are not measuring the right thing for the right reason. People do not want decisions that affect their lives to be made based on misinformation. One bad experience with the use or abuse of metrics can result in a lack of trust, causing people to become reluctant to provide accurate information.

In choreography for the corps de ballet, we make the visual image pleasing to the eye by placing the dancers in line according to height. This is a use of the right metric for the right reason. If the dancers were placed in line according to weight, it wouldn't make sense. But in some cases the wrong metric is used, and dancers become reluctant to provide accurate information. For example, there is a false assumption that younger dancers who have not yet developed bad habits are more likely to be trainable in the style and culture of a dance company. I was once at a dance audition where the artistic director asked a dancer, "How old are you?" Her response was "How old would you like me to be?" Dancers want to be chosen based on talent and ability and not discounted because of age or anything else that has nothing to do with performance.

Software engineers also do not want their performance to be discounted because of irrelevant metrics. There is a false assumption that the software engineer who produces more lines of code is a better performer than one who produces fewer lines of code. This assumption has led to innumerable debates about how to count a line of code. Do you include comments? Do you count non-executable lines? The arguments about what constitutes one line of code are indicative of the reluctance to provide information that could be used for the wrong reason. The right reason to use the line of code count is to improve our foresight—our ability to predict schedule and effort by understanding the relationship between the actual number of lines of code written and the time and effort spent.

Defect Prevention and Change Management

Defect prevention and change management are tools that help us discover insight by using information about our history to make changes that will result in more-effective results now and in the future. By discovering insights about the way we do business, we have the opportunity to develop improved practices. We anticipate what might occur, and we take steps to prevent the results that we don't want and ensure the results that we do want. But we need not wait until we reach Level 4 before we begin to anticipate what might occur. We need not wait until we reach Level 5 before we begin to take steps to prevent the results we don't want and ensure the results we do want. We can take such steps as soon as we begin applying the CMM. This means that preparation for continuous optimization of Level 5 begins at the beginning. It begins at Level 1 and continues throughout every level.

Discovering Level 5 within Each Level of the CMM

A microcosm of Level 5 is expressed within each one of the CMM levels as common features. Common features are attributes that indicate whether the implementation of a key practice is effectively part of the organization's culture (as a repeatable and lasting practice that is part of the normal way to do business). Each of the Key Process Area goals and key practices is aligned with one of the five common features. Table 8.2 describes the common features and the questions that help us gain insight into the organization's software process.

Table 8.2   Common features.

Common Feature	Questions	Key Practices Category Description (Adapted from the CMM)	Visible Aspects
Commitment to perform	What results do we want to achieve?	Actions the organization must take to ensure that the process is established and will endure	Organizational policies and leadership
Ability to perform	Can we achieve those results?	Preconditions that must exist in the project or organization to implement the software process competently	Resources, organizational structures, and training
Activities performed	What do we have to do to achieve the results?	Activities, roles, and procedures necessary to implement a Key Process Area	Plans and procedures, performing the work, tracking it, and taking corrective actions as necessary
Measurement and analysis	What are the current results in comparison to the desired results?	Basic measurements that are necessary to determine process status and used to control and improve the process	Examples of measurements that could be taken
Verifying implementation	How will we know we have achieved the results?	Steps to ensure that the activities are performed in compliance with the established process	Reviews and audits by management and software quality assurance

Mapping the Common Features to a Level 5 System

In Chapter 3, I described what the ideal image of a Level 5 continuously optimizing system would look like. The common features can be mapped to this image, as shown in Table 8.3 and Figure 8.4.

Every level contains the image of Level 5. As we learn to implement the Key Process Areas for each level, these experiences teach us how to perform at Level 5. As we learn how to improve, we are developing our ability to learn, change, and improve, so essentially we are behaving as a Level 5 organization even at Level 1. A beginning dancer starts by learning new steps. A professional dancer continues to learn new steps throughout her career. Continuous learning and continuous optimization for dancers starts at the beginning with the first step. It is the same for software process improvement.

Table 8.3   Mapping the common features to the Level 5 components.

Level 5 Components	Common Features
Standards	Commitment to perform
Preparation	Ability to perform
Activity and results	Activities performed
Results and evaluation	Measurement and analysis
Evaluation	Verifying implementation

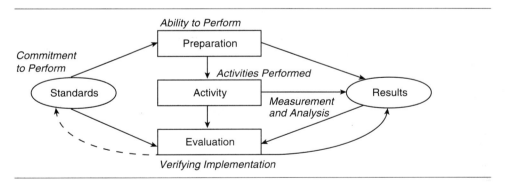

Figure 8.4   Mapping the common features to the image of a Level 5 system.

Mapping the Common Features to a Three-Dimensional Perspective

Looking at the common features from a three-dimensional perspective, we can see a correlation to eyesight, foresight, and insight. This correlation is based on the perspective of the questions that represent those common features.

I put the text of Table 8.4 in this pattern to show how the order of the common features in the CMM moves in a circle starting from insight to foresight, moving to eyesight, moving back to foresight, and then revisiting insight at a new point in time. The results we want to achieve may change over time, and the pattern is repeated whenever we want to achieve a different result. But notice how this pattern starts with a focus on insight and not eyesight. Notice how the progressions of Level 2 through Level 5 start with a focus on eyesight and not insight. Why do some organizations have more difficulty than others in achieving Level 2? I think that those who have an easier time start with insight, and those who have a harder time start with an exclusive focus on Level 2, an exclusive focus on eyesight. This applies to dancers, too. Those who have an easier time learning the steps have insight and understanding about how their bodies move, and those who have a harder time are those who try to imitate what they see without really understanding how their bodies move. But once they "get it," they learn new steps much faster.

Combining the Models

The three dimensions of eyesight, foresight, and insight exist within each component of the Level 5 continuously optimizing system. The order of the movement from one dimension to the next one appears to shift dynamically. Sometimes the movement appears to be happening simultaneously, but technically there is a sequence, and moving out of sequence

Table 8.4   The common features mapped to three dimensions.

	Insight	Foresight	Eyesight
Commitment to perform	What results do we want to achieve?		
Ability to perform		Can we achieve those results?	
Activities performed			What do we have to do to achieve the results?
Measurement and analysis			What are the current results, and how do they compare with the desired results?
Verifying implementation		How will we know we have achieved the results?	

Table 8.5 Movement of the components through each dimension.

Level 5 Component	Dimension	Action
Preparation	Insight	Set the vision, the perspective for the desired state, and the desired results.
	Foresight	Set the strategy, the perspective for the possibilities, and the feasibility of achieving the results.
	Eyesight	Set the tactics, the perspective for action, and the activities and the results.
Activity and results	Foresight	Determine how to measure the gap between the current state and the desired state.
	Eyesight	Measure the gap between the current state and the desired state.
	Insight	Determine what activities in the current state will bring about the desired state.
Evaluation	Eyesight	Determine the current results of the current state.
	Insight	Compare the current results of the current state with the vision of the desired state.
	Foresight	Evaluate the probability of achieving the desired results and make appropriate adjustments.
Standards	Eyesight	Determine what adjustments to the standards might improve performance.
	Foresight	Evaluate the impact of change: the positive and negative possibilities.
	Insight	Determine what must happen to make the change effective.

can cause problems with the dynamics of the system. Such problems cause awkward performance of the steps. What we want is a natural coordination of the movements so that the performance of the steps appears to be natural and becomes natural with practice (see Table 8.5).

Getting Out of the Box

Think of each level of capability maturity as a three-dimensional box; the edge of the box represents the satisfaction of all Key Process Areas for that level and each previous level. At the outer edge of Level 5, all goals for all Key Process Areas for all five maturity levels are satisfied (see Figure 8.5). Once the organization has reached Level 5, it has the capability to "get out of the box." The spiral path in the CMM is one of the paths, but there are many other paths that lead out of the box (see Figure 8.6). There are as many paths as there are people, projects, and organizations, past, present, and future.

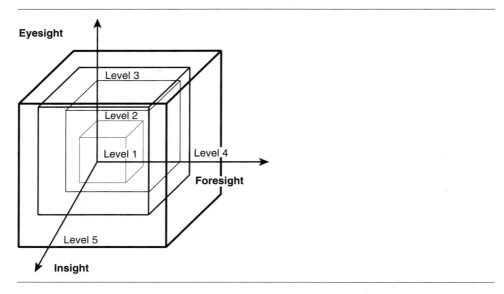

Figure 8.5   The maturity level boxes. Each box represents the satisfaction of the Key Process Area goals for each successive level. The ultimate improvement goal is to get out of the box.

Encouraging Words

Oliver Wendell Holmes said, "The great thing in this world is not so much where we are, but in what direction we are moving." The effects of capability maturity improvement can be like growth spurts. You don't notice any results for a long time, and then suddenly you notice a big difference. As young dancers go through growth spurts, they often experience a sudden lack of coordination because of the changes in their muscles and bones. Typically, turning and jumping steps become awkward and uncoordinated until dancers relearn the techniques and readjust to the changes in their bodies. It seems that every time an organization goes through a reorganization and the organizational muscles change, there is a sudden lack of coordination because of all the changes. The steps become awkward until people relearn the techniques for running the business and readjust to the changes in the organization.

The effects of capability maturity improvement are difficult to see, because external and internal changes are involved. When you find that you have been working hard for a long time to reach the next maturity level and the outward signs show that you are not yet at that next level, it is easy to get discouraged. It's tempting to stop trying, but that's the surest way to ensure that you won't get there. I get through this difficult time by reflecting on how far we really have come, even if there is no maturity level label to mark the progress we have made. I remind myself, "Where we are is where we are. The important thing is

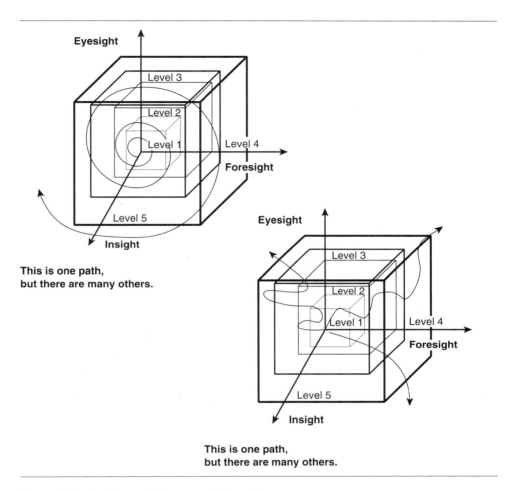

Figure 8.6   Getting out of the maturity level boxes.

that we continue to work at improving. As long as we continue to improve, we won't be where we are for very long." I must encourage myself first, or I won't be any good at encouraging others to improve.

The important thing is not so much where we are but in what direction we are moving and whether we are making progress at the rate we want to move. The direction for software process improvement and for continuous optimization is circular. It is an infinite loop—continuously processing, always practicing, always learning. It is preparation, activities, results, evaluation, standards, and preparation again. It is insight, foresight, and eyesight, in many combinations, over and over again. It is an outward journey followed by an inward journey, and during the journey we are changed. Our experience as well as our learning from experience changes us.

With continuous optimization, there is no last step. Projects and improvement activities are completed, but after the activities are finished there is one more step.

- Evaluate what worked and what did not work.

Then there is one more step.

- Discover why this activity worked or did not work.

Then there is one more step.

- Determine what to do better next time.

And then new projects and new improvement activities begin. There is always one more step, and the results get better one step at a time.

Some people seem to learn more from the experience than others, and some of us change more dramatically than others, but we are all changed nonetheless. Sometimes we internalize the lessons quickly and do not realize that we have learned something, but we are nonetheless changed. Sometimes we do not realize how much progress we are making. We might not be aware of the learning and changing as they occur, but we can reflect and we will see progress if we practice looking not only with our eyesight but also with foresight and insight.

The maturity level labels that delineate progress are arbitrary but necessary guideposts for those who need to see milestones along the way. The labels are helpful to those who need to measure progress and to those who need to become aware of the progress they are making. But even though the guideposts mark the path, they are not the path or the journey. There are many paths between the guideposts, but it is the same journey for all of us. It is a journey that leads from the point of origin to the freedom to work in a creative discipline with the capability of reaching toward our full human potential.

Appendix

A

Assumptions Worksheet

Culture can be defined as a pattern of shared basic assumptions that the people in an organization have learned as they have solved the problems of relating to the outside world and of learning to work together. These assumptions lead to solutions that work well enough to be considered valid, so the organization considers the assumptions to be valid. These assumptions are taught to new members as the correct way to think, feel, and behave in relation to those problems.

Culture change can be defined as a change in the pattern of shared basic assumptions or an expansion to include new shared basic assumptions that lead to improvements.

The following worksheet provides a method for examining an organization's assumptions in relationship to some of the assumptions underlying the key practices of the CMM. Where these desired assumptions are considered valid and are reflected in the organization's practices, we can expect to find a strength relative to the CMM practices. Where these desired assumptions are not reflected, perhaps some overriding assumptions are being reflected instead, and we can expect to find a weakness relative to the CMM practices.

Use the worksheet to capture and compare the current assumptions and the desired assumptions. In this way, you can identify a gap that needs to be closed by changing an assumption or expanding the pattern of assumptions to include the desired assumptions in addition to the existing assumptions.

Assumptions Worksheet

Consider each assumption in relationship to your organization.
Is this assumption considered valid in your organization,
and do the practices in your organization reflect this assumption?
(Ratings: 1 = Not at all valid, 2 = Somewhat valid, 3 = Completely valid and reflected in practice)
If not, what overriding assumptions affect the activities and practices in your organization?

Assumption	Description	Valid? (1,2,3)	Overriding Assumptions
Assumption 1	Engineering discipline is required to build quality into products of large size and complexity.		
Assumption 2	One person can't track all the details, and error detection is more probable when the work is examined by more than one person.		
Assumption 3	Our success is dependent on other groups and customers.		
Assumption 4	The organization uses process definition to transmit the culture's quality values.		
Assumption 5	The projects use process definition to incorporate the culture's quality values.		
Assumption 6	Process makes a difference in the quality of the activities and the quality of the products.		
Assumption 7	Surviving in a business world that is constantly changing requires constant adaptation and learning.		

Assumptions Worksheet: Hypothetical Composite Example

Consider each assumption in relationship to your organization.
Is this assumption considered valid in your organization,
and do the practices in your organization reflect this assumption?
(Ratings: 1 = Not at all valid, 2 = Somewhat valid, 3 = Completely valid and reflected in practice)
If not, what overriding assumptions affect the activities and practices in your organization?

Assumption	Description	Valid? (1,2,3)	Overriding Assumptions
Assumption 1	Engineering discipline is required to build quality into products of large size and complexity.	2	Discipline always interferes with creativity. Just build it as fast as you can. We can test quality into the product.
Assumption 2	One person can't track all the details, and error detection is more probable when the work is examined by more than one person.	2	Our people are so good at what they do that they don't need to have their work inspected.
Assumption 3	Our success is dependent on other groups and customers.	1	Managing requirements is a waste of time, because the requirements change too frequently. The customers don't really know what they want, so it would be a waste of time to discuss it with them. We know what we are doing, but our other interdependent groups never tell us what they are doing, so we don't know whether we can meet the schedule.
Assumption 4	The organization uses process definition to transmit the culture's quality values.	2	If we define one common process and get everyone to follow it, it will guarantee the quality of the product.
Assumption 5	The projects use process definition to incorporate the culture's quality values.	1	Our project is different. The process doesn't apply to us. The overhead will kill the project.
Assumption 6	Process makes a difference in the quality of the activities and the quality of the products.	1	Our people are so good at what they do that they can do it without a process. We don't have enough time and resources to follow the defined process.
Assumption 7	Surviving in a business world that is constantly changing requires constant adaptation and learning.	2	We always hire qualified people, so we don't need any training. The schedule is fixed, the resources are fixed, the features are fixed, and we don't have any choice. Therefore, the quality level is also fixed.

Appendix

B

CMM Overview Workshop

This workshop provides an opportunity for people to reflect on the relationship between their actual experience and the expectations given by the Key Process Areas in the CMM. This method was developed as a follow-up to an assessment, but it can be used at any time. When used with the management team, this method helps to set realistic expectations about what is done currently and what needs to be done. When used with a project team, this method also fosters communication and teamwork of the project team members.

The facilitator presents an overview of the CMM and a summary of the Key Process Areas. Then the participants discuss what they do today that fits the purpose and scope of the Key Process Area as well as the issues they see relative to meeting the goals of the Key Process Area. The ideas are captured and reviewed to identify recommended actions to address those issues.

CMM Overview Workshop

SEI's Vision:
To bring engineering discipline to the development and
maintenance of software products

Desired Result:
Higher quality – better products for a better price
Predictability – function/quality, on time, within budget

Methodology to Achieve that Desired Result:

1. Identify Current State:
Know your current
Capability Maturity Level

2. Identify Desired State:
Understand the description
of the next level

3. Reduce the Gap:
Plan, implement, and institutionalize
the key practices of the next level.
Repeat until continuous optimization is part of the culture.

CMM Workshop Agenda
Workshop Format: Exchange of Information
Presentation of Information & Request for Opinions and Feedback

1. CMM Maturity Levels
   Test Your Knowledge
   Increase Your Knowledge

2. CMM Level 2 Key Process Areas
   What do we do now that meets the goals?
   In your opinion, what issues remain?

3. Comparison of Level 2 and Level 3
   Basic Differences
   CMM Level 3 Key Process Areas

Part 1

The CMM Maturity Levels

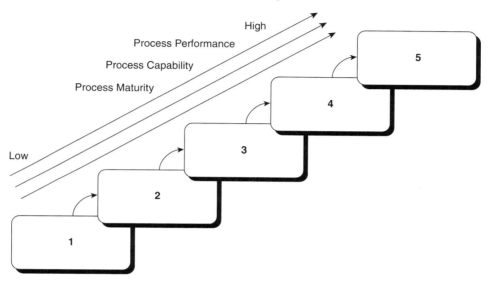

What is the CMM?

- **Concept:** The application of process management and quality improvement concepts to software development and maintenance

- **Model:** A model for organizational improvement

- **Guidelines:** A guide for evolving toward a culture of engineering excellence

- **Basis for Measurement:** The underlying structure for reliable and consistent software process assessments, software capability evaluations, and interim profiles

Maturity Levels: Framework for Process Improvement

- **Based on Continuous Process Improvement:** Based on many small, evolutionary steps rather than revolutionary innovations.

- **Plateau:** A maturity level is a well-defined evolutionary plateau toward achieving a mature software process.

- **Foundation:** Each maturity level provides a layer in the foundation for continuous process improvement.

- **Priority Order:** The levels also help an organization prioritize its improvement efforts.

A Foundation, Not a Destination

- The optimizing level (Level 5) is not the destination of process management.
- The destination is better products for a better price: economic survival.
- The optimizing level is a foundation for building an ever-improving capability.

Maturity Model Inspirations

- **Process management concepts**
  - Crosby
  - Deming
  - Juran
  - etc.

- **Experience**
  - 30 years of similar software problems
  - commonly known software problems
  - solutions exist

- **Application of common sense engineering**

Process Management and the CMM in Context

Process Management	Human Resources	Technical Assets	Customer-Supplier Relationships

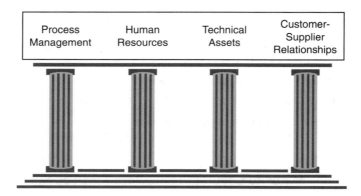

CMM and Business Context

- The CMM is an application of Total Quality Management principles to software engineering.
- Emphasis should be on customer satisfaction.
- The result should be higher-quality software products produced by more-competitive companies.

Common Points in the Quality Movement

- Enabling quality improvement is a management responsibility.
- Quality improvement focuses on fixing the process, not the people.
- Quality improvement must be measured.
- Rewards and incentives are necessary to establish and maintain an improvement effort.
- Quality improvement is a continuous process.

The Five Levels of Software Process Maturity

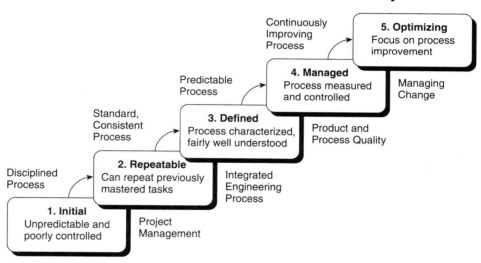

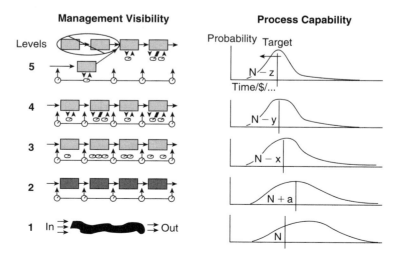

Levels/Process Categories	Management	Organizational	Engineering
5 Optimizing		Technology Change Management	
		Process Change Management	Defect Prevention
4 Managed	Quantitative Software Management		Software Quality Management
3 Defined	Integrated Software Management Intergroup Coordination	Organization Process Focus Organization Process Definition Training Program	Software Product Engineering Peer Reviews
2 Repeatable	Requirements Management Software Project Planning Software Project Tracking and Oversight Software Subcontract Management Software Quality Assurance Software Configuration Management		
1 Initial	Ad Hoc Processes		

Level 1: Just do it.

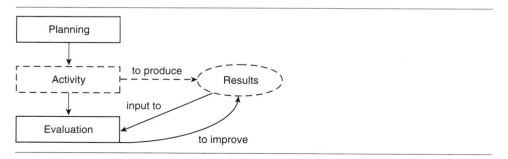

Level 2: Think before you act, and think after you act, just to make sure you did it right.

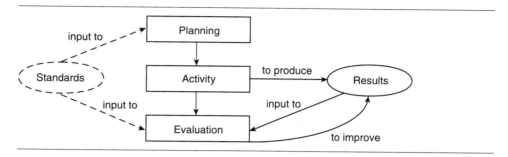

Level 3: Use your lessons learned.

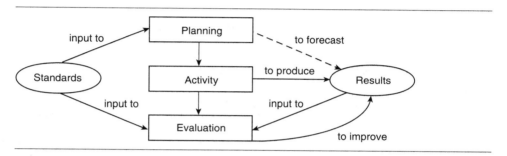

Level 4: Predict the results you need and expect and then create opportunities to get those results.

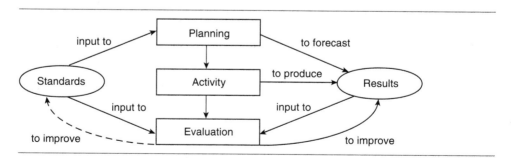

Level 5: Create lessons learned, and use lessons learned to create *more* lessons learned, and use *more* lessons learned to create *even more* lessons learned, and use *even more* lessons learned to create . . . etc.

Level 1—Initial

Activities Performed by the Organization	**Activities Performed by the Projects**	**Resulting Process Capability**
Organization lacks sound management practices	During a crisis, projects abandon planned procedures	Software Process Capability is **unpredictable** because the process is constantly changed or modified as the work progresses (i.e., the process is ad hoc)
Good software engineering practices are undermined by ineffective planning and reaction-driven commitment systems	Even a strong software engineering process cannot overcome the instability created by the absence of sound management practices	Few stable processes in evidence

Level 2—Repeatable

Activities Performed by the Organization	**Activities Performed by the Projects**	**Resulting Process Capability**
Establishes software project management policies and procedures	Make realistic project commitments based on previous project results and current project requirements	Software Process Capability is **disciplined** because project planning and tracking is stable and earlier successes can be repeated
Institutionalizes effective project management processes which allow new projects to repeat successful practices developed on earlier projects, although the specific project's processes may differ	Track software costs, schedules, and functionality to identify problems meeting commitments	Project process is under the effective control of a project management system, following realistic plans
	Control requirements and work products and assure project standards are followed	

Level 3 — Defined

Activities Performed by the Organization

Documents the organization's standard process for developing and maintaining software

Integrates project management and software engineering processes; exploits effective software engineering practices

Provides process support (SEPG) and training program to ensure skills development

Activities Performed by the Projects

Projects tailor the organization's standard software process to develop their own defined software process for the project

Because the software process is well defined, management has good insight into technical progress on all projects

Resulting Process Capability

Software Process Capability is **standard and consistent** because both software engineering and management activities are stable and repeatable

Cost, schedule, and functionality are under control, and software quality is tracked

Level 4 — Managed

Activities Performed by the Organization

Sets quantitative quality goals for both software products and processes

Measures productivity and quality for important software process activities across all projects as part of an organizational measurement program

Provides a foundation for quantitative evaluation

Activities Performed by the Projects

Projects achieve control over their products and processes by narrowing the variation in their process performance to fall within acceptable quantitative boundaries

The risks involved in moving up the learning curve of a new application domain are known and carefully managed

Resulting Process Capability

Software Process Capability is **predictable** because the process is measured and operates within measurable limits

Allows for predictive trends in process and quality within quantitative bounds and allows for corrective action when limits are exceeded

Level 5—Optimizing

Activities Performed by the Organization

Entire organization is focused on continuous process improvement with the goal of defect prevention

Data is used for cost-benefit analysis of new technology and new process changes

Innovations in software engineering practices are transferred to the entire organization

Activities Performed by the Projects

Project teams analyze defects and determine their causes

Project teams evaluate processes to prevent known types of defects from recurring

Resulting Process Capability

Software Process Capability is **continuously improving** because the organization continuously improves the range of capability and process performance of projects

Improvement occurs both by incremental advancement of existing process and by innovations using new technologies and methods

Understanding the Repeatable and Defined Levels (2 & 3)

- **To achieve Level 2, management must focus on its own processes** to achieve a disciplined software process and establish a leadership position.

- **Level 2 provides the foundation for Level 3,** because the focus is on management acting to improve its processes before tackling technical and organizational issues at Level 3.

- Processes may differ between projects in a Level 2 organization; the **organizational requirement for achieving Level 2** is that there are **policies that guide the projects** in establishing the appropriate management processes.

- **Documented procedures provide the foundation** for consistent processes that can be institutionalized across the organization, with training and assurance.

- **Level 3 builds on this project management foundation** by defining, integrating, and documenting the entire software process.

The CMM Structure

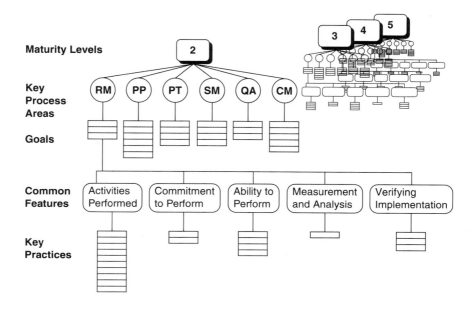

Maturity Levels

Key Process Areas

Goals

Common Features

Key Practices

Common Features: Factors in Implementation and Institutionalization

- **Activities Performed: Implementation**
  Are effective activities performed to satisfy the goals?

- **Commitment to Perform: Institutionalization**
  Are the activities supported by the organization through documented policies, processes, or procedures?

- **Ability to Perform: Institutionalization**
  Are the activities supported by adequate training and resources?

- **Measurement and Analysis: Institutionalization**
  Are measurements used to determine the status of activities, and can those measurements be used to analyze the process for improvement?

- **Verifying Implementation: Institutionalization**
  Are there processes or mechanisms for verifying that the activities are being performed?

Example Assessment Findings:
Process Improvement

- **FINDING**
  - Senior management is not effectively managing the impact of the process improvement program
    - Rate of process change is unregulated
    - Effects of process changes are not measured
    - Improvement efforts are spent on less-critical processes at the expense of key management processes

- **CONSEQUENCES**
  - Pace of process change appears overwhelming
  - Impact of process changes on schedule cannot be determined
  - Environment for developing software remains unstable

Part 2

CMM Level 2 Key Process Areas

Requirements Management	Software Quality Assurance
Software Project Planning	Software Configuration Management
Software Project Tracking and Oversight	Software Subcontract Management

Level 2 Key Process Area:
Requirements Management

Purpose

To establish a common understanding between the customer and the software project of the customer's requirements that will be addressed by the software project

Scope

Involves establishing and maintaining an agreement with the customer on the requirements for the software project

Agreement is the basis for estimating, planning, performing, and tracking the project's software activities

Goals

1. System requirements allocated to software are controlled to establish a baseline for software engineering and management use.
2. Software plans, products, and activities are kept consistent with the system requirements allocated to software.

Example Assessment Findings:
Requirements Management

- **FINDING**
  - Requirements are not sufficiently managed to ensure
    - Adequate definition
    - Thorough analysis
    - Effective change control
    - Usable input for subsequent development steps

- **CONSEQUENCES**
  - Low level of confidence that customer needs are met
  - Design team understanding of requirements is at risk
  - Definition of product content is hard to determine
  - Design and code quality cannot be assured

Brainstorm Exercise for
Requirements Management

What do we do currently that meets the goals for REQUIREMENTS MANAGEMENT?

What issues remain for us to meet the goals and to institutionalize the activities for this KPA?

Level 2 Key Process Area:
Software Project Planning

Purpose

To establish reasonable plans for performing the software engineering and for managing the software project

Scope

Involves:
- developing estimates for the work to be performed
- establishing the necessary commitments
- defining the plan to perform the work

Plan provides the basis for initiating the software effort and managing the work

Goals

1. Software estimates are documented for use in planning and tracking the software project.
2. Software project activities and commitments are planned and documented.
3. Affected groups and individuals agree to their commitments related to the software project.

Example Assessment Findings:
Estimation, Planning, and Commitment Control

- **FINDINGS**
  - Little evidence of formal procedures for estimating project size, cost, and schedule
  - Project plans are not comprehensive
  - Inadequate management review before commitment
    - First-line managers do not have formal approval of schedules
    - Frequently, commitments are not renegotiated when changes occur

- **CONSEQUENCES**
  - Important process tasks are missing from project plans
  - Schedules are unreliable
  - Testing suffers when development schedules slip
  - Resources are overcommitted

Level 2 Key Process Area:
Software Project Tracking and Oversight

Purpose

To provide adequate visibility of progress so that management can take effective actions when performance deviates significantly from the plan

Scope

Involves:

- tracking and reviewing software accomplishments and results against documented estimates, commitments, and plans
- adjusting plans based on actual accomplishments and results

Goals

1. Actual results and performances are tracked against the software plans.
2. Corrective actions are taken and managed to closure when actual results deviate significantly from the software plans.
3. Changes to software commitments are agreed to by the affected groups and individuals.

Example Assessment Findings:
Tracking and Oversight

- **FINDINGS**
  - Project activities are not adequately tracked
  - Product and project interdependencies are insufficiently monitored
  - Inconsistent use of project review procedures
  - Many project plans are not regularly reviewed and updated

- **CONSEQUENCES**
  - Project plans are frequently out-of-date
  - Schedules are often at risk
  - Product content and quality cannot be predicted

Brainstorm Exercise for
Software Project Planning

What do we do currently that meets the goals for PROJECT PLANNING?

What issues remain for us to meet the goals and to institutionalize the activities for this KPA?

Brainstorm Exercise for
Software Project Tracking and Oversight

What do we do currently that meets the goals for PROJECT TRACKING AND OVERSIGHT?	What issues remain for us to meet the goals and to institutionalize the activities for this KPA?

Level 2 Key Process Area:
Software Quality Assurance

Purpose

To provide management with appropriate visibility into the process being used and the products being built

Scope

Involves:
- reviewing and auditing the software products and activities to ensure that they comply with the applicable procedures and standards
- providing the software project and other appropriate managers with the results of those reviews and audits

Goals

1. Software quality assurance activities are planned.
2. Adherence of software products and activities to the applicable standards, procedures, and requirements is verified objectively.
3. Affected groups and individuals are informed of software quality assurance activities and results.
4. Noncompliance issues that cannot be resolved within the software project are addressed by senior management.

Example Assessment Findings:
Software Quality Assurance

- **FINDING**
  - There is minimal product and process assurance
    - Process effectiveness is seldom evaluated
    - Process metrics are often nonexistent or used ineffectively

- **CONSEQUENCES**
  - Data is suspect
  - Confidence in process compliance is limited
  - Process improvement cannot be quantified
  - Product quality is uncertain
  - Management is unable to make informed decisions

Level 2 Key Process Area:
Software Configuration Management

Purpose

To establish and maintain the integrity of the products of the software project throughout the software life cycle

Scope

Involves:
- identifying configuration items/units
- systematically controlling changes
- maintaining integrity and traceability of the configuration throughout the software life cycle

Goals

1. Software configuration management activities are planned.
2. Selected software work products are identified, controlled, and available.
3. Changes to identified software work products are controlled.
4. Affected groups and individuals are informed of the status and content of software baselines.

Level 2 Key Process Area:
Software Subcontract Management

Purpose

To select qualified software subcontractors and manage them effectively

Scope

Involves:
- selecting a software subcontractor
- establishing commitments with the subcontractor
- tracking and reviewing the subcontractor's performance and results

Goals

1. The prime contractor selects qualified software subcontractors.
2. The prime contractor and the software subcontractor agree to their commitments to each other.
3. The prime contractor and the software subcontractor maintain ongoing communications.
4. The prime contractor tracks the software subcontractor's actual results and performances against its commitments.

Brainstorm Exercise for
Software Quality Assurance

What do we do currently that meets the goals for SOFTWARE QUALITY ASSURANCE?

What issues remain for us to meet the goals and to institutionalize the activities for this KPA?

Brainstorm Exercise for
Software Configuration Management

What do we do currently that meets the goals for CONFIGURATION MANAGEMENT?

What issues remain for us to meet the goals and to institutionalize the activities for this KPA?

Brainstorm Exercise for
Software Subcontract Management

What do we do currently that meets the goals for SUBCONTRACT MANAGEMENT?

What issues remain for us to meet the goals and to institutionalize the activities for this KPA?

Part 3

Comparison of Level 2 and Level 3

- Difference between Level 1 and Level 2:
  Level 1 is ad hoc and occasionally chaotic; few processes are defined and success depends on individual effort.

- Level 2: Basic project management processes are established to track cost, schedule, and functionality.

- Level 2: The necessary process *discipline* is in place to *repeat* earlier successes on projects with similar applications.

- Difference between Level 2 and Level 3:
  Level 3 encompasses integrated and standardized management and engineering activities; projects tailor the organization's standard software process to meet their needs.

CMM Level 3 Key Process Areas

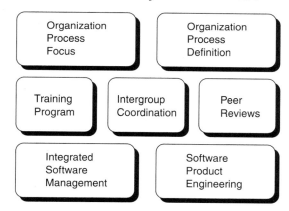

Level 3 Key Process Area: Organization Process Focus

Purpose

To establish the organizational responsibility for software process activities that improve the organization's overall software process capability

Scope

Involves:
- developing and maintaining an understanding of organization and project software processes
- coordinating the activities to assess, develop, maintain, and improve these processes

Goals

1. Software process development and improvement activities are coordinated across the organization.
2. The strengths and weaknesses of the software processes used are identified relative to a process standard.
3. Organization-level process development and improvement activities are planned.

Level 3 Key Process Area:
Organization Process Definition

Purpose

To develop and maintain a usable set of software process assets that improve process performance and provide a basis for cumulative, long-term benefits

Scope

Involves developing and maintaining the organization's standard software process and related process assets

The organization's standard software process describes the fundamental elements that each project incorporates and tailors to fit the project

Goals

1. A standard software process for the organization is developed and maintained.
2. Information related to the use of the organization's standard software process by the software projects is collected, reviewed, and made available.

Level 3 Key Process Area:
Integrated Software Management

Purpose

To integrate the project's software engineering and management activities into a coherent, defined software process tailored from the organization's software process assets

Scope

Involves:
- developing the project's defined software process by tailoring the organization's standard software process
- managing the software project according to this defined software process

Goals

1. The project's defined software process is a tailored version of the organization's standard software process.
2. The project is planned and managed according to the project's defined software process.

Level 3 Key Process Area:
Software Product Engineering

Purpose

To consistently perform a well-defined engineering process that integrates all the software engineering activities to produce correct, consistent software products effectively and efficiently

Scope

Involves performing the engineering tasks to build and maintain the software using appropriate tools and methods

Includes requirements analysis, design, coding, integration, and testing

Goals

1. The software engineering tasks are defined, integrated, and consistently performed to produce the software.
2. Software work products are kept consistent with one another.

Level 3 Key Process Area:
Intergroup Coordination

Purpose

To establish a means for the software engineering group to participate actively with the other engineering groups so the project is better able to satisfy the customer's needs effectively and efficiently

Scope

Involves the disciplined interaction and coordination of the project engineering groups with each other to address system-level requirements, objectives, and plans

Goals

1. The customer's requirements are agreed to by all affected groups.
2. The commitments between the engineering groups are agreed to by the affected groups.
3. The engineering groups identify, track, and resolve intergroup issues.

Level 3 Key Process Area:
Training Program

Purpose

To develop the skills and knowledge of individuals so they can perform their roles effectively and efficiently

Scope

Involves:
- identifying the training needs of the organization, the projects, and individuals
- developing and/or procuring training to address these needs

Goals

1. Training activities are planned.
2. Training for developing the skills and knowledge needed to perform software management and technical roles is provided.
3. Individuals in the software engineering group and software-related groups receive the training necessary to perform their roles.

Level 3 Key Process Area:
Peer Reviews

Purpose

To remove defects from the software work products early and efficiently

To develop a better understanding of the software work products and of defects that might be prevented

Scope

Involves a methodical examination of work products by the producer's peers to identify defects and areas where changes are needed

Goals

1. Peer review activities are planned.
2. Defects in the software work products are identified and removed.

Acknowledgments:

Much of this material is directly obtained from:
Carnegie-Mellon University/Software Engineering Institute—
CMU/SEI's The Capability Maturity Model: A Tutorial, April 1993
CMU/SEI-93-TR-24 Capability Maturity Model for Software, Version 1.1
CMU/SEI-93-TR-25 Key Practices of the Capability Maturity Model, Version 1.1

Appendix

C

Project Manager Interviews

Using this questionnaire, members of the SEPG personally interview each project manager to give the project manager a chance to reflect on actual practices. The project manager identifies any documents or data that provides evidence of satisfying the question. If there is nothing to satisfy the question, the interviewer asks the project manager to identify the issues and actions that could be taken. The project manager can see what they have in place and what to do to get closer to satisfying the question.

The result of this method is a score of the number of questions answered yes and a list of action items for every question answered no. The SEPG then helps the project managers make progress toward closing the action items as soon as possible. Any issues that are beyond the scope of the project manager's responsibility are raised to senior management for resolution.

A typical use of this technique is to gather questionnaire responses monthly for about three to six months following the introduction of project management processes for Level 2. Monthly progress is shown graphically as the number of questions answered yes.

PROJECT MANAGEMENT QUESTIONNAIRE

Project: _____

Instructions:
- Use one questionnaire per project.
- Gather answers by interviewing each project manager.

Project Response:

Yes	Answer "Yes" if you can identify that this is in place. It helps if you have supporting evidence, such as a requirements document, project plan, or whatever is asked for in the question.
No	Answer "No" if you can identify that something needs to be done to get this in place. It may be an awareness issue, it may be a documentation issue, or it may be an implementation issue, but something is still in the way of being able to say this is in place.
Don't Know	Answer "Don't Know" if you don't have enough information to answer yes or no. Maybe you can think of someone else who would have more information, but you don't feel confident to answer one way or the other at this time.
Not Applicable	Answer "Not Applicable" on the Subcontract Management questions if your project does not include a subcontract.

Organizational Support (Policy/Process/Procedure) and/or Project Explanation
Note the evidence of a *Yes* response, or the issue for a *No* response.
For example, indicate the documented process that is being followed, or describe what the project does to address the question or what must occur before the project can satisfy the question.

- Copy the questions answered *No* or *Don't Know* into the Project Action Plan on the last page.
- Determine what actions are necessary to resolve the issues, and assign and track the issues.

PROJECT MANAGEMENT QUESTIONNAIRE

Project: _____

Level 2—Requirements Management

#	Question	Project Response	Organizational Support (Policy/Process/Procedure) and/or Project Explanation
RM-1	Does this project use documented requirements as a baseline for software engineering and management use?		
RM-2	As the requirements change, does the project make necessary adjustments to project plans, deliverables, and activities?		
RM-3	Does the project follow a written organizational policy for managing requirements?		
RM-4	Are the people in the project who manage requirements trained in the procedures for managing requirements?		
RM-5	Does the project track the status of the requirements management activities with measurements (e.g., total number of requirements changes that are proposed, open, approved, and incorporated into the baseline)?		
RM-6	Are the requirements management activities on the project subject to SQA review?		

PROJECT MANAGEMENT QUESTIONNAIRE

Project: _____

Level 2—Software Project Planning

#	Question	Project Response	Organizational Support (Policy/ Process/Procedure) and/or Project Explanation
PP-1	Are estimates (e.g., size, cost, and schedule) documented for use in planning and tracking the project?		
PP-2	Does the project plan document the activities and the commitments for the project?		
PP-3	Are all affected groups and individuals involved in (provide input to) commitment agreements related to the project?		
PP-4	Does the project follow a written organizational policy for project planning?		
PP-5	Are adequate resources provided for planning the project (e.g., funding and experienced individuals)?		
PP-6	Does the project track the status of the project planning activities with measurements (e.g., completion of milestones for the project planning activities)?		
PP-7	Does the project manager review the project planning activities on both a periodic and an event-driven basis?		

PROJECT MANAGEMENT QUESTIONNAIRE

Project: _____

Level 2—Software Project Tracking and Oversight

#	Question	Project Response	Organizational Support (Policy/ Process/Procedure) and/or Project Explanation
PT-1	Are the project's actual results (e.g., size, cost, and schedule) compared with estimates in the project plans?		
PT-2	Is corrective action taken when actual results differ significantly from the project plans?		
PT-3	Are commitment changes negotiated with all affected groups and individuals?		
PT-4	Does the project follow a written organizational policy for project tracking and project reviews?		
PT-5	Is someone on the project assigned specific responsibilities for project tracking (e.g., effort, schedule, and budget)?		
PT-6	Does the project track the status of the project tracking and reviews with measurements (e.g., total effort expended in performing tracking and review activities)?		
PT-7	Does senior management review the project tracking and review activities and results on a periodic basis (e.g., project performance, open issues, risks, and action items)?		

PROJECT MANAGEMENT QUESTIONNAIRE

Project: _____

Level 2—Software Quality Assurance

#	Question	Project Response	Organizational Support (Policy/Process/Procedure) and/or Project Explanation
QA-1	Are SQA activities planned for the project?		
QA-2	Do SQA activities provide objective verification (independent verification that products and activities adhere to applicable standards, procedures, and requirements)?		
QA-3	Are audit results provided to those who performed the work and to those who are responsible for the work?		
QA-4	Does senior management receive and address issues of noncompliance that are not resolved within the project?		
QA-5	Does the project follow a written organizational policy for implementing SQA activities?		
QA-6	Are adequate resources provided for performing SQA activities (e.g., funding and a designated manager who will receive and act on noncompliance items)?		
QA-7	Does the project track the cost and schedule status of the SQA activities with measurements (e.g., work completed, effort, and funds expended compared to the SQA plan)?		
QA-8	Are SQA activities and results reviewed with senior management on a periodic basis?		

PROJECT MANAGEMENT QUESTIONNAIRE

Project: _____

Level 2—Configuration Management

#	Question	Project Response	Organizational Support (Policy/ Process/Procedure) and/or Project Explanation
CM-1	Are software configuration management activities planned for the project?		
CM-2	Has the project identified the deliverables (in-process specifications, documentation, and software) to be placed under configuration management, and are those items controlled and made available?		
CM-3	Does the project follow a documented procedure to control changes to the deliverables under configuration management?		
CM-4	Are standard reports on software baselines (e.g., content definition, change summary, and status reports) available?		
CM-5	Does the project follow a written organizational policy for implementing software configuration management activities?		
CM-6	Are project personnel trained in the tasks they perform for software configuration management?		
CM-7	Does the project (or organization) track the status of software configuration management activities (e.g., effort and funds expended for software configuration management activities)?		
CM-8	Are periodic audits performed to verify that software baselines conform to the documentation that defines them (to verify that it contains what it says it does)?		

PROJECT MANAGEMENT QUESTIONNAIRE

Project: _____

Level 2—Software Subcontract Management

#	Question	Project Response	Organizational Support (Policy/Process/Procedure) and/or Project Explanation
SM-1	Does the project use a documented procedure for selecting subcontractors based on their ability to perform the work?		
SM-2	Are changes to subcontracts made with the agreement of both the prime contractor and the subcontractor?		
SM-3	Are periodic technical interchanges held with subcontractors?		
SM-4	Are the results and performance of the subcontractor tracked against commitments?		
SM-5	Does the project follow a written organizational policy for managing subcontractors?		
SM-6	Are the people responsible for managing software subcontracts trained in managing subcontracts?		
SM-7	Are measurements used to determine the status of software subcontract management activities (e.g., schedule status with respect to planned delivery dates and effort expended for managing the subcontract)?		
SM-8	Are the software subcontract activities reviewed with the project manager on a periodic and event-driven basis?		

PROJECT MANAGEMENT QUESTIONNAIRE

Project: _____

Level 3—Peer Reviews

#	Question	Project Response	Organizational Support (Policy/ Process/Procedure) and/or Project Explanation
PR-1	Are inspections planned for the project?		
PR-2	Does the project track defects until they are removed (e.g., defects in any deliverables that are identified in inspections)?		
PR-3	Does the project follow a written or-ganizational policy for performing inspections?		
PR-4	Do participants of inspections re-ceive the training required to perform their roles?		
PR-5	Does the project (or organization) track the status of inspection activi-ties (e.g., number performed, effort expended, and number of delivera-bles inspected compared to the plan)?		
PR-6	Are inspection activities and delivera-bles subject to SQA review and audit (e.g., to ensure planned inspections are conducted and follow-up actions are tracked)?		
PR-7	Are inspection activities reviewed with senior management on a peri-odic basis?		

PROJECT MANAGEMENT QUESTIONNAIRE

Project: _____

Project Action Plan
(Replace the questions in this example with the specific questions that were answered *No* or *Don't Know* for this project.)

#	Questions that were answered *No* or *Don't Know*	Action to take to resolve the issues	Assigned to	Due date
PT-3	Are commitment changes negotiated with all affected groups and individuals?			
PT-7	Does senior management review the project tracking and review activities and results on a periodic basis (e.g., project performance, open issues, risks, and action items)?			
QA-7	Does the project track the cost and schedule status of the SQA activities with measurements (e.g., work completed, effort, and funds expended compared to the SQA plan)?			
CM-8	Are periodic audits performed to verify that software baselines conform to the documentation that defines them (to verify that it contains what it says it does)?			

Data Entry

	Yes or N/A				Percent Yes or N/A				
	Feb	Mar	Apr	May		Feb: 82%	Mar: 92%	Apr: 91%	May:97%
Project A	30	43	36	40	Project A	68%	98%	82%	91%
Project B	36	37	37	41	Project B	82%	84%	84%	93%
Project C	34	36	41	43	Project C	77%	82%	93%	98%
Project D	39	41	41	44	Project D	89%	93%	93%	100%
Project E	39	42	44	44	Project E	89%	95%	100%	100%
Project F	39	43	40	44	Project F	89%	98%	91%	100%
Interim Goal					Average	82%	92%	91%	97%
	80%								
Total Questions									
	44								

Results Chart

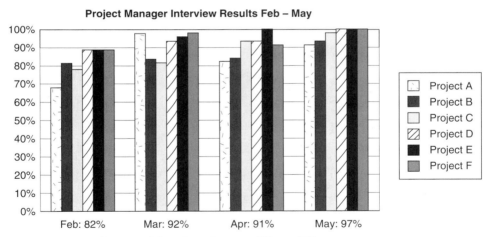

Project Manager Interview Results Feb – May

Legend: Project A, Project B, Project C, Project D, Project E, Project F

Percent of Questions Answered Yes or N/A

Appendix

D

Great Performance Worksheet

This technique is useful after a reorganization to get an idea of what the new management is most interested in for sponsoring improvement initiatives. The SEPG members personally interview representative managers and engineers. These questions are intended to get people to think about what they really want regardless of the limitations. Sometimes people don't say what they really want because they assume that there are limitations that prevent them from getting what they really want. But if we knew what they really want, we might be able to find a way to eliminate the limitations to give them what they really want instead of just what they will settle for.

In our case, setting the expectation that the interviews would take only three minutes time sent an underlying message that we were looking only for the few most important things from their perspective. We were not looking for an exhaustive list of everything we could possibly do for them. We were looking only for what was most important to them, what would make a positive contribution, and what would make a difference. However, you should set your own expectations to take as long as an hour, because some people will find that they have a lot more to say than can be said in three minutes.

Interviewers should follow these steps.

1. Select three key customers (managers or engineers) for separate three-minute interviews.
2. Ask whether they would be willing to give us some information—just some immediate impressions off the top of their heads—to help us determine how to best serve them. We expect it will take only three minutes.

3. If they agree, give them a copy of the worksheet and take notes on another copy. Ask them to answer these questions with whatever comes to mind in any order they want. Note: We are not looking for perfect solutions. We are looking for what it is they want most—their first impressions and impulse reactions. They can say anything, and it doesn't matter whether we agree. We are just capturing the information for consideration.

After the interviews, analyze the information by sorting it into broad categories and looking for recurring themes. Most of the broad categories could be directly related to a Key Process Area from the CMM. Then look for driving actions that could drag other actions along with them. Develop a short list of requirements for the SEPG to initiate improvements to address the few most important needs of the organization.

Great Performance Worksheet

Consider these questions and reply with your first impressions of what you think is most important. Consider answering as if there were no limitations on what could be done.

What is great performance for your clients/customers?
(This means not just meeting their needs, not just mediocrity, but what would be considered great from you?)

What do you want, and what can we do, to provide you with great service?
(This means what would be considered great from us to you?)

What must we do to help you achieve great performance for your clients/customers?
(This means linking the two together. What do you consider to be great from us that would help you achieve what would be considered great from you to your clients/customers?)

Great Performance Worksheet—Sample

Consider these questions and reply with your first impressions of what you think is most important. Consider answering as if there were no limitations on what could be done.

What is great performance for your clients/customers?
(This means not just meeting their needs, not just mediocrity, but what would be considered great from you?)

When the product has a tangible benefit to their business. I'm happy when they want the product to do more than they expected, and when they are pleasantly surprised that it does.

What do you want, and what can we do, to provide you with great service?
(This means what would be considered great from us to you?)

Focusing attention on critical items from a quality standpoint. Clarifying and identifying the key concepts and issues that would aid in our problem solving. Facilitating problem discussions to find solutions.

What must we do to help you achieve great performance for your clients/customers?
(This means linking the two together. What do you consider to be great from us that would help you achieve what would be considered great from you to your clients/customers?)

Requirements analysis and training in how to ask the right questions to get good requirements. Testing and inspections aren't enough to make the product great for our customers. We need to make more improvements at the front end to help us downstream.

Appendix
E

CMM Key Process Area Checklist

This checklist is intended to focus senior management attention on Key Process Areas in relation to business goals.

A typical use for this checklist would be as follows.

1. Review and gather responses to the checklist as part of a quarterly review meeting with senior management.
2. Identify the priorities indicated for areas rating the highest impact and highest urgency.
3. Assign responsibility for investigating specific actions to address issues in those areas.
4. Review the feasibility of the actions and initiate appropriate actions.

Capability Maturity Model (CMM) Key Process Area Checklist

Critical Questions for each Key Process Area:

1. Are we satisfied with our current performance? (Yes or No)
   If not satisfied (No)
   2. What is the negative *impact* on the achievement of our business goals? (H M L)
   3. What is the *urgency* for us to take action to address the relevant issues? (H M L)
      (Next steps: Assign responsibility for investigating specific actions, then review feasibility)

Key Process Area	Purpose	1	2	3
Requirements Management	Establishing and maintaining a *common understanding* between the customer and the project of the *customer's requirements* that will be addressed.	Yes No	H M L	H M L
Software Project Planning	Establishing *reasonable plans* for engineering tasks and for managing the project, developing *estimates,* establishing *commitments,* and defining the plans.	Yes No	H M L	H M L
Software Project Tracking and Oversight	Providing *adequate visibility into actual progress* so that management can *take effective actions* when the project's performance deviates significantly from plan.	Yes No	H M L	H M L
Software Subcontract Management	*Selecting* qualified *subcontractors and managing them* effectively.	Yes No	H M L	H M L
Software Quality Assurance	Providing management with *appropriate visibility through reviews and audits* of products and activities to verify that they comply with applicable procedures.	Yes No	H M L	H M L
Software Configuration Management	Establishing and maintaining the integrity of the products throughout the life cycle, *systematically controlling changes to the configuration.*	Yes No	H M L	H M L

Organization Process Focus	Establishing organizational responsibility for activities to *assess, develop, maintain, and improve processes* that improve the organization's process capability.	Yes No	H M L	H M L
Organization Process Definition	Developing and *maintaining process-related documentation and data* that improve performance across projects and provide a basis for cumulative long-term benefits to the organization.	Yes No	H M L	H M L
Training Program	*Developing the skills and knowledge of individuals* so that they can perform their roles effectively and efficiently, *identifying and procuring needed training.*	Yes No	H M L	H M L

Integrated Software Management	*Integrating the engineering and management activities* into a coherent, defined process, and *managing the project using this defined process.*	Yes No	H M L	H M L
Software Product Engineering	*Consistently performing a well-defined engineering process* that integrates all activities to produce correct, consistent products effectively and efficiently.	Yes No	H M L	H M L
Intergroup Coordination	Establishing *participation with other engineering groups* to establish requirements, plan and manage technical working interfaces, and conduct regular reviews and technical interchanges.	Yes No	H M L	H M L
Peer Reviews	*Removing defects from work products early and efficiently* and, as a side effect, to better understand the products and the defects that might be prevented.	Yes No	H M L	H M L

| Quantitative Process Management | *Controlling the process performance of the project,* identifying the special causes of variation in a measurably stable process, and correcting the circumstances leading to the transient variation. | Yes No | H M L | H M L |
| Software Quality Management | Developing a quantitative understanding of the quality of the project's products and *achieving specific quality goals.* | Yes No | H M L | H M L |

Defect Prevention	Identifying *causes of defects* and *preventing* them from recurring.	Yes No	H M L	H M L
Technology Change Management	*Identifying beneficial new technologies,* tools, methods, and processes and *transferring them into the organization* in an orderly manner.	Yes No	H M L	H M L
Process Change Management	*Continually improving the processes,* incremental improvements, and innovative improvements and providing them to the entire organization.	Yes No	H M L	H M L

Appendix

F

Simple Action Plan

The following template is used to plan and track the action plan details for a specific software process improvement activity. It covers the basic information of who is working on the project, the desired results, the schedule milestones, and issues and risks. You can add other information that you might need as you tailor the template for your organization.

Simple Action Plan

Project or Team Name	
Team Members	
Date Last Revised	

Desired Results (Identify Goals or Objectives)

Description	Source

Schedule Milestones (Activities and Results or Events and Dates)

Description	Original Plan	Current Plan	Actual-Done

Issues and Risks

	Description of Issue or Risk	Actual or Potential Effects	Who is Involved
1.			
2.			
3.			

Appendix

G

Transition Preparation Method Charts

The following charts include the statements of what we have observed in our organization correlated to the stages of transition. You can adapt these statements for your own use by using what you observe in your own organization to tailor this model.

As an informal description, the resulting correlation tables can be used as follows. When you observe a representative statement (question or resistance) in your organization, it indicates a corresponding stage of transition or expresses a corresponding barrier. Then you might use the corresponding leveraging actions to move through the stage of transition. Here are the specific steps for using these charts.

1. Assess the current stage.

- Look at the second column ("The Work") in the first chart and identify the current work. Observe what kind of work or activities are taking place for the change.

- Look at the third column ("Barriers") and identify the representative statement that characterizes what you are observing in the organization relative to the change, and identify the current barriers.

2. Ascertain whether you are making smooth progress or are stuck in a crack or chasm and determine what action to take.

- To accelerate smooth progress, look at the fourth column ("Leveraging Actions") for the corresponding stage, and perform the appropriate actions.

- To recover after progress has slowed or stopped or to start a new stage by anticipating and preventing barriers, look at the second column ("Crossing Criteria") in the second chart. Identify people for each role, and have them fulfill the responsibilities to meet the crossing criteria. Then return to the first chart to continue the work of the next stage, using the leveraging actions.

Transition Preparation Method: Chart 1
Stages, The Work, Barriers, and Leveraging Actions

Stage	The Work	Barriers	Leveraging Actions
Awareness To know about it. *"What is it?"*	Involves training and gathering information	*"What are the Key Process Areas?"* • Lack of knowledge • No perceived need to change	• CMM training • Action Plan Handbook
Understanding To understand how it affects you and your organization. *"What does it mean to me?"* *"What does it mean to us?"*	Involves planning and developing a framework	*"We don't have enough time/ resources for it."* • Resistance to change • Conflicting priorities • Too many changes at once • Resources diverted by other activities • Making unrealistic goals and expectations	• Goals and expectations • Roles/Responsibilities • Framework • Project plans • Change agent • Management support
Definition To define it. *"What do we do?"* *"How do we do it?"*	Involves defining and documenting processes	*"There's no consistent focus."* • Lack of framework • Lack of change management knowledge roles, methods • Lack of focus • Lack of change agent to di-rect/coordinate • Lack of management support	• Implementation approach • Involvement of process users • Constraints for size/effort • Guidelines to meet needs • Planning and tracking to framework • Change agent • Management support
Installation To identify and correct issues by using it. *"Will it work?"*	Involves process pi-lot or preliminary use, postmortems, and updates	*"The problems aren't fixed."* • Lack of monitoring change and issues • Lack of change management knowledge: resistance, spon-sorship, targets • Lack of sustained communi-cation of progress	• Project-level installation • Progress measurement • Proactive monitoring and fa-cilitating to manage transi-tion and resistance
Adoption To adopt it as the new way to do business. *"Are we meeting the goals?"*	Involves active use of process required for all	*"How do we get everyone to use it?"* • Management not creating need for change • Lack of sustained communi-cation of progress • Lack of monitoring	• Share success stories • Share approaches • Compare progress measurements • Address compliance issues
Institutionalization To confirm it as the normal way of doing business. *"Is it good enough?"*	Involves active use of process required for all, with assurance and corrective action	*"Is it working, or do we need to change it?"* • Lack of monitoring • Lack of evaluation activities	• Measure process usage and effectiveness • Capture lessons learned and improvements for next time

Transition Preparation Method: Chart 2
Cracks and Chasms, Crossing Criteria, and Responsibilities

Crack or Chasm	Crossing Criteria	Sponsor Management Responsibilities	Target User Process User Responsibilities	Change Agent SEPG Responsibilities
Understanding Prerequisites to the understanding stage of planning and developing a framework	Defined: • Scope • Deliverables Description • Timeframe	• Scope • Timeframe	• Timeframe Input	• Deliverables Description
Definition Prerequisites to the definition stage of defining and documenting processes	Known: • Current State • Desired State • Roles • Approach • Resource Commitment	• Current State Input • Desired State Input • Roles Input • Resource Commitment	• Current State Input • Desired State Input • Roles Input	• Approach • Desired State Input • Facilitate Agreement on Current State, Desired State, and Roles
Installation Prerequisites to the installation stage of piloting and updating processes	Known: • Roles for Trial Use • Approach for Trial Use • Resource Commitment	• Roles for Trial Use • Resource Commitment	• Roles Input	• Approach for Trial Use
Adoption Prerequisites to the adoption stage of active process use	Obtained: • Management Authorization • User Buy-in • Agreement to Use Process	• Management Authorization • Agreement to Use Process	• User Buy-in • Agreement to Use Process	• Facilitate Agreement
Institutionalization Prerequisites to the institutionalization state of process use with assurance and corrective action	Known: • Approach for Process Assurance • Approach for Corrective Action	• Approach for Corrective Action	• Process Usage • Process Feedback	• Approach for Process Assurance

Appendix
H

Results, Needs, Activities Worksheet

The following worksheet is used for high-level planning and prioritization of improvement activities. The worksheet format helps maintain the alignment of activities and results. Related results, needs, and activities are placed in the same row across the page. If you already have existing improvement activities or a detailed improvement plan, you can use this worksheet to organize the activities or identify flaws in your plan. For example, you might find that you have a high-priority desired result with no activities defined, or you might have an activity defined with no corresponding desired result. This worksheet helps you find and correct these discrepancies in your plans.

The prioritization scheme can consist of these kinds of ratings:

- Major or minor
- High, medium, or low
- Scale of 1 to 5

Those who use the form can decide which scheme is most practical for their use.

The prioritization columns are aligned so that

- Results are prioritized by impact
- Needs are prioritized by urgency
- Activities are prioritized by feasibility

Results, Needs, Activities Worksheet

Results What desired results do we want to achieve? What current result is not meeting desired expectations?	Impact How much improvement can we expect?	Needs What are the current results and how do they compare with the desired results? What do we need to change to affect this result?	Urgency How soon do we need this result to improve?	Activities What do we have to do to achieve the desired results? What tasks do we expect to be done to effect the needed change?	Feasibility Can the tasks be done, and done in time, to get the desired result?

Appendix

I

Is This Project Worthwhile? Worksheet

This worksheet provides a method for examining the questions "What's in it for me?" and "Is this project worthwhile?"

Use these ten questions to help ensure that the people on the project team have a vested interest in the success of the project. The questions help to reveal both the positive and the negative aspects of "What's in it for me?" so that people can see the project from a more balanced perspective. The results of answering these questions might also have an impact on how the project will be performed.

Is This Project Worthwhile?

Consider each question for you personally in relationship to the project or goal for the team.

1. What do you *hope* to *achieve* by doing this project?

2. What do you *hope* to *gain personally* by doing this project?

3. What do *you offer to others* by doing this project?

4. What do *others offer to you* by doing this project?

5. What does *"success" look like* on this project?

6. What *concerns* you about the *success/failure* of this project?

7. What *attracts* you to this project?

8. In what ways might this project *detract from your energies*?

9. In what ways might this project *be of benefit* to another current or future project?

10. Is this project *worthwhile*?

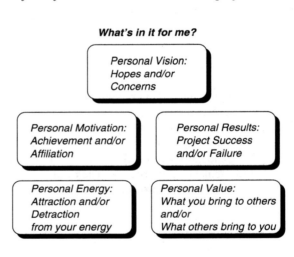

Appendix

J

Sample Processes for Level 2

The following are samples of processes written to address the Key Process Areas of Level 2. These processes represent some early steps toward addressing these Key Process Areas but do not necessarily meet every key practice. The people who collaborated to write the processes defined what they could agree on with the expectation that the processes would be continuously improved. In a sense, we could consider these processes to be a "starter set" having enough information and enough agreement to begin continuous process improvement using the CMM as a guideline.

These samples are not intended to be implemented directly in another organization, but they can be used as a basis for discovering what will work and deciding what can be implemented in your organization.

Project Management Policy

Effective Date:
Authorizing Manager:

Purpose

To provide direction for using these project management processes:

Project Level Processes	Business Unit Level Processes
Requirements Management Process	Commitment Control Process
Project Planning Process	Project Management Review Process
Estimation Process	Software Quality Assurance Process
Project Tracking Process	Project Management Processes Overview

As of the effective date above, these processes are required for use.

As of three months after the effective date above, all quality records for these processes are required to be available.

Scope

Applies to all projects that meet the following criteria:

- The project commitment is external to the business unit and either
- exceeds $20K of departmental resources or
- exceeds 10 elapsed weeks.

Policy

The project management processes form a management system directed toward meeting software delivery commitments. These processes are required to ensure the following objectives:

Requirements Management

1. The requirements are documented.
2. The requirements are reviewed by managers and affected groups.
3. When requirements change, project plans, deliverables, and activities are also changed.

Software Project Planning

1. The requirements and estimates are the basis of project plans.
2. Commitments are negotiated among the project manager, department manager, director, and managers of affected groups.
3. Interdependencies with other business units are negotiated and documented.
4. Affected groups review project plans and estimates.
5. The director reviews all commitments made external to the business unit.
6. The project plans are documented, managed, and controlled.

Software Project Tracking and Oversight

1. The project plans are the basis for project tracking and are maintained to current status.
2. The project manager is kept informed of the project status and issues.
3. Corrective actions are taken when the project plan is not being achieved, either by adjusting performance or by adjusting the plan.
4. Changes to commitments are renegotiated with all affected parties.

Software Quality Assurance

1. The SQA function is performed on all projects.
2. Those performing SQA activities are independent of the project's management reporting chain.
3. The director and department managers periodically review SQA activities and results.

Software Configuration Management

1. SCM responsibility is explicitly assigned.
2. SCM is implemented throughout the life cycle.
3. SCM is implemented for all externally deliverable software products, designated internal software deliverables, and designated support tools (such as compilers).
4. The projects have the ability to store the elements under SCM.
5. The software baselines and SCM activities are audited on a periodic basis.

Project Management Processes Overview

Effective Date:
Authorizing Manager:

Purpose

This document describes how the project management processes work together to form a management system directed toward meeting software delivery commitments.

Introduction

This document describes an overview of how to follow the project management processes defined in this organization. These project management processes work together to form a management system directed toward meeting software delivery commitments.

Everyone in the organization has a role to perform in these processes.

Role	Description/Responsibilities
Director	Head of the business unit Approval authority for all commitments outside the business unit
Department Manager	Directly reports to the director Owner of departmental resources with approval authority for delegation of resources to support committed programs
Project Manager	Usually a section manager or team leader assigned to a project Responsible for project management activities, such as planning and tracking
Project Team Member	Software engineer or writer assigned to a project Responsible for completing project tasks, providing input to plans, and providing status
Program Manager	Staff to director Responsible for tracking commitments and providing the marketing perspective
SEPG	Responsible for support of software quality assurance and process improvement activities

These processes are designed to satisfy the SEI Capability Maturity Model goals for Level 2. See *Relationship to SEI CMM v1.1*, for a description of how these project management processes address Level 2 process maturity.

Scope

The scope covers the processes necessary to support software delivery commitments at the business unit level. These processes include organization-wide processes at the business unit level and project-based processes at the project level.

Project Level Processes	Business Unit Level Processes
Requirements Management Process	Commitment Control Process
Project Planning Process	Project Management Review Process
Estimation Process	Software Quality Assurance Process
Project Tracking Process	Project Management Processes Overview

Conceptual Flow

The objective of this management system is to establish basic project management processes to track size, cost, schedule, and functionality and to establish the necessary process discipline to repeat delivery within budget, on time, with required functionality and quality, on projects with similar applications. The conceptual flow of these processes is depicted in the following Management System Processes Pyramid.

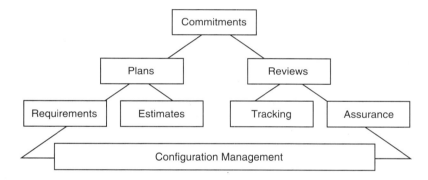

To meet commitments, it is necessary to

- Understand REQUIREMENTS
- ESTIMATE the work
- PLAN the work so that the original commitment is achievable
- Control the COMMITMENT approvals
- TRACK status against the plans
- REVIEW status toward commitments and initiate changes if necessary
- ASSURE product quality and process compliance and initiate corrective action if necessary
- Control CONFIGURATION of deliverables and records

From a top-down view, initial commitments are supported by project plans, which in turn are supported by requirements and estimation activities. After initial commitments are made, commitment status monitoring is supported by reviews, which in turn are supported by tracking and assurance activities.

From a bottom-up view, requirements are gathered and estimates of the work effort are made. The results feed into plans, and the plans receive commitment approval. Then the plans are tracked, and the products and processes are assured. The results feed into reviews, and reviews report status or issues on progress toward commitments.

Throughout, configuration management is applied to prevent loss of important project information such as deliverables and records.

Process Flow

The overall process flow given below shows the interaction and flow between the processes. More details about the process steps can be found in each process document. The overall process begins with a request to the business unit to provide some functionality. This may be indicated by a Program Statement from marketing, a request from another business unit with an interdependency, or a Custom Engineering Request.

1. **Requirements Management Process**
   Definition
   Analysis
   Proposal and Project Planning

The process steps of definition and analysis result in a Requirements Specification. The Requirements Specification is the basis for the proposal and project planning step.

2. **Project Planning Process**
   Initial Planning

Project planning is initiated. If the Requirements Specification is to be addressed by more than one project, the requirements are divided among the projects. The Multiproject Development Plan and Individual Project Plans are started.

3. **Estimation Process**
   Create Estimates
   Review Estimates

Estimates are generated using inputs from the Requirements Specification or Proposal and resource and schedule constraints from project planning.

4. **Project Planning Process**
   Initial Planning

The estimates are incorporated into the plans. The plans are prepared for approval and commitment negotiation.

5. **Commitment Control Process**
   Commitment Negotiation
   Approval Forms
   (Commitment Point)
   Commitment Tracking

The plans and estimates are reviewed and discussed during commitment negotiation. When all parties have agreed, the commitment is made and the approval form is signed. This is the commitment point. Information about the commitment is recorded in the Commitment Change Record, and the product roadmap is updated.

6. Project Tracking Process
Compare Actuals to Plan
Evaluate Status and Performance

The project status is tracked and compared against the plans, and deviations are identified. The impact of the deviation is evaluated to determine whether corrective action is required.

7. Requirements Management Process
Requirements Status Tracking

The status of requirements is tracked to ensure that requirements are addressed and met throughout the development life cycle.

8. Software Quality Assurance Process
Annual SQA Plan
Conduct Audits

Annually, an SQA Plan is prepared with input from the Quality Plans from individual projects. This plan shows the resources and schedule of assurance activities, such as audits. After approval, the plan is performed and the audits are conducted.

9. Project Management Review Process
Status Meetings
Project Reviews
Commitment Reviews

Management review of project status and performance is performed at two levels. Status meetings are held at the project level, and project reviews are held at the business unit level. In addition, commitment reviews are held to review status of all commitments on the product roadmap.

At this point, the process flow is redirected if replanning is needed. If replanning is needed, then do steps 10–13. Otherwise, return to the commitment point to continue the project tracking process and project management review process. If the project is complete, go to the delivery point, step 14.

10. Project Planning Process
(Replanning needed?)
Replanning

Update project plans. If necessary, get input from requirements changes and estimation changes. Prepare a revised plan for approval and commitment negotiation.

11. Requirements Management Process
Requirements Change Control

Perform the requirements change control step if the revised plan involves a change to requirements.

12. Estimation Process
Additional Estimates

Create additional estimates as required from project planning. This may be needed for replanning (requirements change or significant deviation from plan) or for refinement of estimates for the next phase of development.

13. Commitment Control Process
New Commitment Negotiation
(Return to commitment point or go to delivery point)
(Delivery Point)

The updated plans and estimates are reviewed and discussed during commitment negotiation. When all parties are agreed, the new commitment is made and the approval form is signed. This is a new commitment point. Information about the commitment is recorded in the Commitment Change Record, and the product roadmap is updated. From this new commitment point, continue the project tracking process and project management review process against the updated plans. If the project is complete, go to the delivery point, step 14.

14. Project Tracking Process
Postmortem

Shortly after delivery, a postmortem evaluation is held to capture information and lessons learned from the project.

15. Estimation Process
Update Historical Database

The actual performance data is collected, compared against the estimates, and stored in a historical database for use in future project estimation activities.

Process Flow Diagram

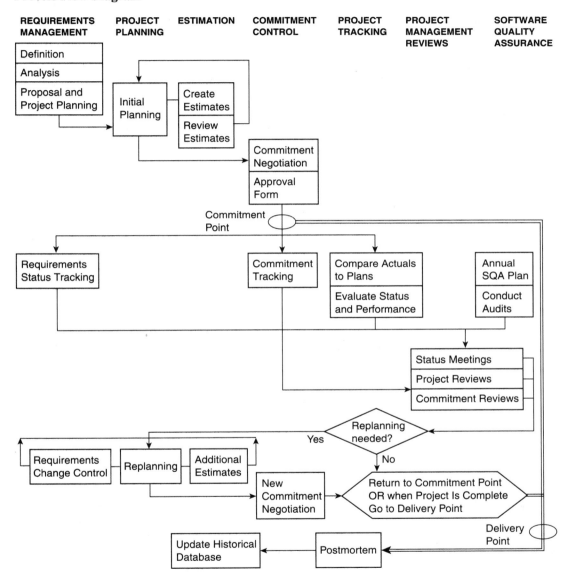

Quality Records

Quality records are the documents that report and demonstrate use of the process. Where process problems exist, the quality records may indicate the need for process improvement. Quality records must be archived for the supported life of the product.

Project notebooks are set up to store the following documents from the project management processes. If the record is stored outside the notebook, there should be an entry in the notebook to identify the location of that record.

Notebook Section	Document/Record	Controlling Process	Traceability to KPA/Key Practice
1.0	Project Management Policy		*/C-1,*/C-2
1.1	Project Management Processes Overview		*/C-1,*/C-2
2.0	Requirements Management Process		2RM
2.1	Requirements Specification	Requirements Management	2RM/AB-2
2.2	Proposal	Requirements Management	2PP/AB-1
2.3	Requirements Traceability Tool/Matrix	Requirements Management	2RM/AC-2, M-1
3.0	Project Planning Process		2PP, 2CM
3.1	Multiproject Development Plan	Project Planning	2PP/AC-7, 2PT/AB-1
3.2	Individual Project Plan	Project Planning	2PP/AC-7, 2PT/AB-1
3.3	Quality Plan	Project Planning	2PP/AC-8, AC-13, 2PT/AB-1, 2QA/AC-3, 2CM/AC-4
4.0	Estimation Process		2PP
4.1	Estimation Factors Checklists	Estimation	2PP/AC-15
4.2	Software Estimates	Estimation	2PP/AC-15
5.0	Commitment Control Process		2PP, 2PT
5.1	Commitment Approval Forms	Commitment Control	2PP/AC-4, 2PT/AC-3
6.0	Project Tracking Process		2PT
6.1	Staffing Tracking Report	Project Tracking	2PT/AC-6, */M-1
6.2	Schedule Tracking Report	Project Tracking	2PT/AC-8, */M-1
6.3	Equipment, Tools, Supplies Report	Project Tracking	2PT/AC-7, */M-1
6.4	Issues, Risks, Opportunities Report	Project Tracking	2PT/AC-10

Notebook Section	Document/Record	Controlling Process	Traceability to KPA/Key Practice
6.5	Quality Plan Status Report	Project Tracking	2PT/AC-5, AC-9
6.6	Postmortem Report/Actual Measurements	Project Tracking	2PT/AC-11
7.0	Project Management Review Process		2PT
7.1	Status Meeting Minutes	Project Management Reviews	2PT/V-2, AC-12, */V-2
7.2	Project Review Minutes	Project Management Reviews	2PT/V-1, */V-1
7.3	Project Review Schedule	Project Management Reviews	2PT/V-1, */V-1
7.4	Project Review Presentations	Project Management Reviews	2PT/V-1, */V-1
8.0	Software Quality Assurance Process		2QA
8.1	SQA Plan	Software Quality Assurance	2QA/AC-1
8.2	SQA Audit Reports	Software Quality Assurance	2QA/AC-4, AC-5, */V-3
8.3	SQA Status Reports	Software Quality Assurance	2QA/AC-6, */V-3
9.0	(Other Documents/Records (optional))	(Other Processes)	2CM/AC-3

Other quality records maintained for the organization-wide processes are listed below. The master copies are maintained by the controlling group listed.

Controlling Group	Document/Record	Controlling Process	Traceability to KPA/Key Practice
Program Management	Product Roadmap	Commitment Control	2PP/AC-4, 2PT/AC-4
Program Management	Commitment Change Record	Commitment Control	2PP/AC-4, 2PT/AC-3
Program Management	Commitment Approval Forms	Commitment Control	2PP/AC-4, 2PT/AC-3
SEPG	Project Review Schedule	Project Management Reviews	2PT/V-1
SEPG	SQA Plan	Software Quality Assurance	2QA/AC-1
SEPG	SQA Audit Reports	Software Quality Assurance	2QA/AC-4
SEPG	SQA Status Reports	Software Quality Assurance	2QA/AC-6
SEPG	Metric Reports	(Various Processes)	*/M-1

Relationship to SEI CMM v1.1 for Level 2

Table 1: KPA Goals to Processes

This table shows which processes address the specific Key Process Area (KPA) goals. In some cases more than one process is necessary to cover the intent of the goal.

KPA	GOAL	From Capability Maturity Model for Software	PROCESS
2RM	Goal 1	System requirements allocated to software are controlled to establish a baseline for software engineering and management.	Requirements Management
2RM	Goal 2	Software plans, products, and activities are kept consistent with the system requirements allocated to software.	Requirements Management, Project Planning
2PP	Goal 1	Software estimates are documented for use in planning and tracking the software project.	Estimation
2PP	Goal 2	Software project activities and commitments are planned and documented.	Project Planning, Commitment Control
2PP	Goal 3	Affected groups and individuals agree to their commitments related to the software project.	Commitment Control
2PT	Goal 1	Actual results and performance are tracked against the software plans.	Project Tracking
2PT	Goal 2	Corrective actions are taken and managed to closure when actual results and performance deviate significantly from the software plans.	Project Tracking, Project Management Reviews
2PT	Goal 3	Changes to software commitments are agreed to by the affected groups and individuals.	Commitment Control
2QA	Goal 1	Software quality assurance activities are planned.	Software Quality Assurance
2QA	Goal 2	Adherence to software products and activities to the applicable standards, procedures, and requirements is verified objectively.	Software Quality Assurance
2QA	Goal 3	Affected groups and individuals are informed of software quality assurance activities and results.	Software Quality Assurance
2QA	Goal 4	Noncompliance issues that cannot be resolved within the software project are addressed by senior management.	Project Management Reviews Software Quality Assurance

KPA	GOAL	From Capability Maturity Model for Software	PROCESS
2CM	Goal 1	Software configuration management activities are planned.	Project Planning
2CM	Goal 2	Selected software work products are identified, controlled, and available.	Project Planning
2CM	Goal 3 Goal 4	Changes to identified software work products are controlled. Affected groups and individuals are informed of the status and content of software baselines.	(Separate procedures for the software release process and tools)
2SM	Goal 1	The prime contractor selects qualified software subcontractors.	(Separate procedures in corporate policies and guidelines)
	Goal 2	The prime contractor and the software subcontractor agree to their commitment to each other.	
	Goal 3	The prime contractor and software subcontractor agree to maintain on-going communication.	
	Goal 4	The prime contractor tracks the software subcontractor's actual results and performance against its commitments.	

Relationship to SEI CMM v1.1 for Level 2

Table 2: KPA Key Practices to Processes

This table shows which processes address the specific key practices of the CMM v1.1. In most cases, the key practice is addressed by a process or quality record from a process. However, in some cases, the key practice is addressed by assigning responsibility or by providing adequate resources or adequate training.

KPA	Key Practice	Process	KPA	Key Practice	Process
2RM	C-1	Project Management Policy	2PT	AC-2	Project Planning
2RM	AB-1	(assign responsibility)	2PT	AC-3	Commitment Control
2RM	AB-2	Requirements Management	2PT	AC-4	Commitment Control
2RM	AB-3	(adequate resources)	2PT	AC-5	Project Tracking
2RM	AB-4	Requirements Management	2PT	AC-6	Project Tracking
2RM	AC-1	Requirements Management	2PT	AC-7	Project Tracking
2RM	AC-2	Requirements Management	2PT	AC-8	Project Tracking
2RM	AC-3	Requirements Management	2PT	AC-9	Project Tracking
2RM	M-1	Requirements Management	2PT	AC-10	Project Tracking
*	V-1	Project Management Review	2PT	AC-11	Project Tracking
*	V-2	Project Management Review	2PT	AC-12	Project Management Review
*	V-3	Software Quality Assurance	2PT	AC-13	Project Management Review
2PP	C-1	(assign responsibility)	2PT	M-1	Project Tracking
2PP	C-2	Project Management Policy	2QA	C-1	Project Management Policy
2PP	AB-1	Software Development	2QA	AB-1	(assign responsibility)
2PP	AB-2	(assign responsibility)	2QA	AB-2	(adequate resources)
2PP	AB-3	(adequate resources)	2QA	AB-3/4	(adequate training)
2PP	AB-4	(adequate training)	2QA	AC-1	Software Quality Assurance
2PP	AC-1	Commitment Control	2QA	AC-2	Software Quality Assurance
2PP	AC-2	Project Planning	2QA	AC-3	Software Quality Assurance
2PP	AC-3	Project Planning	2QA	AC-4	Software Quality Assurance
2PP	AC-4	Commitment Control	2QA	AC-5	Software Quality Assurance
2PP	AC-5	Software Development	2QA	AC-6	Software Quality Assurance
2PP	AC-6	Project Planning	2QA	AC-7	Software Quality Assurance
2PP	AC-7	Project Planning	2QA	AC-8	Software Quality Assurance
2PP	AC-8	Project Planning	2QA	M-1	Software Quality Assurance
2PP	AC-9	Estimation	2CM	C-1	Project Management Policy
2PP	AC-10	Estimation	2CM	AB-1/2	(assign responsibility)
2PP	AC-11	Estimation	2CM	AB-3	(adequate resources)

KPA	Key Practice	Process	KPA	Key Practice	Process
2PP	AC-12	Estimation	2CM	AB-4/5	(adequate training)
2PP	AC-13	Project Planning	2CM	AC-1	Project Planning, Software Release
2PP	AC-14	Project Planning	2CM	AC-2	Project Planning, Software Release
2PP	AC-15	Estimation	2CM	AC-3	Software Release
2PP	M-1	Project Tracking	2CM	AC-4	Project Planning
2PT	C-1	(assign responsibility)	2CM	AC-5	Software Development
2PT	C-2	Project Management Policy	2CM	AC-6	Software Development
2PT	AB-1	Project Planning	2CM	AC-7	Software Release
2PT	AB-2	(assign responsibility)	2CM	AC-8	Software Release
2PT	AB-3	(adequate resources)	2CM	AC-9	Software Release
2PT	AB-4/5	(adequate training)	2CM	AC-10	Software Release
2PT	AC-1	Project Planning	2CM	M-1	Project Tracking

Requirements Management Process

Effective Date:
Authorizing Manager:

Purpose

This document describes the process for managing requirements to ensure delivery of agreed functionality and quality attributes.

Scope

This process applies to software projects where an initial set of requirements is given by one or more requestors, and these requirements are managed and controlled so that the resulting product meets the requirements.

This process does not directly apply to advanced development projects since there is no requestor with whom to negotiate agreement to requirements.

This process does not cover specific activities for gathering the initial set of requirements, but it assumes that an initial set is gathered by some means and is documented for negotiation and approval.

Introduction

The requirements management process is a parallel process to the software development process. The requirements management process is described in this document in the context of the software development process, so the following summary of the software development process is presented as background information.

The software development process can be divided into stages of requirements, proposal, design, code, and verification.

> The requirements stage covers program initiation and program definition. The deliverables are a program statement and a requirements specification. The requirements specification includes both customer requirements and technical requirements.
>
> The proposal stage covers the engineering proposal to address the requirements specification. The proposal document is the basis of subsequent design.
>
> The design stage covers both functional description and design. The deliverables are one or more functional specifications addressing the proposal and design specifications adding further details. These designs are the basis of subsequent implementation.
>
> The code stage covers implementation of source code and unit testing of object code. The deliverable is the actual software and documentation or product information.
>
> The verification stage covers various testing activities. The deliverables are test descriptions, test plans, and test run results based on designs and technical or customer requirements.

The requirements management process borrows principles from Quality Function Deployment (QFD), a proactive requirements management technique. QFD as it applies to software seeks to deploy the "voice of the user" (what the user values) throughout the software development process. Using QFD concepts, the user's values are translated into customer requirements, which in turn are translated into technical requirements. The technical requirements are deployed to designs, which in turn are deployed to code. In this way, the requirements are built-in and not tested in, and testing activities are a simple verification. Products that meet their requirements provide value to the user.

The requirements management process provides a framework to ensure that products meet their requirements and provide value to the user.

Objectives

The objectives of the requirements management process are

- To ensure that requirements for the software product are defined and understood
- To establish and maintain agreement on the requirements with the requestor (external customer, marketing, or another internal organization)
- To ensure that the requirements are met

In addition, requirements shall be documented and controlled to establish a basis for software development and project management use. Changes to requirements shall be documented and controlled to ensure that plans, deliverables, and activities are consistent with requirements.

Definitions

Requestor. External customer, marketing, or another internal organization that requests the product or functionality. This concept does not apply to advanced development where there is no requestor.

Requirement Types. There are three types of requirements: customer, technical, and project requirements. Some customer requirements and all technical requirements drive software development. Some customer requirements and all project requirements are input to project management.

Customer Requirements. Customer requirements state what the customer needs, usually expressed in customer terms. These requirements include actual customer requests, market-driven requirements, such as delivery dates, exciting requirements, or differentiators, and unstated but expected requirements, such as acceptable performance and reliability.

Technical Requirements. Technical requirements state the technical functionality and quality attributes needed to satisfy the customer requirements. These requirements shall be traceable back to customer requirements and traceable forward to designs and tests. The technical requirements identify what must be provided and not how it is to be provided.

Project Requirements. Project requirements, such as resource and schedule requirements or constraints, are used for project planning and tracking activities. Project requirements may be related to customer requirements, such as a delivery date requested by a customer. Project requirements are managed through project planning and project tracking, which are outside the scope of this document.

Requirement Categories. In terms of customer satisfaction, requirements usually address one or more categories of functionality or quality attributes desired by customers. Categorizing requirements helps uncover undefined or hidden requirements.

This Checklist for a Requirements Specification provides the following list of categories. One of these is product attributes, which may include suggested categories or additional categories as appropriate to the project.

Checklist

- Marketing
- Functionality
- Performance
- Reliability and Availability
- Serviceability (Service Architecture)
- Migration
- Coexistence
- Installability
- Environmental
- Internationalization/Localization
- Configurability
- Professional Services
- Support
- Architecture Compliance
- Interdependency
- Platform Requirements

Product Attribute (suggested categories)

- Security
- Portability
- Interoperability
- Extensibility/Limits
- Warnings/Error Handling
- Recovery
- Standards Conformance

Needs and Expectations

The engineers need an initial set of requirements to form the basis for software development and project management activities and deliverables. The engineers also need requirements as a basis for verification of the resulting deliverables.

The project manager needs to be able to determine the status of the requirements. The status can be used to assess risk and to determine resulting capability. Each requirement must be uniquely identified, such as with a numbering scheme, for status tracking purposes.

The requestors need reassurance that the resulting product will meet their requirements. Where possible, the requestors should be included in definition, validation, and prioritization of requirements.

The requestors and engineers need change control for requirements to ensure that any changes are agreed upon and then reflected in the project.

Activities

The activities are presented under the appropriate process steps from the process flow diagram. These activities cover gathering and managing requirements throughout the software development life cycle. Some of these activities may overlap or be performed in parallel. See *Recommendations* for suggestions regarding how to perform these steps.

1. Definition

During the requirements stage, the project manager and project team gather requirements and develop a draft requirements specification. These requirements are defined and validated with the requestors. The requirement requestor or source should be tracked to direct approval and change requests to the requestor. See *Recommendations* for suggested methods for gathering requirements.

At this point, the status of each requirement in the draft requirements specification is set to "defined."

2. Analysis

During the requirements stage, the requirements are analyzed to ensure that they are clear, precise, meaningful, and measurable and can be used for development and testing. Relationships between customer and technical requirements are established to ensure adequate coverage and decomposition. The requirements are categorized to expose insufficient or incomplete areas to address. Then the requirements are prioritized, and the requirements specification is updated. See *Recommendations* for suggested methods for analyzing requirements.

The requirements specification is reviewed and approved by the requestors. The result is an approved requirements specification that is the basis for software development and project management activities.

At this point, the status of each requirement in the approved requirements specification is updated to "approved."

3. Proposal and Project Planning

During the proposal stage, the proposal and project plans are developed according to the appropriate processes. The proposal might not address all approved requirements, and some requirements may be addressed in another project's proposal or in a later delivery. The proposal and project plans are reviewed, approved, and committed.

At this point, the status of each requirement in the proposal is updated to "committed." Any requirements not addressed in the proposal remain at approved status to be addressed later.

4. Design

During the design stage, the technical requirements are addressed in one or more design specifications. The requirements are traceable forward to the designs, and the designs are inspected to determine whether the requirements have been adequately addressed.

At this point, the status of each requirement addressed in a design is updated to "designed." The project manager ensures that all committed requirements are addressed by one or more designs.

5. Code

During the code stage, the designs are implemented. The designs are traceable forward to the software and documentation, which are then inspected. If the designs are not adequately implemented, some requirements might not be met. This indicates the need for rework.

At this point, the status of each requirement covered in the software and documentation is updated to "implemented." The project manager ensures that all committed requirements are addressed in the product.

6. Verification

During the verification stage, requirements are verified through testing the product. The requirements are traceable forward to the test descriptions, and the test descriptions should be inspected at the design or code stage. During testing, the test results are tracked to identify which requirements have been met.

At this point, the status of each requirement verified in the product is updated to "completed." The project manager ensures that all committed requirements are addressed by the product.

7. Change Control

After the proposal stage, requirements are expected to change as a result of information gained in later stages. Changes to requirements must be controlled, and the change must be reflected in the related plans, deliverables, and activities.

The requirements change may take effect starting with either the requirements specification or the proposal. Various scenarios are described below.

Situation	Action
The change is to drop a requirement as no longer required.	**Requirements specification** is updated to delete the requirement, and the requirements specification is updated and approved. The change is reflected in the proposal, project plans, and deliverables.
The change is to drop a requirement from the current proposed implementation, but the requirement is expected to be met in a subsequent delivery.	**Proposal** is updated to reflect the change. The status of the requirement is dropped back to "approved." The change is reflected in the project plans and deliverables.
The change is to add new requirements to an approved requirements specification.	The new requirements are validated, analyzed, and prioritized. **Requirements specification** is updated and approved. The change is reflected in the proposal, project plans, and deliverables.
The change is to add a requirement to the current proposed implementation, and the requirement is already approved in the requirements specification.	**Proposal** is updated to reflect the change. The status of the requirement is changed to "committed." The change is reflected in the project plans and deliverables.

Data Flow

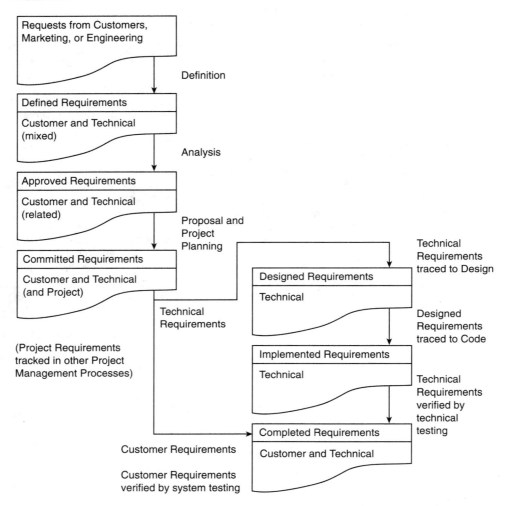

Process Flow

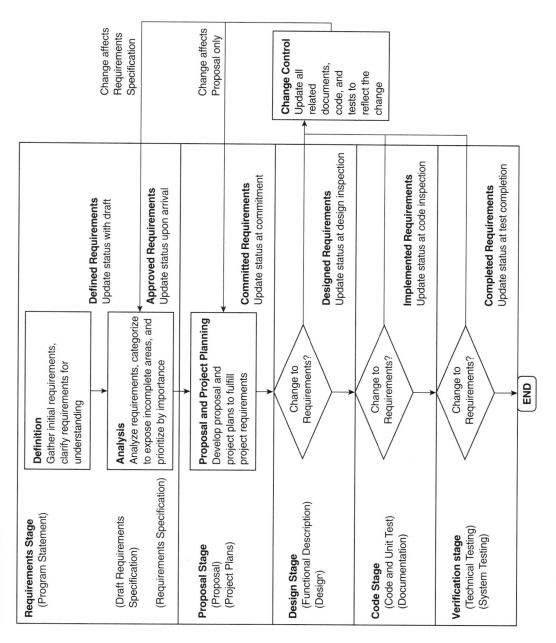

Process Inputs/Outputs, Customers/Suppliers

Inputs	From	To	For (Outputs)
Customer Discussions, Custom Engineering Requests, New Feature Suggestions	Customers	Engineering	Draft Requirements Document *(proposed requirements)*
Market-Driven Requirements	Marketing		
Competitive Comparisons, Reverse Engineering, Quality Guidelines, Technical Innovations	Engineering		
Draft Requirements Document	Engineering	Customers, Marketing, Engineering	Requirements Document *(approved requirements)*
Requirements Document	Engineering	Customers, Marketing, Engineering	Proposal, Project Plans *(committed requirements)*
Proposal *(committed requirements)*	Engineering	Project Manager and Project Team	Design Documents, Test Descriptions
Design Documents, Proposal *(committed requirements)*	Author	Inspectors	Design Inspection *(designed requirements)* Code
Code or Documentation, Design Documents *(designed requirements)*	Author	Inspectors	Code or Document Inspection *(implemented requirements)* Unverified Product
Test Descriptions, Unverified Product, Test Runs *(implemented requirements)* *(committed requirements)*	Testers	Testers	Test Results and Final Verification *(completed requirements)* Verified Product
Requirements Document, Requirements Change	Customers, Marketing, or Engineering	Project Manager and Project Team	Controlled Changes to: Requirements Document, Proposal, Project Plans, Design Documents, Code, Test Descriptions

Note: The phases and steps that produce these inputs and outputs may overlap or cycle back. However, each output should be complete at the end of the project.

Interdependencies

Interdependent processes include the following.

- Project Planning Process

Metrics

1. Requirements Completion Status

Goal   Fulfill all committed requirements.

Question   How many committed requirements are there?
What is the status of the requirements?
Are we progressing toward completed status?

Metric   Percentage of requirements of each status and level
Pareto chart

Measures   (Optionally, weight the number of requirements by priority.)
1. Total technical requirements: committed to completed
   Number at committed status/ Total
   Number at designed status/ Total
   Number at implemented status/ Total
   Number at completed status/ Total
2. Total customer requirements: committed to completed
   Number at committed status/ Total
   Number at completed status/ Total

Frequency Quarterly

2. Progress Metrics

These metrics are optional, based on project size and need.

Goal   For each step, determine progress toward step completion. (This data can be input to project planning and estimating.)

2.1 Analysis Step Progress

Goal   Eliminate unrelated requirements (customer without related technical, or technical without related customer) by relating, further defining, or removing them.

Question   How many unrelated requirements exist?
Are we progressing toward the goal?

Metrics/   Number of unrelated requirements over time.
Measures   (Goal: decreasing to 0.)

Frequency Action as needed per metric results.

2.2 Proposal Step Progress

Goal   Eliminate undecided requirements (requirements that we have not decided whether to address or not address in the proposal).

Question   How many requirements are still undecided?
                Are we progressing toward the goal?

Metrics/   Number of undecided requirements over time.
Measures   (Goal: decreasing to 0.)

Frequency   Action as needed per metric results.

2.3 Design Step Progress

Goal   Eliminate undesigned requirements (requirements not covered in a design).

Question   How many undesigned requirements exist?
                Are we progressing toward the goal?

Metrics/   Number of undesigned requirements over time.
Measures   (Goal: decreasing to 0.)

Frequency   Action as needed per metric results.

2.4 Implementation Step Progress

Goal   Eliminate unimplemented requirements (requirements not covered in implementation).

Question   How many unimplemented requirements exist?
                Are we progressing toward the goal?

Metrics/   Number of unimplemented requirements over time.
Measures   (Goal: decreasing to 0.)

Frequency   Action as needed per metric results.

2.5 Verification Step Progress

Goal   Eliminate untested and unverified requirements (requirements not verified through testing).

Question   How many untested and unverified requirements exist?
                Are we progressing toward the goal?

Metrics/   Number of untested and unverified requirements over time.
Measures   (Goal: decreasing to 0.)

Frequency   Action as needed per metric results.

Recommendations

1. Gathering Requirements

The method for gathering and validating the requirements will vary depending on the situation. Possibilities include the following.

- Direct customer negotiation. Input from customer contact and discussions.
- Market and business analysis/no direct customer. Input from phase review process and competitive comparisons.
- Reverse engineered requirements/no direct customer. Requirements defined by what already exists.

2. Analysis and Prioritization

Customer requirements and technical requirements: The requirements are categorized as customer or technical. Relationships and traceability should be defined between the customer and technical requirements, and unrelated requirements should be eliminated.

Situation	Action
A customer requirement has no related technical requirements (unsupported or underdeveloped).	Develop supporting technical requirements or negotiate with requestor to drop requirement.
A technical requirement has no related customer requirement (unnecessary or unsubstantiated).	Determine a related customer requirement or drop technical requirement.

A method to establish the relationships is requirements decomposition.

Requirements Decomposition. Initial requirements may be decomposed into child requirements that are more clear, precise, meaningful, and testable. The decomposition task results in parsed, interpreted, or derived requirements.

- Parsed requirements break an initial requirement into separate parts.
- Interpreted requirements rephrase an initial requirement to remove ambiguity or vagueness.
- Derived requirements collapse two or more requirements into a single statement.

Requirement Categories. The requirements should be categorized to analyze for undefined or missing requirements. For recommended categories, see *Definitions*.

Prioritization. Customer requirements are prioritized, and the priorities are inherited by the related technical requirements. The priority scheme may be simple or complex, as appropriate to the project. For example:

- Mandatory or discretionary
- High, medium, or low priority
- QFD-style matrices with priority weights

3. Status Tracking

Suggested status tracking methods include the following.

- Use a requirements database tool.
- Maintain a matrix of related customer and technical requirements and status levels.

Require-ment	Defined	Approved	Committed	Designed	Implemented	Complete
CR1	x	x	x	-	-	x
TR1.1	x	x	x	x	x	x
CR2	x	x	x	-	-	
TR2.1	x	x	x	x	x	
TR2.2	x	x	x	x		

Legend: CRn = Customer Requirement
TRn.m = Technical Requirements related to CRn

- Customer requirements would not be tracked in "designed" and "implemented" status.
- Project requirements are not tracked by this tracking method but are tracked through other project management processes.
- Variation: Instead of recording an "x" in the matrix columns, record the document number of the document that addresses the requirement.

4. Traceability

When creating the proposal and project plans, keep the following in mind.

- Customer requirements form the basis of final validation tests.
- Technical requirements form the basis of designs and tests.
- Technical requirements are inputs to project planning estimates.

Suggested methods for traceability of requirements in designs include the following.

- In the overview section of the design, include a matrix of requirements addressed and page number or section of design.
- At the beginning of each design section, include a list of each requirement addressed by the section.

It is not necessary to trace requirements in the code itself, only to ensure that the code covers the design. If the code does not adequately implement the design, some of the requirements might not be met. This indicates the need for rework. Suggested methods for traceability of requirements in test plans and test descriptions include the following.

- In the overview section of the test plan, include a matrix of requirements addressed and test description name/number.
- At the beginning of each test description, include a list of each requirement addressed by the test.

Requirements Management Example

This example follows a subset of requirements through the requirements management process.

Legend: CR-Customer Requirement, TR-Technical Requirement, PR-Project Requirement

Definition. The customer request is as follows.

The system shall load our entire database within three weeks, running on a U6000/65 machine with operating system level SVR4, and delivery is required by <date>.

Analysis. The requirements include

- CR1—The system shall load 45,360,000 records within three weeks.
- TR1.1—The system shall load input data at an average rate of 25 records per second or better.
- CR2—The system shall run on a U6000/65 machine with operating system level SVR4.
- PR2.1—Obtain a U6000/65 machine with SVR4 for development by <date>.
- CR3—Deliver system by <date>.
- PR3.1—Staff 14 people for six months.

Requirements Specification. The requirements include

- CR1—The system shall load 45,360,000 records within three weeks.
- TR1.1—The system shall load input data at an average rate of 25 records per second or better.
- CR2—The system shall run on a U6000/65 machine with operating system level SVR4.
- CR3—Deliver system by <date>.

Proposal and Requirements Tracking. The proposal includes these requirements.

- CR1—The system shall load 45,360,000 records within three weeks.
- TR1.1—The system shall load input data at an average rate of 25 records per second or better.
- CR2—The system shall run on a U6000/65 machine with operating system level SVR4.

Project Plans and Project Tracking. The project plan includes these requirements.

- PR2.1—Obtain a U6000/65 machine with SVR4 for development by <date>.
- CR3—Deliver system by <date>.
- PR3.1—Staff 14 people for six months.

Design Stage. The design addresses the technical requirement(s):

- TR1.1—The system shall load input data at an average rate of 25 records per second or better, with:
- Cache algorithm
- Input processing algorithm

Code Stage. The design is implemented by:

- Cache algorithm
- Input processing algorithm

Verification Stage. The test descriptions address the requirement(s):

- CR1—The system shall load 45,360,000 records within three weeks.
- TR1.1—The system shall load input data at an average rate of 25 records per second or better.
- CR2—The system shall run on a U6000/65 machine with operating system level SVR4.

With test descriptions:

- Load database of 25 records in 1 second (after loading, verify stored data matches input data).
- Load database of 1/5 of the customer database in four days.
- Load entire database of 45,360,000 records in three weeks.

Project Planning Process

Effective Date:
Authorizing Manager:

Purpose

This document describes the process for project planning to support commitment control.

Objectives

The project planning process supports establishing and maintaining product development commitments.

After commitments are established, project plans represent the commitment to schedule and costs, and corporate plans and resources are allocated on the assumption that the commitments will be met.

Project plans are a requirement for establishing an acceptable business case. The development effort must be sized to determine the cost involved. The cost must be in line with the marketing forecast to establish the business case prior to a product commitment.

Project plans are also a tool for managing the development effort. The plans are tracked to determine whether the project commitments are on track or at risk. The plans are living documents, updated regularly to reflect the current project status and revised estimates.

The project planning process is integrated with the corporate phase review process, and the project plans support the Phase Review Project Status Report. Also, the project planning process is flexible to be tailored for use in custom engineering requests and special projects not covered by phase reviews as well.

Needs and Expectations

The director, department managers, and marketing need project plans to support commitment control and reduce risk to the commitments of the organization.

Project managers need a framework for managing and organizing project planning information in a general overall manner. The process should be flexible yet unambiguous so that expectations are clear. The contents of project plans need to be defined for complete coverage of activities and interdependencies.

To support the corporate phase review process, project managers need to be able to reference details with pointers to internal project plans so that information is easily accessible and not unnecessarily repeated in multiple places. Also, for ease of use, the planning documents should be easy to update.

Process Inputs/Outputs, Customers/Suppliers

Inputs	From	To	For (Outputs)
Commitment Constraints	Director, Marketing	Project Managers	Project Plans
Project Planning Resources	Department Managers	Project Managers	Planning Activities
Estimation and Planning Input and Commitment	Section Managers, Team Leaders, Team Members, Interdependencies	Project Managers	Project Plans
Project Plans	Project Managers	Department Managers, Director, Marketing	Commitment Control
Quality Plans	Project Managers	SQA Personnel	Verifying Process Compliance

Project Planning Activities

Project Planning Phases

Initial Planning		Replanning
Develop inputs to Project Plans	Develop initial version Project Plans	Develop revisions to Project Plans

Initial Planning

Entrance Criteria:
Completion of Proposal Step – Market Analysis and Strategic Assessment

Exit Criteria:
Approval and Commitment of Project Plans

Inputs: → **Project Planning Process** → Outputs: →

Identification of:
1. Program/Projects
2. Functionality
3. Delivery Dates

Gross Estimates of:
1. Size
2. Cost
3. Labor

Initial Version of:
1. Multiproject Development Plan
2. Individual Project Plan
3. Quality Plan

Replanning

Entrance Criteria:
Replanning indicated due to changes in Project Status, Functionality, Staffing, Budget, etc.

Exit Criteria:
Approval and Commitment of Project Plans

Inputs: → **Project Planning Process** → Outputs: →

Changed Conditions

Current version of Project Plans

Revision of:
1. Multiproject Development Plan
2. Individual Project Plan
3. Quality Plan

Project Planning Process Flow

Multiproject Development Plan

| **Propose Multiproject Schedule** |
| Get estimated commitment dates |

↓

| **Create Interdependencies Matrix** |
| Get estimated commitment dates |

→

Individual Project Plan

| **Identify Constraints** |
| Functionality, Resource, and |
| Schedule Constraints |

↓

| **Identify Tasks** |
| Work Breakdown Structure |
| Create Quality Plan |

→

Quality Plan

| **Identify Processes and Procedures** |

↓

| **Identify Deliverables and Quality Records** |

↓

| **Identify Goals, Criteria, and Metrics** |

| **Update Multiproject Schedule** |
| Update Plan to Reflect |
| Approved Commitment Dates |

←

| **Estimate Work Effort** |
| Use Estimation Process for Size, |
| Resource, and Schedule Estimates |

↓

| **Check and Balance** |
| Compare Estimates to Constraints, |
| Determine Alternatives or |
| Contingency Plans |

↓

| **Create Integration Plan** |
| Identify Project Integration |
| Milestones and Reviews |

↓

| **Negotiate Commitment Approval** |
| Receive Approval or Renegotiate |
| Constraints and Replan the Project |

| **Identify Milestones** |
| Use Project Review Guidelines to |
| Schedule Milestones and Reviews |

Project Plan Contents

Multiproject Development Plan	*covers interdependencies and integration* *only needed when a set of projects will be released together*
Multiproject Master Schedule	high-level schedule of all projects
Interdependencies Matrix	matrix of project interdependencies
Integration Plans	integration plans/milestones of all projects
List of **Individual Project Plans**	list of pointers to project summaries and where to find them/whom to contact

Individual Project Plan	*covers tasks, resources, and schedule for a single project*
Project Schedule	schedule including tasks and staff resources
Functionality Summary	list of major features and functionality
Staffing Summary	total labor months and names of assigned staff
Interdependencies List	list of project's interdependencies
Equipment/Materials Summary	list of equipment/materials resource requirements
Quality Plan	pointer to (or section in project plan containing) the project's Quality Plan

Quality Plan	*covers planning assumptions* *and configuration management and quality control information*
Processes/Procedures List	list of standard or special processes for this project
Deliverables/Quality Records	list of all deliverables and quality records and their location
Goals/Criteria/Metrics	goals and/or entrance and exit criteria for critical tasks, metrics to measure and determine product content and quality
Other Assumptions and Risks	other assumptions and risks to capture for review

Activities

The activities are divided based on the three minimum component documents of project plans:

    I.   Multiproject Development Plan
   II.   Individual Project Plan
  III.   Quality Plan

I. Multiproject Development Plan

Managing the multiproject development plan is the responsibility of a multiproject manager. The multiproject manager coordinates with the project managers of interdependent projects to provide initial constraints and then to consolidate integration plans. *(The steps below may overlap or repeat.)*

1. Create Master Schedule

Estimate an initial master schedule as input constraints for further project planning. In early stages, provide a rough schedule estimate of delivery date within ½ year.

2. Create Interdependencies Matrix

Identify the individual projects for the program and identify the interdependencies between the projects. This matrix becomes input to the projects and input to integration plans.

3. Create Integration Plan

Identify the integration sequence and the test sequence for all projects in the program. Determine milestones and review points to check the progress of the integration efforts and identify risks.

4. Negotiate Commitment Approval

This step has two possible outcomes.

(A) Approval—The plan is approved; the commitment process proceeds.
(B) Replanning—Constraints are renegotiated, and replanning proceeds based on the new constraints.

Approval of the plan requires the signature of all interdependent managers. After initial approval, the plan is regularly reviewed and updated. Changes to the plan also require approval signatures. If commitments are affected, the commitment control process is invoked.

II. Individual Project Plan

Managing the individual project plan is the responsibility of a project manager. The project manager may change the plan without external approval if there is no effect on interdependencies or commitments (such as changing the order of tasks or adding an inspection without affecting the critical path). If changes affect interdependencies, approvals from interdependencies are required. If changes affect commitments (delivery date, functionality, or resource levels), the commitment control process is required. *(The following steps may overlap or repeat.)*

1. Identify Constraints

Inputs to begin planning are as follows.

- First cut at functionality (Requirements/Proposal Document)
- First cut at schedule constraints (expected delivery date)
- First cut at resource constraints

The goal is to balance these three variables. If they do not balance, risk is indicated for delivery of the project on time within budget with required functionality. Changes are negotiated to reduce the risk to an acceptable amount.

2. Identify Tasks

Create a work breakdown structure of all tasks needed to satisfy the requirements. Identify the processes and deliverables for the project in the Quality Plan, and map the product requirements to processes and deliverables to identify tasks within the work breakdown structure.

3. Estimate Work Effort

Create the following estimates based on the estimation process.

Size—Create size estimates for the deliverables of each task. The initial size estimation is used for comparing this task to previous tasks to determine resource and schedule estimations. Example size estimates are "number of pages," "lines of code (LOC)," or "function points."

Resource—Create resource estimates based on task size. Get input from team members and interdependencies, and consider background and capabilities. Example resource estimates are "Two people for two weeks," or "Nine labor months."

Schedule—Create schedule estimates based on resource estimates and calendar work days with overhead and slack allowances. Get input from team members and interdependencies, and consider availability. Create an initial project schedule with tasks to required granularity using a project management tool.

4. Check and Balance

Check to see whether the variables balance (i.e., does the schedule overrun the schedule constraints?). If the variables do not balance, risk is indicated. Determine alternatives to reduce the risk, and negotiate agreement to changes in functionality, resources, or schedule if necessary.

5. Identify Critical Path and Milestones

Identify the critical path and milestones for update and review. Identify tentative dates at those milestones for project status reviews by the project manager. Identify tentative dates for project management review meetings by senior management. The plan should be updated regularly, at a minimum, prior to reviews.

6. Negotiate Commitment Approval

This step has two possible outcomes.

(A) Approval—The plan is approved; the commitment process proceeds.
(B) Replanning—Constraints are renegotiated, and replanning proceeds based on the new constraints.

Approval of the plan requires the signature of the section managers or team leaders of the project team and all interdependent managers. Also, if changes occur as the plan is tracked, renegotiating and replanning are necessary to determine and evaluate risks. Changes to the plan also require approval signatures. If commitments are affected, the commitment control process is invoked.

III. Quality Plan

Managing the Quality Plan is the responsibility of a project manager. The Quality Plan contains information for configuration management and for quality control, including SQA assuring the project. *(The steps below may overlap or repeat.)*

1. Identify Processes and Procedures

Identify standard or special processes and procedures that will be followed for the project. The selection of processes provides basic assumptions for estimating the work effort. It also provides a basis for process assurance.

2. Identify Deliverables and Quality Records

Identify and maintain a list of deliverables and quality records related to the project. The list should also indicate the location of these documents. The list provides a basis for configuration management, auditing, and tracking the progress of deliverables.

3. Identify Goals, Criteria, and Metrics

At a minimum, identify release criteria. Identify other goals, process step entrance and exit criteria, and metrics for tracking the quality of the project.

4. Capture Other Assumptions and Risks

If there are known assumptions or risks that are not captured elsewhere, include them in this section. Assumptions may be added during the planning process (such as product size estimates).

Interdependencies

Interdependent processes include the following.

- Commitment Control Process
- Project Tracking Process
- Requirements Management Process
- Estimation Process

Metrics

1. Project Planning Usage

Goal   Increase percentage of projects using project planning techniques. Target is 100%.

Question   How many project plans vs. total projects?
Are we making progress toward the goal?

Metric   Percentage of project plans = Project plans/Total projects.

Measures   Number of project plans in place this quarter.
Number of total projects this quarter.

Frequency   Quarterly

Estimation Process

Effective Date:
Authorizing Manager:

Purpose

This document describes the process for estimating size, resources, and schedules of projects to support project planning and commitment control. Estimates are inherently sensitive to the input data, and results must be framed within a range and not considered exact answers. However, with process improvement and calibration to historical data, estimates can become more reliable over time.

Objectives

The objective of the estimation process is to provide input to establish and maintain product development commitments. Project plans are based on estimates of project size, resources, and schedule, reflecting past performance on similar project efforts.

In relation to the project planning process, the estimation process provides a framework for

- When estimates should be done
- Who should be involved
- What data should be used as input to the estimate

At a minimum, estimates should be done three times in the life cycle.

1. Near approval of requirements or proposal to cover design through delivery (using estimation based on requirements and planned tasks)
2. Near approval of design to cover implementation through delivery (using current project data and estimation of planned tasks)
3. Near completion of implementation to cover integration test through delivery (using current project data and estimation of planned tasks)

The project planning process may require additional estimates as needed. Because an estimate is based on requirements, if requirements change, the estimates are invalid, and new estimates are needed.

Historical data of recent projects should be used for better reliability of estimates. This historical data should be gathered as projects are completed.

Needs and Expectations

Project managers and team members need to have historical data as a basis for estimating current project size, resources, and schedule. They need a repeatable, easy method for producing an estimate.

The director, department managers, and marketing need to review the estimates as part of commitment negotiation to be aware of the cost and time involved.

As the project progresses, project managers and team members need to refine the estimates based on current data for the project. Other interdependent managers need to review the estimates to identify risks. Overall, there is a need to improve the accuracy of our estimates with tools and process improvements.

Process Inputs/Outputs, Customers/Suppliers

Inputs	From	To	For (Outputs)
Staffing or Schedule Constraints	Director, Department Manager, Marketing	Project Manager	Estimates
Historical Project Data Profiles	SEPG	Project Manager	Estimates
Estimation Factors Checklist	Project Manager, Project Team	Project Manager	Estimates
Estimates	Project Manager, Project Team	Project Manager	Project Plans
Actual Project Data	Project Manager	SEPG	Historical Project Data Profiles

Estimation Process Inputs and Outputs

Entrance Criteria:
Estimates required by
Project Planning Process

Exit Criteria:
Estimation inputs and outputs
recorded in project plans

Inputs: **Estimation**   **Outputs:**
⟶ **Process** ⟶

1. Requirements and Tasks to Perform
2. Staffing or Schedule Constraints
3. Historical Project Data Profiles
4. Estimation Factors Checklist Data

Estimates for:
1. Size
2. Resource
3. Schedule

Process Flow

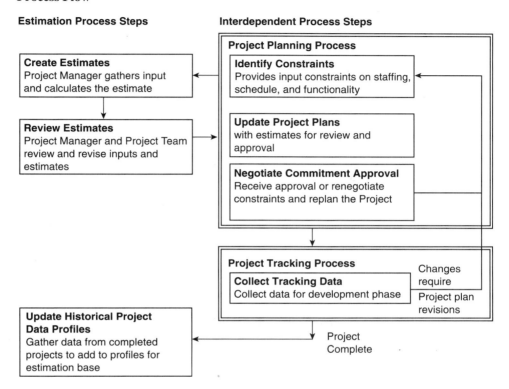

Estimation Process Steps   **Interdependent Process Steps**

Project Planning Process

Create Estimates
Project Manager gathers input
and calculates the estimate

Identify Constraints
Provides input constraints on staffing,
schedule, and functionality

Review Estimates
Project Manager and Project Team
review and revise inputs and
estimates

Update Project Plans
with estimates for review and
approval

Negotiate Commitment Approval
Receive approval or renegotiate
constraints and replan the Project

Project Tracking Process

Collect Tracking Data
Collect data for development phase

Changes
require
Project plan
revisions

**Update Historical Project
Data Profiles**
Gather data from completed
projects to add to profiles for
estimation base

Project
Complete

Activities

Creating an Estimate. Project managers are responsible for creating estimates. The project team should be consulted in creating the estimate; however, the project manager may create an initial estimate for review by the team. If there are input constraints from the director, department manager, or marketing (such as staffing or schedule limitations), the constraints are provided from the project planning process prior to this step.

The estimate can be generated using a tool package or by following the comparative estimate guidelines provided in the attachments. If the estimates overrun the constraints, provide alternative estimates, favoring some constraints over others, so that management can make data-driven trade-off decisions. The alternatives might include changes to requirements. Regardless of the estimation method used, the inputs and outputs must be documented so that they can be reviewed and added to the project plans.

Reviewing an Estimate. The project team members (or potential team members) review the inputs and outputs of the estimate. The team should concur with the estimate or provide reasons for changing the inputs. If the inputs are not correct, the project manager uses the new information to generate another estimate. This step iterates until the project team agrees. Then the estimate becomes part of the project plans in the project planning process to be approved in that process.

Update Historical Project Data Profiles. When a project is complete, the project manager provides the SEPG with data to create a Historical Project Data Profile. The profiles are used for estimating future projects by finding a profile project with similar attributes and using the sizes and productivity rates as input to the estimate. The data includes the following.

	Item	Description
1	Project Name	Name of project
2	Coding Language	Programming language
3	Size (KLOC)	KLOC (thousand lines of code), %new, % modified
4	Peak Staff	Maximum number of people on the project at one time
5	Total Months	Elapsed months from start to delivery
6	Total Staff Months (SM)	Sum of number of months each person worked on the project
7	Productivity Rate	Thousand lines of code per staff month (KLOC/SM)
8	Features List	Features that identify this project
9	Documentation Size	Pages or screens, %new, % modified
10	Document Productivity Rate	Pages or screens per staff month
11	Document List	Books or helptext created or modified
12	Contacts and References	Names of people to contact for more information
13	Estimation Factors Descriptions	*Relative to the Estimation Factors Checklist*
a	Skill/Experience	Rate and describe team mix from novice to expert
b	Desired Quality Level	Defects/KLOC, rate and describe defect removal tasks
c	Product Complexity	Rate and describe level of code structure, control flow
d	Process/Tools	Rate and describe impact from learning new processes/tools, impact from tools reliablility level
e	Project Management	Rate and describe impact from project management tasks

Estimation Factors Checklist—For Software:

In comparison to the Historical Project Data:

a. Skill/Experience
Expert/Average/Novice

What is the skill mix of the team with regard to:

1 2 3 4 5

- Experience in the same type of application
- Experience with the programming language
- Experience with platform/environment
- Experience with the existing product (for enhancements or portation)
- Design/Design Analysis capabilities
- Programming/Debugging capabilities
- Testing capabilities

b. Desired Quality Level
Less/Same/More

How reliable/maintainable does the product need to be?
What level of defects will be tolerated?
(Defects/KLOC target: same or decrease percentage)
How will that affect productivity with regard to:

1 2 3 4 5

- Design and code detail level
- Use of inspections or reviews
- Rigor of testing
- Performance, memory, or stress testing

c. Product Complexity
Less/Same/More

How complex is the design and code structure and control flow?
(from simple batch reports to complex timing and communications)
How will that affect productivity with regard to:

1 2 3 4 5

- Design and code detail level
- Use of inspections or reviews

d. Process/Tool Changes
Less/Same/More

Will the processes or tools used be different?
How will that affect productivity with regard to:

1 2 3 4 5

- Are the processes well defined?
- Is there a learning curve to account for new processes/tools?
- Are the tools stable/reliable?
- Do you expect an increase/decrease in machine availability?
- Do you expect the processes/tools to be less/more time-consuming?

e. Project Management
Low/Average/High

Rate the impact on productivity of:

1 2 3 4 5

- Teamwork Skills/Leadership Skills
- Meetings/Project Management Tasks—size and location(s) of team
- External assignments/Training
- Requirements Stability
- How much definition and rework expected?
- How accessible is the "customer" for clarifying requirements?

Estimation Factors Checklist—For Documentation:

In comparison to the Historical Project Data:

a. Skill/Experience

What is the skill mix of the team with regard to:

- Experience writing the same type of document
- Familiarity with the type of product (system s/w, compilers, database, applications, etc.)
- Experience with the tools (including graphics)
- Experience with the existing product and documents
- Design/Library Analysis capabilities
- Document Planning and Design capabilities
- Writing capabilities
- Editing/Testing capabilities

Expert/Average/Novice

1 2 3 4 5

b. Desired Quality Level

What level of defects will be tolerated?
(Defects/KLOC or documentation defects: same or decrease percentage)
How will that affect productivity with regard to:

- Design/organization of the documents (or suite)
- Completeness of the documents
- Use of inspections or reviews
- Rigor of testing, usability testing

Less/Same/More

1 2 3 4 5

c. Product Complexity

How complex is the type of document (or suite)?
How will that affect productivity with regard to:

- Design and writing level
- Completeness of the document
- Use of inspections or reviews, and testing

Less/Same/More

1 2 3 4 5

d. Process/Tool Changes

Will the processes or tools used be different?
How will that affect productivity with regard to:

- Are the processes well defined?
- Is there a learning curve to account for new processes/tools?
- Are the tools stable/reliable?
- Do you expect an increase/decrease in machine availability?
- Do you expect the processes/tools to be less/more time-consuming?

Less/Same/More

1 2 3 4 5

e. Project Management

Rate the impact on productivity of:

- Teamwork Skills/Leadership Skills
- Meetings/Project Management Tasks—size and location(s) of team
- External assignments/Training
- Requirements Stability
- How much definition and rework expected?
- How accessible is the "customer" for clarifying requirements?

Low/Average/High

1 2 3 4 5

Interdependencies

Interdependent processes include

- Project Planning Process
- Project Tracking Process

Metrics

1. Estimation Accuracy

Goal   Project estimate error margins should be no more than X%.

Question How far off were the estimates compared to the actuals?
Are we making progress toward the goal?

Metric   Bar chart of each project on X-axis and error margins in ascending order on
Y-axis, with goal line displayed on the chart.
Error margin = (actual − estimate)/actual

Measures Number of completed projects.
Error margin for each completed project.

Frequency Quarterly if there are completed projects.

Commitment Control Process

Effective Date:
Authorizing Manager:

Purpose

This document describes the process for negotiating, approving, and recording all high-level commitments of functionality, resources, and schedule made by the organization to anyone outside the business unit. This process is intended to document the activities of commitment control so that a commitment discipline can be sustained within the organization.

Scope

The scope of this document is the commitment control activities of negotiating, approving, and recording commitments. The supporting activities of planning and review are not covered in this document.

Objectives

The commitment control process provides a framework to establish and monitor product commitments to allow the delivery of products

- With agreed functionality
- On time
- Within budget

The objectives of the process are to

- Provide a primary mechanism for efficient commitment management
- Facilitate the approval process for change requests
- Identify and track the source of commitment changes
- Facilitate analysis of short and medium-term implications of deviations from plan

Needs and Expectations

All high-level commitments made by the organization must be formally approved by the director after negotiation and concurrence of those involved. This applies to all commitments to anyone outside the business unit.

The program managers maintain ownership of the commitment control records (the commitment change record and the product roadmap) to ensure that this process is followed for every change. The program managers assure commitment negotiation and approval by requiring a form with the director's signature for every change to the commitment control records.

Process Inputs/Outputs, Customers/Suppliers

Inputs	From	To	For (Outputs)
Commitment Request	Requester	Project Manager	Project Planning
Project Plan/Status	Project Manager	Director	Negotiation
Resource Levels	Department Manager	Director	Negotiation
Business Case	Program Managers	Director	Negotiation
Needs/Expectations	Requester	Director	Negotiation
Negotiation	All involved	Director	Commitment Approval
Commitment Approval Form	Department Manager	Program Managers	Commitment Control Records
Commitment Control Records	Program Managers	Director, Department Managers, Project Managers	Project Reviews

Commitment Control Process Flow, Inputs and Outputs

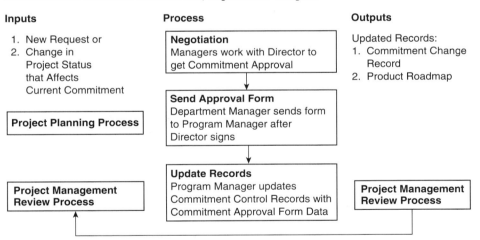

Inputs

1. New Request or
2. Change in Project Status that Affects Current Commitment

Project Planning Process

Project Management Review Process

Process

Negotiation
Managers work with Director to get Commitment Approval

Send Approval Form
Department Manager sends form to Program Manager after Director signs

Update Records
Program Manager updates Commitment Control Records with Commitment Approval Form Data

Outputs

Updated Records:
1. Commitment Change Record
2. Product Roadmap

Project Management Review Process

Commitment Control Records

Commitment Change Record

Description	Data
• Captures change control information for original commitment and all changes • Contains consolidated data from commitment approval forms to develop product roadmaps and metrics reports • Used for tracking all high-level commitments made by the business unit • Maintained up-to-date	A table of commitment control information • Project name • Commitment description • Delivery date • Date signed • Type of commitment • Who requested • Who committed • Project manager • For changes: Description and reason for change

Product Roadmap

Description	Data
• Provides overall picture of product delivery commitments • Used mainly for program reviews • Maintained up-to-date	A matrix of delivery dates • by program (rows) • by quarter (columns) Commitment categories: (P) Planned: in planning phase (C) Committed: committed functionality, resources, and delivery date

Summary Product Roadmap Change Record

Description	Data
• Summarizes commitment changes affecting the product roadmap since the last program review • Used only for the program review • Produced for the meeting and discarded	A table of commitment control information • Date (date when the change was made) • Change (project, description of the change) • Reason (why the change was made)

Activities

The activities cover negotiation, approval of commitments, and maintaining the commitment change record and the product roadmap. These activities are initiated whenever a new commitment or commitment change is requested. The request may come from customers, project managers, department managers, interdependencies, or even the director or VP. Regardless of who makes the request, the process must be followed to guard against the risk of making commitments that are impossible to meet.

Negotiation. The project managers and/or department managers work with the director to get commitment approval. Changes to commitments cannot be announced externally prior to approval.

The negotiation with the director is done face-to-face or by phone. The steps, information, and additional people involved in negotiation will differ from project to project. Where appropriate, consider the following.

- Estimation of resources and schedule to meet the commitment
- Project team and interdependencie's support for the commitment
- Potential impact to other commitments
- Potential impact to revenue and market share

If necessary, the director informs the VP and marketing prior to making the decision.

When agreement is reached, perhaps in the same meeting, the department manager completes a Commitment Approval Form with appropriate information about the commitment and obtains the director's signature.

Send Approval Forms. After obtaining the director's signature on the Commitment Approval Form, the department manager forwards the form to the program manager. The department manager also forwards copies to the project manager. Also after approval, the project manager informs affected organizations and requesters of the resulting approved commitment.

Update Commitment Records. The program manager maintains the master copy of the commitment change record and product roadmap for consistency. This includes recording changes and distributing dated copies monthly to keep managers informed of the status of commitments.

The program manager updates the commitment change record after receiving a Commitment Approval Form signed by the director. The program manager retains the Commitment Approval Form on file for the extent of the commitment.

Commitment reviews provide a sanity check for the process. The commitment control records are reviewed by the director, department managers, program managers, and project managers to identify discrepancies or risks. The data for metrics is extracted from the commitment control records.

Interdependencies

Interdependent processes include

- Project Planning Process
- Project Tracking Process

Metrics

1. Commitment Control Effectiveness

Goal   Increase percentage of commitments met, delivered with required functionality, on time, and within budget, based on the last commitment made. Target is 100% commitments met.

Question   How many commitments met vs. commitments not met?
Are we making progress toward the goal?

Metric   Percentage of commitments met over time = Commitments met / (Commitments met + Commitments not met)

Measures
- Commitments met: Number of commitments met for delivery dates this quarter, including decommitments that were requested by the original requester (i.e., they backed out)
- Commitments not met: Number of commitments not met for delivery dates this quarter, including decommitments that were requested by the organization (i.e., we backed out)

Frequency   Quarterly

2. Root Cause Analysis Data

Goal   Determine causes for the metric results to identify issues or possible process changes.

Question   What types of changes are being made?
When are changes being made?

Metrics/
Measures   Type of change (percentages):
1. Internally generated changes vs. externally generated changes
internal/(internal + external)
external/(internal + external)
2. Schedule vs. resource vs. functionality
schedule/(schedule + resource + functionality)
resource/(schedule + resource + functionality)
functionality/(schedule + resource + functionality)

Frequency   Action as needed per metric results.

Project Tracking Process

Effective Date:
Authorizing Manager:

Purpose

The purpose of the process is to monitor a project's actual progress against its plan, throughout the life of the project. Monitoring is accomplished by collecting significant information about schedule, resources, costs, features, and quality. This information, reflecting the current status of the project, is compared to the original and/or currently approved project plan.

Comparing the project's progress against its plan allows management to identify deviations from the plan so that appropriate adjustments can be made to the project's objectives, plans, or resources. It also ensures that significant deviations, which can determine the viability of the project, are evaluated and raised to upper-level management's attention in a timely manner.

Objectives

- The process should produce the information needed to conduct periodic project status meetings and project reviews.
- The process should provide the project manager and higher-level management with enough information to make data-based business decisions.
- The process should provide information to assist future projects in their estimation and planning efforts.

The adequacy of a project's tracking process will be reviewed as a byproduct of the normal project management review process.

Needs and Expectations

- Only useful, meaningful data is collected.
- Timely, accurate, relevant data is available.
- All issues and risks are identified and addressed in a timely manner.
- Sufficient information is collected to determine the current project status, to propose adjustments to the plan and/or resources, and to determine whether upper-level management needs to be notified.
- Historical data is available and accessible to assist in making more accurate plans, improve the tracking process, and determine trends.

Customers/Suppliers

The project tracking process is part of a complete management system directed toward meeting software delivery commitments. Everyone in the organization has a role to perform in this process.

Process Inputs/Outputs, Customers/Suppliers

Inputs	From	To	For (Outputs)
Data Collection Requirements, Tracking Frequency, and "planned" values	Project Plan(s)	Project Manager	Data Requirements and Decision Template which quantify the project plan
Task status, i.e., "actual" values	Project Team Members	Project Manager	Project Status Meetings, project replanning, Project Tracking Report
Project Tracking Report	Project Managers	Department Manager, Director, Program Manager, Project Reviewers, Interdependencies	Project Review, project replanning
Project Tracking Report	Project Managers	Interdependencies and functional organizations	Planning and scheduling
Project Tracking Report	Project Managers	SQA	SQA process evaluation
Project Tracking Report	Project Managers	Project Archives	Postmortem evaluation to aid future projects

Input

Tracking information comes from two immediate sources.

(1) The original and/or revised project plan
(2) The current status of the project

The tracking process assumes that the following project planning information is documented and that the current status can be measured.

- Requirements (all types, including technical, quality, and marketing)
- The defined feature content
- The defined frequency of project tracking
- The estimated size of the project in measurable terms, e.g.
  (a) LOC (thousand lines of code), function points, or feature points
  (b) Pages of documentation or screens of help text
  (c) Number of test cases
- The resource usage plan, including staffing, equipment, tools, and supplies
- The approved schedule, which usually includes a list of major activities necessary to complete the project
- Commitments
- Interdependencies
- Assumptions, issues, risks, and opportunities

Activities

(1) From the project plan, identify the data collection requirements for project tracking, and obtain management agreement regarding when deviations need to be escalated to upper levels of management.

(2) From the project plan, obtain the "planned" values.

(3) Collect and store the current actual values of the tracking data, and compare them to the planned values.

(4) Evaluate the project's performance and status relative to the plan. Identify the reasons for deviations from the plan; identify both delays and accelerations.

(5) Determine whether the project's objectives, plan, or resources need to be adjusted. If adjustments are required and the project manager can make those adjustments without higher-level management approval, the project manager makes the adjustments. For adjustments that require higher-level management approval, the project manager recommends adjustments.

(6) Report the status of the project and store a copy of the report for postmortem evaluation.

(7) Invoke the project planning process if adjustments were made to the project's objectives, plan, or resources (either before or after issuing the tracking report). Make the changes and update the appropriate documents to reflect the currently approved plan for use during the next tracking cycle.

Output

The output of the process is a report of the project's status relative to the plan.

The report should identify reasons for deviations from the plan, document what adjustments have already been made by the project manager, and recommend adjustments to the plan as appropriate. Adjustments include both corrective actions and optimizations. It is recommended that more than one person evaluate the tracking data.

The items that should be tracked and reported upon are schedule, resources, cost, features, quality, and others as defined in the project plan. Resources include people, equipment, tools, training, and purchased software as appropriate to the project.

The project tracking report may take many forms. It may be a separate report, or it may be included in the minutes of project status meetings or the monthly operating letter. The primary reporting requirement is that the status is assessed and documented on a regular basis. A copy of the report shall be stored as part of the project's quality records.

Metrics

1. Process Usage

Goal   Better meet software delivery commitments by evaluating project status and adjusting the project plan on a regular basis.

Question What percentage of the planned and/or required tracking reports are actually being prepared?

Metric   Percent Tracking Usage = Number of reports prepared/Number of planned or required reports *100

Measures Number of planned or required reports.
Number of reports prepared.

2. Tracking Frequency

Goal   After establishing our current baseline frequency, be able to adjust the tracking frequency in order to optimize the effectiveness of the process.

Question How frequently are we preparing tracking reports now?

Metric   Tracking Frequency = Number of reports prepared/Number of months in the reporting period

Measures Number of reports prepared.

3. Effectiveness

Goal   Better meet software delivery requirements by adjusting the project plan in a timely manner in response to both issues and opportunities.

Question TBD

Metric   TBD

Measures TBD

Interdependencies

Interdependent processes include

- Project Planning Process
- Commitment Control Process
- Project Management Review Process

The project tracking process relies upon the project planning process to provide an approved project plan, which includes the items listed below.

- The resourcing plan (staffing, equipment and materials, and subcontractors)
- The task list
- The schedule

- Assumptions
- Risks
- Interdependencies
- Frequency of tracking

Note: The project plan must be maintained in a current state, and changes to the plan must be captured for postmortem analysis.

The project tracking process provides input to the project planning process in the form of recommendations or requirements to modify the project plan.

The commitment control process may constrain the modifications to the project plan that are recommended by the project tracking process.

The scope of the project tracking process must be sufficient to satisfy the requirements of the project management review process.

Exit Criteria

The frequency of preparing tracking reports should be defined in a project's development plan. Tracking reports must be prepared on a regular basis and must be prepared at least monthly during the latter phases of the software development life cycle. These reports must to be stored along with a project's other quality records.

The Project Tracking Report will contain the following information.

1. An Executive Summary of one page maximum length, including
   - Status relative to plan
   - Status of critical path tasks
   - Impact of current status on project outcome (i.e., impact on commitments, interdependencies, or quality)
   - Adjustments already made by project management
   - Opportunities
   - Recommendations for adjustments and/or requests for decisions requiring higher-level management approval
2. Tracking data for
   - Staffing
   - Schedule
   - Equipment, tools, supplies
   - Issues, risks, opportunities
   - Quality Plans

At the end of the project, an evaluation of tracking process usage and effectiveness should be included in the project's postmortem report. In addition to usage and effectiveness, the evaluation should consider such things as how the data was gathered, how the data was validated, and who managed the tracking process.

Even for projects that are too small to require tracking, a postmortem report is recommended.

Process Flow

Project Tracking Process   **Project Planning Process**

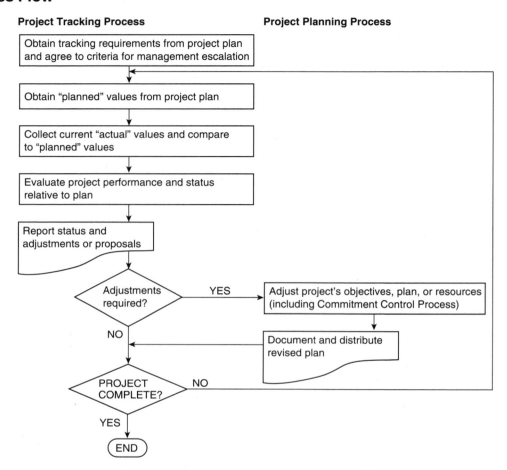

Project Management Review Process

Effective Date:
Authorizing Manager:

Purpose

This document describes the process for project management reviews to support program management, project management, and commitment control.

Objectives

The project management review process supports establishing and maintaining product development commitments. To ensure monitoring of progress and management assistance with project issues, the following meetings are held, and action items are tracked to closure. To support a more team-centered approach for information exchange and review, the model for the meetings is a "round table" approach, where participants provide their perspective and data for other members to evaluate and determine actions. Checklists ensure that the exchange of information covers all the needs of the team members.

The following table lists the frequency and content of each type of review and key participants. Other managers or team members involved may attend if desired.

Review/Meeting	Frequency	Content	Participants
Program Review	Quarterly	Marketing, financial, and development progress reports at the program level	Program Managers, Finance, Department Managers, Director, Facilitator, and Scribe
Project Review	Quarterly	Requirements, quality, and progress reports at the project level	Project Managers, Program Managers, Department Managers, SQA, Facilitator, and Scribe
Commitment Review	Monthly	Product Roadmap, Major Project Milestones	Program Managers, Department Managers
Status Meeting	As needed	Project Team status updates	Project Manager, Project Team

Program Reviews

Agenda and Content

The checklists at the end of this document provide standard agendas for quarterly program reviews. Prior to the meeting, the program manager determines what can be checked off and removed from the agenda due to information exchanged prior to the review. The remaining items are the program review agenda. The facilitator should keep the meeting on track and on time. Any items not covered by the end of the meeting must be handled through contact outside the meeting.

The agenda should finish with

- Review of open action items
- Review of new action items (what, who, by when)
- Comments from the floor (open forum information exchange)

Information Format

Each person brings data and reports as needed to cover the agenda. Formal overhead projection cells are not required; however, handouts of the relevant information are required.

Minutes and Action Items

A continuous log of action items will be located on a LAN file server. Prior to the meeting, the program manager will print the open actions for review at the meeting. After the meeting, the scribe will update the file with new action items from the meeting. Everyone will have access to the list, and as action items are marked closed by the program manager they should be moved to the end of the list. Materials distributed at the meeting will be kept in a central file by the SEPG.

Scheduling

Program managers are responsible for scheduling program reviews. To facilitate scheduling, each program will be designated for review during a specified month. Reviews should be scheduled for one-hour or two-hour meetings depending on the agenda. A master schedule of both program reviews and project reviews will be maintained on a LAN file server to facilitate scheduling and notification.

Program reviews may be canceled or rescheduled one week in advance with the consent of the director.

Project Reviews

Agenda and Content

The checklists at the end of this document provide standard agendas for quarterly project reviews. Prior to the meeting, the project manager determines what can be checked off and removed from the agenda due to information exchanged prior to the review. The remaining items are the project review agenda. The facilitator should keep the meeting on track and on time. Any items not covered by the end of the meeting must be handled through contact outside the meeting.

The agenda should finish with

- Review of open action items
- Review of new action items (what, who, by when)
- Comments from the floor (open forum information exchange)

Information Format

Each person brings data and reports as needed to cover the agenda. Formal overhead projection cells are not required; however, handouts of the relevant information are required. Supporting information, such as project notebooks, should be brought to the meeting.

Minutes and Action Items

A continuous log of action items will be located on a LAN file server. Prior to the meeting, the project manager will print the open actions for review at the meeting. After the meeting, the scribe will update the file with new action items from the meeting. Everyone will have access to the list, and as action items are marked closed by the project manager they should be moved to the end of the list. Materials distributed at the meeting will be kept in a central file by the SEPG.

Scheduling

Project managers are responsible for scheduling project reviews. To facilitate scheduling, each project will be designated for review during a specified month. Reviews should be scheduled for one-hour or two-hour meetings depending on the agenda. A master schedule of project reviews will be maintained on a LAN file server to facilitate scheduling and notification.

Project reviews may be canceled or rescheduled one week in advance with the consent of the department manager if all the following criteria are met.

1. The project is on target for schedule and resources.
2. There are no outstanding action items.
3. There are no issues regarding the checklist items.

Commitment Reviews

Agenda and Content

The product roadmap and major project milestones are reviewed to discuss issues, risks, potential changes, and trade-offs. The relevant questions are as follows.

- Is the information correct?
- Does everyone have the same understanding of the commitment?
- Are we making commitments at the right level of detail?
- Are we balancing the resources?
- Are we considering the impact after emergencies?
- Are the current commitments realistic?
- Were commitments (that were due this quarter) met?

Information Format, Minutes, and Action Items

The business manager prepares copies of the current product roadmap and major project milestones for review and update at the meeting. Updates to these records will be posted on the LAN file server for final review prior to approval and submission to the corporate database system.

Scheduling

The business manager is responsible for scheduling commitment reviews. These meetings will be held approximately two weeks in advance of submission of the data to the corporate database system to ensure adequate time for approval of changes.

Status Meetings

Agenda and Content

The agenda is set by the project manager to exchange information with the project team about

- Requirements status
- Task and schedule status
- Quality status (defect tracking, inspection and test completion, and so on)
- Action items

The project manager ensures that project plans are updated based on the status.

Information Format, Minutes, and Action Items

Each person brings data and reports as needed to cover the agenda. This is generally an informal exchange of information. Status meeting minutes are recommended to capture key information for future reference. If action items or issues are found that need to be raised to the project review, the project manager adds these items to the continuous log of action items located on the LAN file server and ensures that those responsible are notified prior to the review.

Scheduling

Project managers are responsible for scheduling status meetings weekly to monthly based on the needs of the project.

Metrics

1. Project Management Review Coverage

Goal   All programs must be reviewed quarterly.
            All projects must be reviewed quarterly.
            All commitments must be reviewed monthly.
            All project plans (major project milestones) must be updated at least monthly.

Question   How many reviews of each type were held this year?
            Are we progressing toward the goal?

Metric   Percentage of program reviews, project reviews, commitment reviews = Number of reviews held/Number of reviews planned

Measures   Number of reviews held
            Number of reviews planned

Frequency Quarterly

2. Program Review and Project Review Checklist Data Coverage

Goal   100% of checklist data items covered each quarter.

Question   How many checklist items were covered per quarter?
            Are we progressing toward the goal?

Metric   Percentage covered = Number of checklist items covered/total items

Measures   Checklists maintained by program managers and project managers, audited by SQA.

Frequency Quarterly

Interdependencies

Interdependent processes include

- Project Planning Process
- Commitment Control Process
- Project Tracking Process
- Software Quality Assurance Process

Quality Record	Responsibility	Frequency
Matrix of Programs and Projects	Business Manager	Maintained to current status
Master Schedule	Program Managers, Project Managers	Maintained to current status
Log of Action Items from Program Reviews	Program Managers	Maintained to current status
Log of Action Items from Project Reviews	Project Managers	Maintained to current status
Program Level Checklists	Program Managers	Reported Quarterly
Project Level Checklists	Project Managers	Reported Quarterly
Status Meeting Minutes	Project Managers	Optional, as needed
Materials and Attendees List	SEPG	Filed per Review
Coverage Metrics	SQA	Reported Quarterly

These checklists are used quarterly to track and ensure that management needs are met.

Goal—To minimize risk, cover 100% of the items each quarter.

Procedure—Cover all checklist items by the end of the quarter. If information is exchanged off-line prior to the meeting, coverage at the review can be minimized. Information skipped at the review must be covered off-line prior to the end of the quarter.

Checklist items are checked off the list ("X" in the lead column) when they are covered.

Program Level Checklist

Program managers are responsible for updating/completing the Program Level Checklist. For agendas estimate 15–30 minutes per segment.

Program:	Program Manager:
Review Date:	Quarter:

	X	Agenda Checklist Item	Responsibility
1.1		Market data, competitive positioning, differentiators	Program Manager
1.2		Requirements over time, bill of materials	Program Manager
1.3		Packaging, pricing, distribution channel	Program Manager
1.4		Marketing rollout, conferences, marketing plans	Program Manager
1.5		Third-party contract (or suppliers) plans and issues	Program Manager

		Agenda Checklist Item	Responsibility
2.1		Revenue plan	Program Manager
2.2		Unit and revenue data	Program Manager, Finance
2.3		Labor loading	Finance
2.4		Project issues stopping progress	Department Manager
2.5		Cross-team or cross-project issues	Department Manager
2.6		Engineering excellence data, quality concerns	Department Manager

		Agenda Checklist Item	Responsibility
3.1		Strategic direction affirmation or changes and why	Director
3.2		Priorities, commitment status, perspectives, insights	Director
3.3		Upper management issues	Director

The following items are typically covered through other meetings or contacts prior to the review meetings, and any issues with these items should be added to the review agendas.

		Agenda Checklist Item	Responsibility
4.1		Features planned	Program Manager
4.2		External liaisons defined	Program Manager, Department Manager
4.3		Software capitalization plans and timing	Finance
4.4		Recommended use of metrics	SQA
4.5		Audit plan	SQA

Project Level Checklist

Project managers are responsible for updating/completing the Project Level Checklist. For agendas estimate 15–30 minutes per segment.

Project:	Project Manager:
Review Date:	Quarter:

	X	Agenda Checklist Item	Responsibility
1.1		Brief status against plan, resource/planning needs	Project Manager
1.2		Project/product definition, requirements from project's perspective	Project Manager
1.3		Problems meeting spec. understanding of limitations	Project Manager
2.1		Customer and competitive product information	Program Manager
2.2		Interorganization program activities	Program Manager
2.3		Training requirements for CSCs, collateral material required	Program Manager
3.1		Project issues stopping progress	Department Manager, Project Manager
3.2		Cross-team or cross-project issues	Department Manager, Project Manager
3.3		Labor loading and resource and staffing requirements plans and issues	Department Manager, Project Manager
3.4		Quality concerns, assessment	SQA
3.5		Compliance data, quality initiatives required, exceptions	SQA
4.1		Concerns (areas to audit), priority shifts affecting SQA plan	Department Manager, Project Manager
4.2		Strategic direction affirmation or changes and why Priorities, commitment status, perspectives, insights	Department Manager, Program Manager

The following items are typically covered through other meetings or contacts prior to the review meetings, and any issues with these items should be added to the review agendas.

		Agenda Checklist Item	Responsibility
5.1		Software capitalization plans and timing	Finance
5.2		Ensure correct time reporting	Project Manager
5.3		Process exceptions	Department Manager, Project Manager
5.4		Recommended use of metrics	SQA
5.5		Audit plan	SQA

Action Item Log

This is a template for recording the action items from review meetings.

Project Review History Log
Filename:

Project	Project Manager	Program Manager	Department Manager

	Review Date and Time	Review Location (Meeting Room)	Participants in attendance
1			
2			
3			
4			

Open Action Items

Action Number	Assigned to	Action Description	Due Date

Issues, Risks, Opportunities

Number	Identified by	Description	Date Identified

Closed Action Items

Action Number	Assigned to	Action Description	Closure Date

Software Quality Assurance Process

Effective Date:
Authorizing Manager:

Purpose

The Software Quality Assurance (SQA) process provides independent verification that software development activities are being performed in an approved manner.

The phrase "software development activities" refers to activities of the entire organization and includes the activities of development, product information, continuation engineering, and the various support functions. It includes management activities as well as nonmanagement activities.

"In an approved manner" means that the activities and resulting products are in compliance or accord with applicable policies, processes, procedures, plans, and standards.

Scope

Although all software projects and most software development activities are potentially subject to SQA review, not all software development activities require a formal SQA process, and applying SQA to some activities will result in greater benefits than applying it to others. In order to derive maximum benefit, the SEPG and the Steering Committee need to monitor and review the SQA process so that the available SQA resources are always being directed toward those areas that management deems most important for ensuring quality.

The Steering Committee and SEPG will formulate and agree to an annual SQA Plan that identifies line management's SQA priorities and resource commitments to accomplish the plan, and will jointly review the SQA status, results, and plans quarterly.

Objectives

The objectives of the SQA process are as follows.

- To independently verify that software development activities, such as code and document inspections, are being performed in an approved manner
- To ensure that process and product deficiencies are brought to management's attention and resolved satisfactorily
- To maximize the benefit of SQA activities by reviewing results and adjusting SQA plans on a regular basis
- To minimize SQA resources while maximizing assurance by establishing a clearly defined set of SQA activities
- To minimize SQA resources while maximizing assurance by documenting assurance procedures, allowing line management to more easily assure their own activities

Customer Needs and Expectations

The customer of the SQA process is any manager or group responsible for complying with various policies, processes, procedures, plans, and standards. SQA auditors are the primary users of the process.

The customer of the SQA process expects an independent, objective evaluation against clearly defined evaluation criteria. (Personnel will conduct SQA evaluations only outside their own departments.)

The customer needs an SQA process that is nonthreatening—that is, a process involving clearly understood criteria and requiring little or no preparation time by the group(s) being audited.

A list of a project's applicable policies, processes, procedures, plans, and standards must be available. It is recommended that projects prepare this list during the project planning process and include it in the project's Quality Plan. Projects need to maintain adequate quality records in the areas that SQA audits.

To help meet these expectations, the organization's annual SQA plan will identify the following as accurately as possible.

- What areas are subject to SQA audit
- When, or in which development stage, SQA will conduct an evaluation or audit
- What general procedures and/or criteria SQA will use to evaluate compliance
- What additional personnel resources, if any, the SQA group will require in order to carry out the annual plan

SQA will develop and distribute copies of the detailed evaluation procedures and criteria based upon the requirements identified in the annual SQA plan. The SEPG may need to train those assisting in conducting audits. If necessary, include such training in the annual SQA plan.

The SEPG and the Steering Committee will evaluate how well the process is working using feedback obtained from users in the process of preparing the annual SQA plan and from periodic reviews of SQA activities.

Input

The process involves two types of input: input to the annual SQA plan and input to the auditing process.

Input to the Annual SQA Plan

The SQA group will create an annual SQA plan and review and revise it periodically based upon input from various sources, including

- Line management's SQA priorities conveyed via the Steering Committee
- Feedback based upon the results of previous SQA activities
- ISO 9000 requirements and Software Engineering Institute (SEI) CMM recommendations

Input to the SQA Audit Process

The input to the audit process will vary depending upon which process, project, or product deliverable is being audited. In general, an SQA auditor must have access to the following material in order to conduct an audit.

- A definition of the scope of the audit (usually specified in the annual SQA plan)
- A list and copies of all applicable policies, processes, procedures, plans, and standards (usually specified in the project's Quality Plan)
- The auditing procedures and/or criteria developed by the SQA group to evaluate compliance
- The quality records or other forms of supporting material that indicate compliance or noncompliance

Activities

The SQA process includes the following types of activities.

- Providing independent confirmation that applicable policies, processes, procedures, plans, and standards are being followed
- Identifying deviations from the applicable policies, processes, procedures, plans, and standards and notifying the group that has been audited so that it may initiate corrective actions
- Working with the groups that have been audited to ensure that process and product deficiencies are tracked and resolved satisfactorily
- Escalating problems to higher levels of management if corrective actions are not completed as agreed upon

The SQA audit is the primary mechanism used by the SQA group to perform the activities listed above. An SQA audit might not always involve interaction with project personnel, and to the extent it is practical, SQA will conduct audits without interaction with project personnel. For example, an audit might consist only of evaluating process data from a database or reading a project's local process or project documents.

In conducting an SQA audit of any type, the SQA auditor will

- Determine the scope of the audit
- Acquire and study the applicable policies, processes, procedures, plans, and standards
- Inspect the deliverables of a process and/or review other documents that indicate compliance or noncompliance, and record the results of the audit
- Re-audit at a later date to determine the status of corrective actions if an audit indicates that corrective actions are needed

Output

Audit Reports

In cases where SQA audits specific projects, SQA will provide an audit report to the project manager, section manager, or team leader. The report will identify the processes audited and itemize each area of noncompliance. SQA will assign a unique identifier to each noncompliance item it finds so that it can track the item to closure. SQA will present the findings to the project manager, section manager, or team leader within one week of an audit. The manager will have 30 days to respond to a noncompliance item, and 45 days to resolve the noncompliance, before SQA escalates the item to the Steering Committee.

Monthly Status Reports

The SQA group will produce a monthly SQA status report and distribute it to all project managers, section managers, team leaders, and department managers. The monthly report will include a list of all outstanding noncompliance items.

Steering Committee Reviews of SQA Activities

The SQA group will present status and results to the Steering Committee quarterly. The Steering Committee will assign each past-due, unresolved noncompliance item to a Steering Committee member for action and will review the resolution of each item at the subsequent quarterly SQA review meeting. The Steering Committee member will escalate a noncompliance item to the director if it cannot be resolved by the agreed date.

Metrics

To assist in assurance tracking, the SQA auditor will record the following for each noncompliance item.

- A description of the item, its cause, and the correction needed
- The auditor and the date the item was found
- The manager responsible for correcting the item
- The date by which the item is to be corrected
- The date the item is actually corrected
- The manager responsible for approving closure
- The date and name of the auditor verifying closure

The data tracked and reported includes

(1) Number of noncompliance items found during each audit
(2) Percentage of noncompliance items closed by the agreed date

Interdependencies

Interdependent processes include

- Project Planning Process
- Project Tracking Process

Process Flow

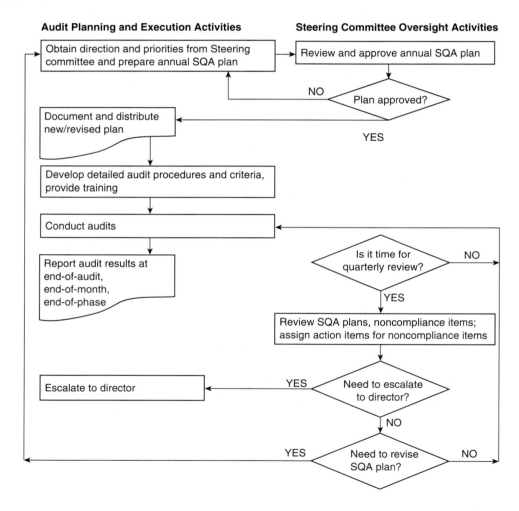

Appendix

K

Project Notebook Table of Contents

This file provides a Table of Contents and notebook tabs for a project notebook. The project notebook contains copies of the process documents and sections for each of the quality records associated with each process. The organization of the notebook makes it easy to find the documents and easy to audit the use of the processes with the process and records located together. For color-coded Table of Contents and notebook tabs, print the first two pages of the file. For black-and-white Table of Contents and notebook tabs, print the last two pages of the file.

Some project managers use an electronic version of the project notebook; instead of printing these pages, they establish links from the table of contents to their on-line records. Some project managers use a combination of electronic and physical project notebooks when they have a combination of on-line and hard-copy-only documents.

Project Notebook—Table of Contents

1.0 Project Management Policy
      1.1 Project Management Processes Overview

2.0 Requirements Management Process
      2.1 Requirements Specification
      2.2 Proposal
      2.3 Requirements Traceability Matrix

3.0 Project Planning Process
      3.1 Multiproject Development Plan
      3.2 Individual Project Plan
      3.3 Quality Plan

4.0 Estimation Process
      4.1 Estimation Factors Checklist
      4.2 Software Estimates

5.0 Commitment Control Process
      5.1 Commitment Approval Forms

6.0 Project Tracking Process
      6.1 Staffing Tracking Report
      6.2 Schedule Tracking Report
      6.3 Equipment, Tools, Supplies Report
      6.4 Issues/Risks/Opportunities Report
      6.5 Quality Plan Status Report
      6.6 Postmortem Report

7.0 Project Management Review Process
      7.1 Status Meeting Minutes
      7.2 Project Review Minutes
      7.3 Project Review Schedule
      7.4 Project Review Presentations

8.0 Software Quality Assurance Process
      8.1 SQA Plan
      8.2 SQA Audit Reports
      8.3 SQA Status Reports

1.0 Project Management Policy	1.0 Project Management Policy	5.0 Commitment Control Process	5.0 Commitment Control Process
1.1 Process Management Processes Overview	1.1 Process Management Processes Overview	5.1 Commitment Approval Forms	5.1 Commitment Approval Forms
2.0 Requirements Management Process	2.0 Requirements Management Process	6.0 Project Tracking Process	6.0 Project Tracking Process
2.1 Requirements Specification	2.1 Requirements Specification	6.1 Staffing Tracking Report	6.1 Staffing Tracking Report
2.2 Proposal	2.2 Proposal	6.2 Schedule Tracking Report	6.2 Schedule Tracking Report
2.3 Requirements Traceability Matrix	2.3 Requirements Traceability Matrix	6.3 Equipment, Tools, Supplies Report	6.3 Equipment, Tools, Supplies Report
3.0 Project Planning Process	3.0 Project Planning Process	6.4 Issues/Risks/ Opportunities Report	6.4 Issues/Risks/ Opportunities Report
3.1 Multiproject Development Plan	3.1 Multiproject Development Plan	6.5 Quality Plan Status Report	6.5 Quality Plan Status Report
3.2 Individual Project Plan	3.2 Individual Project Plan	6.6 Postmortem Report	6.6 Postmortem Report
3.3 Quality Plan	3.3 Quality Plan	7.0 Project Management Review Process	7.0 Project Management Review Process
4.0 Estimation Process	4.0 Estimation Process	7.1 Status Meeting Minutes	7.1 Status Meeting Minutes
4.1 Estimation Factors Checklist	4.1 Estimation Factors Checklist	7.2 Project Review Minutes	7.2 Project Review Minutes
4.2 Software Estimates	4.2 Software Estimates	7.3 Project Review Schedule	7.3 Project Review Schedule
		7.4 Project Review Presentations	7.4 Project Review Presentations
		8.0 Software Quality Assurance Process	8.0 Software Quality Assurance Process
		8.1 SQA Plan	8.1 SQA Plan
		8.2 SQA Audit Reports	8.2 SQA Audit Reports
		8.3 SQA Status Reports	8.3 SQA Status Reports
		Other	Other

Appendix

L

Process Definition Templates

These templates provide an easy structure for process documents.

Some groups prefer very short documents and might be content with the single-page summary as a one-page process document.

Other groups would not be content with a one-page document and would want additional details. The table formats help to organize the information in a smaller amount of space. For example, we took an existing 50-page process document and reduced it to 20 pages containing the same information simply by using the table formats provided here. By using these formats, we were able to identify places in the document that did not specify who performed the task (such as in a sentence in passive voice). These issues were made visible by the table format, in which each task is identified with each role. The structure also made it easier to reference the information and find the answer to questions much faster than before.

Make a copy of the template that you would like to use and fill in the blanks.

Sample Format for a Single-Page Summary

Single Page Summary:

Process Objective:	Key Milestones:

People Involved:
    Primary:
    Secondary:
	Data Records Required:
	    Tools or Databases:
	    Forms or Deliverables:

When to Perform These Activities: 1. 2. 3.	Input Data: 1. 2. 3.
Communication Activities: 1. 2. 3.	Recording Activities: 1. 2. 3.
Results (Closure Agreements or Decisions): 1. 2. 3.	Results (Output Data): 1. 2. 3.

Sample Format for Process Guide

Cover Page and Single-Page Summary

Table of Contents

1. Document Control
    1.1 Changes Since Previous Revision
    1.2 Document Cross Reference

2. Introduction
    2.1 Purpose, Scope, and Audience
    2.2 Organization of This Guide

3. Process Overview
    3.1 ⟨Descriptions/Specific Terminology⟩
    3.2 Schedule Milestones

Milestone Name	Description

    3.3 Process Timelines
        (Timeline Charts)
    3.4 Roles and Responsibilities

Function or Functional Role	Responsibilities and Expectations

4. Activities
    4.1 Basic Process Activities

From Whom	Activity/Document	To Whom For What

    4.2 Additions for ⟨Alternative Case 1⟩

From Whom	Activity/Document	To Whom For What

    4.3 Additions for ⟨Alternative Case 2⟩

From Whom	Activity/Document	To Whom For What

5. Standard Deliverables and Templates

Document	From Whom To Whom	Purpose	Content

6. Additional Process Details

Sample Format for Supporting Document—Tailorable Process

Cover Page and Single-Page Summary

Table of Contents

1. Purpose, Scope, and Audience

2. Standard Process
   2.1 Standard Process Flow
        (Timeline Chart or Flowchart)
   2.2 Standard Activities

Step	Objectives	Guidelines for Activities

   2.3 Standard Roles and Responsibilities

Role	Responsibilities

   2.4 Standard Documents and Quality Records

Document or Data Type	Objectives	Contents

Document or Data Type	Data Recording Requirements

3. Tailoring the Standard Process
    3.1 Methods

Methods	Description	Conditions

    3.2 Additional Tailoring Guidelines
        (Describe recommendations for limits, selection criteria, special cases)

4. Task List
    4.1 ⟨Name 1⟩ Method

From Whom	Activity/Document	To Whom For What

    4.2 ⟨Name 2⟩ Method

From Whom	Activity/Document	To Whom For What

    4.3 ⟨Name 3⟩ Method

From Whom	Activity/Document	To Whom For What

5. Data Definitions
    (Tables of data items, definitions, acronyms, explanations, checklist items, etc.)

Sample Format for Supporting Document—Procedure

Cover Page and Single-Page Summary

Table of Contents

1. Document Control
    1.1 Changes Since Previous Revision
    1.2 Document Cross Reference

2. Introduction
    2.1 Purpose, Scope, and Audience
    2.2 Organization of This Guide

3. Overview
        ⟨Descriptions/Specific Terminology⟩

4. Task List

Condition	⟨Role 1⟩ Task	⟨Role 2⟩ Task

5. Forms for ⟨Role⟩

Condition	Forms provided from ⟨Role 1⟩ to ⟨Role 2⟩	Using template(s)
		⟨actual link to form⟩
		⟨actual link to form⟩

6. Database and Metrics

Goal	
Questions	
Metrics	
Measurements	
Sample Report	

Appendix
M

CMM Action Planning Workshop Technique

These presentation materials are designed to be used for a series of four one-hour workshops for project team members. Each workshop covers one or more of the CMM Level 2 Key Process Areas and what the project team does in relationship to the goals. The project team identifies issues and actions to take to improve its performance.

The same pattern of a standard agenda is used for all four meetings.

- A 10-minute team warm-up.
- A 20-minute review of the goals and current practices (desired state and current state).
- A 30-minute team discussion of issues and actions.
  - 15 minutes to discuss in small groups of two or three
  - 15 minutes for sharing the results

Following this pattern, you can change the materials to meet your needs. For example, you can change the warm-up exercises to whatever else you like that makes a good point or helps the team members learn something about themselves and others on the team. For your use, change the materials that mention our processes and quality records to reflect your own processes and quality records. If you have other goals or initiatives, you can change the "desired state" materials.

Breaking into small groups at first helps get ideas from everyone in a shorter period of time. Some people are more comfortable sharing their ideas with one or two people first before sharing their ideas with the entire team, so this method helps build their confidence in their good ideas. It also helps to eliminate the weaker ideas in the smaller group to save the time and attention of the entire group.

After the meeting, the actions are consolidated for use in planning and tracking. Various methods can be used for this, such as the Simple Action Plan in Appendix F, the Results, Needs, Activities Worksheet in Appendix H, or whatever your organization currently does to track action items. For each action, at a minimum determine the following:

- Who is involved now
- Who should be involved
- What priority it should have (impact of results, urgency of the needs, feasibility of the activities)

CMM Action Planning
Meeting #1

- Purpose of the Meetings:
  - To identify actions in response to issues relative to CMM Level 2 Key Process Areas
  - To increase project team awareness of the project management processes
  - To increase project team involvement in using and improving the processes
- Today's Topic:
  - *Software Project Tracking and Oversight*

Standard Agenda

- Mental Warm-up and Guidelines Review
  10 minutes
- Today's Topic
  20 minutes
  - Desired State
    Key Process Area Goals
  - Current State
    Our Processes and Quality Records
- Brainstorm: Issues and Actions
  30 minutes

Mental Warm-up
Why do a Mental Warm-up?

Centering	Focus on the task at hand. Leave everything else outside the door.
Stimulate creative thinking for problem solving	Problem solving requires a combination of left-brain (logical, rational, sequential) thinking and right-brain (holistic, intuitive, out-of-the-box) thinking.
Self-awareness and team awareness	Become more aware of what your opinions are and how they compare with others. Identify individual and team strengths and weaknesses.
Lighten up!	Don't get too serious. Depression is not conducive to change.

The STAIRS

Service	Remember who your customers are and what they need and expect.
Teamwork	**T**ogether **E**veryone **A**chieves **M**ore
Action	Leadership is *not* about doing things *right*, it's about doing the *right* things.
Involvement	If you're not part of the solution, you're part of the problem. The best solution involves everyone.
Responsiveness	You may not always be able to control the situation, but you can control your reaction and your response.
Stop the Insanity	Insanity is doing the same thing over and over and expecting a different result. If you want a different result, you have to change what you do.

Personal Results

	S	T	A	I	R	S
F						
W						
S						

Team Results

	S	T	A	I	R	S
F						
W						
S						

F: your favorite
W: your weakness
S: your strength

Guidelines
(From Team Training)

- Key Principles for Effective Communication
    - Maintain or enhance self-esteem.
    - Listen and respond with empathy.
    - Ask for help and encouragement.

- Differences and Conflict
    - Differing points of view can promote creativity and innovation.
    - Discussing differing opinions can lead to unique approaches to solving a problem.

- The Weather Forecast
    - Forming
    - Storming
    - Norming
    - Performing

Guidelines
(States of Transition)

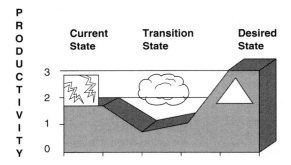

Desired State—Key Process Area:
Software Project Tracking and Oversight

Purpose

To provide adequate visibility into actual progress so that management can take effective actions when performance deviates significantly from the plan

Scope

Involves:

- tracking and reviewing software accomplishments and results against documented estimates, commitments, and plans

- adjusting plans based on actual accomplishments and results

Goals

1. Actual results and performances are tracked against the software plans.
2. Corrective actions are taken and managed to closure when actual results deviate significantly from the software plans.
3. Changes to software commitments are agreed to by the affected groups and individuals.

Software Project Tracking and Oversight
Our Processes and Quality Records

- PROJECT TRACKING PROCESS
  - Staffing Tracking Report
  - Schedule Tracking Report
  - Equipment, Tools, and Supplies Report
  - Issues, Risks, and Opportunities Report
  - Quality Plan Report
  - Postmortem Report

- PROJECT MANAGEMENT REVIEW PROCESS
  - Status Meetings
  - Project Reviews
  - Commitment Reviews

Brainstorm Issues and Actions

First 15 minutes (alone and then in groups of 2–3)
1. Alone—Review background material
2. Alone—Take 1 minute to select 3–5 issues
3. Alone—Take 2 minutes to think about actions to address the issues
4. Group—Make a combined list of each member's issues and actions
5. Group—Each member clarifies ideas for understanding
6. Group—Discuss/develop ideas as a group
7. Group—Reduce the list (eliminate or combine actions)
8. One Person—Write the final list on overhead cells or flip chart

Second 15 minutes (Everyone)
Share results with the Project Team
(Each group presents its list and clarifies its ideas)

Next Steps

- Consolidate the actions in a Project Team Action Plan
- Determine who is involved and who should be involved
- Determine the priority of the action
- Initiate action, track progress and results

CMM Action Planning
Meeting #2

- Purpose of the Meetings:
  - To identify actions in response to issues relative to CMM Level 2 Key Process Areas
  - To increase project team awareness of the project management processes
  - To increase project team involvement in using and improving the processes

- Today's Topic:
  - *Requirements Management*

Standard Agenda

- Mental Warm-up and Guidelines Review
  10 minutes

- Today's Topic
  20 minutes
  - Desired State
    Key Process Area Goals
  - Current State
    Our Processes and Quality Records

- Brainstorm: Issues and Actions
  30 minutes

Mental Warm-up
Why do a Mental Warm-up?

Centering	Focus on the task at hand. Leave everything else outside the door.
Stimulate creative thinking for problem solving	Problem solving requires a combination of left-brain (logical, rational, sequential) thinking and right-brain (holistic, intuitive, out-of-the-box) thinking.
Self-awareness and team awareness	Become more aware of what your opinions are and how they compare with others. Identify individual and team strengths and weaknesses.
Lighten up!	Don't get too serious. Depression is not conducive to change.

Skills and Preferences

Of the following tasks, which do you prefer, and which would you rather avoid?

+	Prefer:	Something that you do well and get a lot of satisfaction from doing well.
−	Avoid:	Something that you don't get much satisfaction from doing and would like to rely on others who have this as a strength.
○	Neutral:	Doesn't matter—Take it or leave it.

+ − ○	1.1 Determining Requirements		+ − ○	4.1 Communicating in Meetings
+ − ○	1.2 Surveying/Talking to Customers		+ − ○	4.2 Communicating by E-mail
+ − ○	1.3 Designing/Drawing Design Diagrams		+ − ○	4.3 Facilitating Meetings
+ − ○	1.4 Writing Documents		+ − ○	4.4 Taking Meeting Minutes
+ − ○	1.5 Reading/Reviewing Documents		+ − ○	4.5 Tracking Time/Meeting Agenda
+ − ○	2.1 Writing Code		+ − ○	5.1 Working Alone
+ − ○	2.2 Inspecting Code		+ − ○	5.2 Working in Small Groups (2–4)
+ − ○	2.3 Writing Tests		+ − ○	5.3 Working in Large Groups (5 or more)
+ − ○	2.4 Running Tests		+ − ○	5.4 Expressing Opinions
+ − ○	2.5 Debugging Code		+ − ○	5.5 Finding Facts
+ − ○	3.1 Organizing/Keeping Records			
+ − ○	3.2 Estimating Time/Tasks			
+ − ○	3.3 Tracking Features/Requirements			
+ − ○	3.4 Tracking Defects			
+ − ○	3.5 Tracking Schedule/Time/Cost			

Guidelines
(From Team Training)

- Key Principles for Effective Communication
    - Maintain or enhance self-esteem.
    - Listen and respond with empathy.
    - Ask for help and encouragement.

- Differences and Conflict
    - Differing points of view can promote creativity and innovation.
    - Discussing differing opinions can lead to unique approaches to solving a problem.

- The Weather Prediction
    - Forming
    - Storming
    - Norming
    - Performing

Guidelines
(States of Transition)

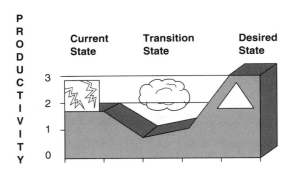

Desired State—Key Process Area:
Requirements Management

Purpose

To establish a common understanding between the customer and the software project of the customer's requirements that will be addressed by the software project

Scope

Involves establishing and maintaining an agreement with the customer on the requirements for the software project

Agreement is the basis for estimating, planning, performing, and tracking the project's software activities

Goals

1. System requirements allocated to software are controlled to establish a baseline for software engineering and management use.
2. Software plans, products, and activities are kept consistent with the system requirements allocated to software.

Requirements Management
Our Processes and Quality Records

- REQUIREMENTS MANAGEMENT PROCESS
  - Requirements Specification
      Definition and Analysis
      Understanding of Requested Functionality
  - Proposal
      Defines Requirements Committed for Delivery
  - Requirements Traceability Matrix:
      Tracks Requirements Status:
      Approved, Committed,
      Designed, Implemented,
      Test Written, Completed

Brainstorm Issues and Actions

First 15 minutes (alone and then in groups of 2–3)
1. Alone—Review background material
2. Alone—Take 1 minute to select 3–5 issues
3. Alone—Take 2 minutes to think about actions to address the issues
4. Group—Make a combined list of each member's issues and actions
5. Group—Each member clarifies ideas for understanding
6. Group—Discuss/develop ideas as a group
7. Group—Reduce the list (eliminate or combine actions)
8. One Person—Write the final list on overhead cells or flip chart

Second 15 minutes (Everyone)
Share results with the Project Team
(Each group presents its list and clarifies its ideas)

Next Steps

* Consolidate the actions in a Project Team Action Plan
* Determine who is involved and who should be involved
* Determine the priority of the action
* Initiate action, track progress and results

CMM Action Planning
Meeting #3

* Purpose of the Meetings:
  - To identify actions in response to issues relative to CMM Level 2 Key Process Areas
  - To increase project team awareness of the project management processes
  - To increase project team involvement in using and improving the processes

* Today's Topic:
  - *Software Project Planning*

Standard Agenda

* Mental Warm-up and Guidelines Review
  10 minutes

* Today's Topic
  20 minutes
  - Desired State
       Key Process Area Goals
  - Current State
       Our Processes and Quality Records

* Brainstorm: Issues and Actions
  30 minutes

Mental Warm-up
Why do a Mental Warm-up?

Centering	Focus on the task at hand. Leave everything else outside the door.
Stimulate creative thinking for problem solving	Problem solving requires a combination of left-brain (logical, rational, sequential) thinking and right-brain (holistic, intuitive, out-of-the-box) thinking.
Self-awareness and team awareness	Become more aware of what your opinions are and how they compare with others. Identify individual and team strengths and weaknesses.
Lighten up!	Don't get too serious. Depression is not conducive to change.

High-Tech Marketing Model—Psychographic Profiles

- Where do you see yourself in the model?
- Where do you see other members of your team?
- Where do you see our company's markets? Your product's markets?

Likes to figure out how a technology works and why. Wants to be the first to adopt the new stuff. Enjoys "the latest and greatest"– pushing the edge of the envelope Interested in learning and evaluating new things. *Technology Enthusiasts:*	Highly motivated and driven by a "dream". Seeks quantum leap breakthroughs, not just improvement. Willing to take risks to achieve goals– sees potential, but not always practical. "Big Picture" view, matching emerging technology to a strategic opportunity or business need. *Visionaries:*	Does not want to be a pioneer– too much risk. Seeks to gain a percentage improvement. Values the opinions of and reference from others like them. Practical, prefers standards, loyal once won over. *Pragmatists:*	Believes more in tradition than in progress. Not looking for improvement, but doesn't want to be left behind to get stung. Prefers "whole solutions" with every element thought through and packaged. Buys when the price drops. *Conservatives:*	Believes new technology doesn't deliver on promises made. Tends to see through the marketing hype and point out discrepancies. Continually points out flaws and costs, and doesn't see the benefits as justified. *Skeptics:*
Innovators	**Early Adopters**	**Early Majority**	**Late Majority**	**Laggards**

Adapted from *Crossing the Chasm* by Geoffrey A. Moore, Harper Business, 1991.

Guidelines
(From Team Training)

- Key Principles for Effective Communication
  - Maintain or enhance self-esteem.
  - Listen and respond with empathy.
  - Ask for help and encouragement.

- Differences and Conflict
  - Differing points of view can promote creativity and innovation.
  - Discussing differing opinions can lead to unique approaches to solving a problem.

- The Weather Prediction
  - Forming
  - Storming
  - Norming
  - Performing

Guidelines
(States of Transition)

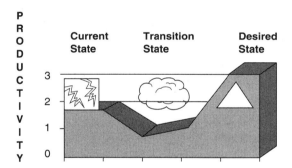

Desired State—Key Process Area:
Software Project Planning

Purpose

To establish reasonable plans for performing the software engineering and for managing the software project

Scope

Involves:
- developing estimates for the work to be performed

- establishing the necessary commitments

- defining the plan to perform the work

Plan provides the basis for initiating the software effort and managing the work

Goals

1. Software estimates are documented for use in planning and tracking the software project.
2. Software project activities and commitments are planned and documented.
3. Affected groups and individuals agree to their commitments related to the software project.

Software Project Planning
Our Processes and Quality Records

- ESTIMATION PROCESS
  - Estimate and collect historical data for future estimates

- PROJECT PLANNING PROCESS
  - Multiproject Development Plan
  - Individual Project Plan
  - Quality Plan

- COMMITMENT CONTROL PROCESS
  - Product Roadmap, Approval Forms
  - Monthly Commitment Reviews

Brainstorm Issues and Actions

First 15 minutes (alone and then in groups of 2–3)
1. Alone—Review background material
2. Alone—Take 1 minute to select 3–5 issues
3. Alone—Take 2 minutes to think about actions to address the issues
4. Group—Make a combined list of each member's issues and actions
5. Group—Each member clarifies ideas for understanding
6. Group—Discuss/develop ideas as a group
7. Group—Reduce the list (eliminate or combine actions)
8. One Person—Write the final list on overhead cells or flip chart

Second 15 minutes (Everyone)
Share results with the Project Team
(Each group presents its list and clarifies its ideas)

Next Steps

- Consolidate the actions in a Project Team Action Plan
- Determine who is involved and who should be involved
- Determine the priority of the action
- Initiate action, track progress and results

CMM Action Planning
Meeting #4

- Purpose of the Meetings:
    - To identify actions in response to issues relative to SEI Level 2 Key Process Areas
    - To increase project team awareness of the project management processes
    - To increase project team involvement in using and improving the processes
- Today's Topic:
    - *Software Quality Assurance (SQA)*
    - *Software Configuration Management*
    - *Software Subcontract Management*

Standard Agenda

- Mental Warm-up and Guidelines Review
  10 minutes
- Today's Topic
  20 minutes
    - Desired State
        Key Process Area Goals
    - Current State
        Our Processes and Quality Records
- Brainstorm: Issues and Actions
  30 minutes

Mental Warm-up
Why do a Mental Warm-up?

Centering	Focus on the task at hand. Leave everything else outside the door.
Stimulate creative thinking for problem solving	Problem solving requires a combination of left-brain (logical, rational, sequential) thinking and right-brain (holistic, intuitive, out-of-the-box) thinking.
Self-awareness and team awareness	Become more aware of what your opinions are and how they compare with others. Identify individual and team strengths and weaknesses.
Lighten up!	Don't get too serious. Depression is not conducive to change.

Cultural Patterns (Weingerg)

From the *engineering* view, NOT the *management* view

Pattern	Classification	Description
0	Oblivious	We don't even know that we're performing a process
1	Variable	We do whatever we feel like at the moment
2	Routine	We follow our routines (except when we panic)
3	Steering	We choose among our routines based on the results they produce
4	Anticipating	We establish routines based on our past experience with them
5	Congruent	Everyone is involved in improving everything all the time

What pattern are we using when we perform the following processes?

Pattern	Process	Pattern	Process
	Software Development Processes		Project Management Processes
	Inspection Processes		Strategic Planning Processes
	Testing Processes		Process Management Processes
	Documentation Processes		People Management Processes
	Continuation/Support Processes		Customer Satisfaction Processes

Note: Material reprinted by permission of Dorset House publishing, from Gerald M. Weinberg, *Quality Software Management Vol. 1: Systems Thinking* (p. 23). Copyright © 1992 by Gerald M. Weinberg. Published by Dorset House Publishing, 353 W. 12th St., New York, NY 10014. All rights reserved.

Guidelines
(From Team Training)

- Key Principles for Effective Communication
  - Maintain or enhance self-esteem.
  - Listen and respond with empathy.
  - Ask for help and encouragement.

- Differences and Conflict
  - Differing points of view can promote creativity and innovation.
  - Discussing differing opinions can lead to unique approaches to solving a problem.

- The Weather Prediction
  - Forming
  - Storming
  - Norming
  - Performing

Guidelines
(States of Transition)

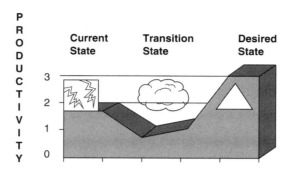

Desired State—Key Process Area:
Software Quality Assurance

Purpose

To provide management with appropriate visibility into the process being used and the products being built

Scope

Involves:
- reviewing and auditing the software products and activities to ensure that they comply with the applicable procedures and standards

- providing the software project and other appropriate managers with the results of those reviews and audits

Goals

1. Software quality assurance activities are planned.
2. Adherence of software products and activities to the applicable standards, procedures, and requirements is verified objectively.
3. Affected groups and individuals are informed of software quality assurance activities and results.
4. Noncompliance issues that cannot be resolved within the software project are addressed by senior management.

Software Quality Assurance
Processes and Quality Records

- SOFTWARE QUALITY ASSURANCE PROCESS
  - Organization-wide Record Audits
  - Project Notebook Audits
  - Annual Plan, Project Review Reporting
  - Independent SQA Staffing:
    current—from Software Process Management team
    future—may draw part-time resources from projects

- PRODUCT ASSURANCE
  - Inspection Processes and Records
  - Testing Processes and Records
  - Quality Plans

- QUALITY SYSTEM MANAGEMENT REVIEWS
  - Quarterly Steering Committee Review of Process Metrics and Results

Desired State—Key Process Area:
Software Configuration Management

Purpose

To establish and maintain the integrity of the products of the software project throughout the software life cycle

Scope

Involves:
- identifying configuration items/ units
- systematically controlling changes
- maintaining integrity and traceability of the configuration throughout the software life cycle

Goals

1. Software configuration management activities are planned.
2. Selected software work products are identified, controlled, and available.
3. Changes to identified software work products are controlled.
4. Affected groups and individuals are informed of the status and content of software baselines.

Software Configuration Management
Processes and Quality Records

- PROJECT PLANNING PROCESS
  - All Deliverables and Quality Records are identified in Project Plans (Quality Plan)

- SOFTWARE DOCUMENT CONTROL
  - ISO 9000 Document Control
    - Product Documents: Design Review Database
    - Process Documents: "Red Binders"
    - Project Management Documents: Project Notebooks

- SOURCE CODE CONTROL

Desired State—Key Process Area:
Software Subcontract Management

Purpose

To select qualified software sub-contractors and manage them effectively

Scope

Involves:

- selecting a software subcontractor

- establishing commitments with the subcontractor

- tracking and reviewing the sub-contractor's performance and results

Goals

1. The prime contractor selects qualified software subcontractors.
2. The prime contractor and the software subcontractor agree to their commit-ments to each other.
3. The prime contractor and the soft-ware subcontractor maintain ongoing communications.
4. The prime contractor tracks the soft-ware subcontractor's actual results and performances against its commitments.

Brainstorm Issues and Actions

First 15 minutes (alone and then in groups of 2–3)
1. Alone—Review background material
2. Alone—Take 1 minute to select 3–5 issues
3. Alone—Take 2 minutes to think about actions to address the issues
4. Group—Make a combined list of each member's issues and actions
5. Group—Each member clarifies ideas for understanding
6. Group—Discuss/develop ideas as a group
7. Group—Reduce the list (eliminate or combine actions)
8. One Person—Write the final list on overhead cells or flip chart

Second 15 minutes (Everyone)
Share results with the Project Team
(Each group presents its list and clarifies its ideas)

Next Steps

- Consolidate the actions in a Project Team Action Plan
- Determine who is involved and who should be involved
- Determine the priority of the action
- Initiate action, track progress and results

Feedback

- Did these sessions satisfy the objectives?
    - To identify actions in response to issues relative to CMM Level 2 Key Process Areas
    - To increase project team awareness of the project management processes
    - To increase project team involvement in using and improving the processes

- Were the warm-up exercises effective (for centering, stimulating creative thinking and self and team awareness, and lightening up)?

- Were these sessions effective for team-building?

- Were the number and length of the sessions adequate and effective?

- Would you recommend these sessions for a "kick-off" of each new project/project team?

- Other comments on effectiveness or improvements?

Appendix

N

Postmortem Process Techniques

The methods for these templates are described in Chapter 7.

For the structured meeting postmortem method, the postmortem report template can be filled in directly from the notes captured at the meeting.

For the software process postmortem method, the questions can be used directly or can be tailored to meet your needs. The Software Process Postmortem Report template can be used to sort and analyze the information gathered in the interviews or meeting discussions.

For starting a new project, you can use the new project questions directly or tailor them to meet your needs.

Structured Meeting Postmortem Report Template

1. Executive Summary

Members of the (project name) Project met on (date) to discuss and evaluate the process and issues relative to (project deliverable). The purposes of the postmortem were to

- Assess what happened
- Assess what worked and did not work
- Make recommendations for the benefit of future projects

Postmortem Participants:

Name	Role

Postmortem Agenda:

1. Scope—What timeframe to cover
2. Process—What events and activities took place in that timeframe
3. Hot Areas—Each participant selected the area he or she most wanted to discuss
4. Prioritize/Affinitize—List of areas selected, order for discussion decided
5. Brainstorm—Each area: What worked or didn't work
6. Major Strengths and Major Weaknesses—Selected from brainstorm data
7. Recommendations—Recommendations for action

Major Strengths:

1. (comment)
2. (comment)
3. (comment)
4. (comment)
5. (comment)

Major Weaknesses:

1. (comment)
2. (comment)
3. (comment)
4. (comment)
5. (comment)

Recommendations Summary:

1. (recommendation)
2. (recommendation)
3. (recommendation)
4. (recommendation)
5. (recommendation)

2. Summary of Process

The following chart represents a history of events and activities for the project from (start date) to (end date):

Dates	Events and Activities	Discussion Topics Relative to These Events and Activities

Of these items and issues relative to these items, the team chose to discuss the following:

1. (Topic #1)
2. (Topic #2)
3. (Topic #3)
4. (Topic #4)

3. Findings Data

For each topic, participants gave their impression of what worked and what did not work relative to the topic. Items in **boldface** indicate strong mutual feeling of the group for that item.

3.1 (Topic #1)

	What Worked		What Didn't Work
1		1	
2		2	
3		3	

3.2 (Topic #2)

	What Worked		What Didn't Work
1		1	
2		2	
3		3	

3.3 (Topic #3)

	What Worked		What Didn't Work
1		1	
2		2	
3		3	

3.4 (Topic #4)

	What Worked		What Didn't Work
1		1	
2		2	
3		3	

4. Recommendations

The following recommendations were made by the team:

Category	Recommendation

Software Process Postmortem Questions

Please consider these 14 questions to assess the process used on this project, and, in contrast to prior practices, what was better and/or what was worse?

1. Communication and Information

What was done to ensure communication and definition of the project (internally? with interdependencies? with marketing and clients?)?

2. Software Life Cycle

What was the overall sequence of events or milestones for the project?

3. Program Statement and Requirements

How did you know "what was in and what was out" for requirements and features?
If requirements changed, how was this communicated?

4. Requirements Verification and Release Criteria

How did you determine a requirement was met or a feature was complete?
How did you determine the product was ready?

5. Design and Design Verification

How were product functions designed (prototype? formal designs?)?
How were the designs evaluated (reviews? inspections? approvals?)?
How were design errors identified and removed?

6. Code and Code Verification

How was the software code developed?
How was code evaluated, and how were defects discovered (inspections? unit test?)?
If multiple evaluation methods were used, what selection criteria were used?
How were software defects identified and removed?

7. Integration and Qualification

How was the software integrated and tested?
How was the testing planned?
How were defects handled (tracked to closure? deciding who gets to fix the defect?)?

8. Preparation for Support

How were regression tests developed and maintained?
How were test results reported and to whom?
What information is available to those who will maintain or interface with the product in the future (training materials? designs? documentation?)?

9. Packaging and Delivery

How was user documentation designed and integrated with the product?
How was the product packaged and delivered for release?

10. Project Planning and Tracking

How were the project tasks determined, estimated, communicated, and tracked?
How was status evaluated (such as "schedule on track" or "behind schedule")?
How were impacts of changes accounted for on the project (for example, requirements changes, defect levels, staffing changes)?

11. Configuration Management

How was the code managed and controlled for version control (tracking the "current levels" or current files or patches? patch reviews or approvals? source code control tools?)?

12. Project Coordination and Risk Management

How were commitments managed and communicated?
How were risks managed and communicated?
How were corrective actions identified, planned, and tracked?
How were project activities reviewed or verified?
How were the needs for tools or training identified, planned, and tracked?

13. Process Effectiveness

What was most effective about doing the project in this way?
What would you recommend to keep or change about the process based on this?

14. Process Risk

What was most risky about doing the project in this way?
What would you recommend to keep or change about the process based on this?

Software Process Postmortem Final Report Template

Software Process Postmortem Report

Summary

In (month, year), the following people were interviewed to discuss the process used for the (project name) project:

Name	Role

Postmortem Objective

We need to evaluate what happened, what was effective, and what risks are involved in this approach for future projects.

Summary of Recommendations

based on what was "most effective" and "most risky" about the actual practices:

Most Effective	Most Risky
• (from question #13) • • • •	• (from question #14) • • • •

What should be done based on these "most effective" and "most risky" practices:

What should continue	What should be discontinued or improved next time
• (from question #13) • • • •	• (from question #14) • • • •

Report Details: Individual Questions and Summarized Responses

1. Communication and Information

Activity Statements	Evaluation Statements
• (what was done) • • • •	• (positive and negative aspects about what was done) • • • • •

2. Software Life Cycle

Activity Statements	Evaluation Statements
• • •	• • •

3. Program Statement and Requirements

Activity Statements	Evaluation Statements
• • •	• • •

4. Requirements Verification and Release Criteria

Activity Statements	Evaluation Statements
• • •	• • •

5. Design and Design Verification

Activity Statements	Evaluation Statements
• • •	• • •

6.   Code and Code Verification

Activity Statements	Evaluation Statements
•	•
•	•
•	•

7.   Integration and Qualification

Activity Statements	Evaluation Statements
•	•
•	•
•	•

8.   Packaging and Delivery (including Configuration Management and Support Preparation)

Activity Statements	Evaluation Statements
•	•
•	•
•	•

9.   Project Coordination (Planning and Tracking and Risk Management)

Activity Statements	Evaluation Statements
•	•
•	•
•	•

New Project Questions

Please consider these 14 questions to determine the process to use on this project.

1. Communication and Information
What will be done to ensure communication and definition of the project (internally? with interdependencies? with marketing and clients?)?

2. Software Life Cycle
What will the overall sequence of events or milestones for the project be?

3. Program Statement and Requirements
How will you know "what is in and what is out" for requirements and features? If requirements change, how will this be communicated?

4. Requirements Verification and Release Criteria
How will you determine a requirement has been met or a feature has been completed? How will you determine the product is ready?

5. Design and Design Verification
How will product functions be designed (prototype? formal designs?)? How will the designs be evaluated (reviews? inspections? approvals?)? How will design errors be identified and removed?

6. Code and Code Verification
How will the software code be developed? How will the code be evaluated, and how will defects be discovered (inspections? unit test?)? If multiple evaluation methods are used, what selection criteria will be used? How will software defects be identified and removed?

7. Integration and Qualification
How will the software be integrated and tested? How will the testing be planned? How will defects be handled (tracked to closure? deciding who gets to fix the defect?)?

8. Preparation for Support
How will regression tests be developed and maintained? How will test results be reported and to whom? What information will be available to those who will maintain or interface with the product in the future (training materials? designs? documentation?)?

9. Packaging and Delivery
How will user documentation be designed and integrated with the product? How will the product be packaged and delivered for release?

10. Project Planning and Tracking

How will the project tasks be determined, estimated, communicated, and tracked?
How will status be evaluated (such as "schedule on track" or "behind schedule")?
How will impacts of changes be accounted for on the project (for example, requirements changes, defect levels, staffing changes)?

11. Configuration Management

How will the code be managed and controlled for version control (tracking the "current levels" or current files or patches? patch reviews or approvals? source code control tools?)?

12. Project Coordination and Risk Management

How will commitments be managed and communicated?
How will risks be managed and communicated?
How will corrective actions be identified, planned, and tracked?
How will project activities be reviewed or verified?
How will the needs for tools or training be identified, planned, and tracked?

13. Process Effectiveness

What do you expect to be most effective about doing the project in this way?

14. Process Risk

What do you expect to be most risky about doing the project in this way?

Appendix

O

Risk Management Tracking Techniques

The methods for using these templates are described in Chapter 7.

For risk analysis, postmortem issues are converted into risk statements and are entered into the template for a Risk Analysis Survey.

For risk tracking and control, the Risk Management Tracking and Control template is seeded with the highest-ranking risks. The list is reviewed and updated at each project team meeting; additional risks are identified, and the status of probability and impact is changed when appropriate.

Risk Analysis Survey

Instructions:
Rate from 0 to 10 the probability and severity of the risk occurring,
where a rating of 0 means it can't happen or it has no impact,
lower numbers indicate low probability or low severity, and
higher numbers indicate high probability or high severity.
Or indicate "DK" if you don't know or don't have enough information.

ID#	Risk Description	Probability	Impact
1			
2			
3			
4			
5			
6			
7			
8			
9			
10			

Write in any additional known risks:

Risk Management Tracking and Control

Instructions:
Track the current risks and rate the probability and impact as High, Medium, or Low. When the probability is zero, close the risk. If the risk should become an actual problem, close the risk and assign action items to address the problem.

Item Identifier	Risk Description	Probability	Impact	Mitigation Action(s)	Assigned to
Track the item by date and number.	Describe risk conditions in terms of the chance that it might happen and the cost incurred if it does. Classify the item as a risk only if you have a choice to influence the outcome.	Rate the probability or likelihood that the event will occur.	Rate the impact of the loss if the event were to occur.	Describe what is being done or will be done to reduce the probability and/or impact of the risk.	Track who is involved in the mitigation action.

References

ami consortium (application of metrics in industry). *Metric User's Handbook.* London: ami consortium, 1992.

Belasco, James A. *Teaching the Elephant to Dance.* New York: Crown, 1990.

Belasco, James A., and Ralph C. Stayer. *The Flight of the Buffalo: Soaring to Excellence, Learning to Let Employees Lead.* New York: Warner Books, 1993.

Boehm, Barry. *Software Engineering Economics.* Englewood Cliffs, NJ: Prentice Hall, 1981.

Bolton, Robert. *People Skills.* New York: Simon & Schuster, Inc., 1979.

Bridges, William. *Managing Transitions: Making the Most of Change.* Reading, MA: Addison Wesley Longman, 1991.

Bridges, William. *Transitions: Making Sense of Life's Changes.* Reading, MA: Addison Wesley Longman, 1980.

Brooks, Fred. *The Mythical Man-Month: Essays on Software Engineering,* Anniversary ed. Reading, MA: Addison Wesley Longman, 1995.

Brown, Mark Graham. *Baldrige Award Winning Quality: How to Interpret the Baldrige Criteria for Performance Excellence,* 7th ed. New York: Quality Resources, 1997.

Brown, Mark Graham. *The Pocket Guide to the Baldrige Award Criteria,* 4th ed. New York: Quality Resources, 1997.

Burden, Richard L., and J. Douglas Faires. *Numerical Analysis,* 3rd ed. Boston: Prindle, Weber & Schmidt, 1985.

Burns, David D., M.D. *Feeling Good: The New Mood Therapy.* New York: Avon Books, 1980.

Butler, Kelley. "Process Lessons Learned While Reaching Level 4," *CrossTalk: The Journal of Defense Software Engineering* 10, 5 (May 1997), pp. 4–8.

Caputo, Kim. "Level 3 Culture Is More Than Just the Artifacts," 9th Software Engineering Process Group Conference, San Jose, CA, March 1997.

Caputo, Kim. "Level 3 Culture Is More Than Just the Artifacts," 9th Software Technology Conference, Salt Lake City, UT, April 1997.

Caputo, Kim. "Measuring the Pulse of Change," 8th Software Technology Conference, Salt Lake City, UT, April 1996.

Caputo, Kim. "Measuring the Pulse of Change," 9th Software Engineering Process Group Conference, San Jose, CA, March 1997.

Caputo, Kim. "Postmortem Evaluations and Risk Management: Practical Connections," 10th Software Engineering Process Group Conference, Chicago, IL, March 1998.

Caputo, Kim. "Software CMM Maturity Levels: Can You See Beyond the Labels," *CrossTalk: The Journal of Defense Software Engineering* 9, 8 (Aug. 1996), pp. 28–30.

Caputo, Kim, and Michael Sturgeon. "Facilitating CMM Culture Change: Clarifying Communications, Expectations, and Assumptions," 10th Software Technology Conference, Salt Lake City, UT, April 1998.

Carnegie Mellon University / Software Engineering Institute. *The Capability Maturity Model: Guidelines for Improving the Software Process.* Reading, MA: Addison Wesley Longman, 1995.

Carr, Marvin, et al. *Taxonomy-Based Risk Identification.* CMU/SEI-93-TR-6, Pittsburgh, PA: Software Engineering Institute, Carnegie Mellon University, June 1993.

Charette, Robert N. *Software Engineering Risk Analysis and Management.* New York: McGraw Hill, 1989.

Conner, Daryl. *Managing at the Speed of Change: How Resilient Managers Succeed and Prosper Where Others Fail.* New York: Villard Books, 1993.

Conner, Daryl R., and Robert W. Patterson. "Building Commitment to Organizational Change," *Training and Development Journal,* April 1982, pp. 18–30.

Covey, Stephen R. *The Seven Habits of Highly Effective People: Restoring the Character Ethic.* New York: Simon & Schuster, 1989.

Crosby, Philip B. *Quality Is Free.* New York: McGraw Hill Book Company, 1979.

Cusamano, Michael A., and Richard W. Selby. *Microsoft Secrets.* New York: Free Press, 1995.

DeMarco, Tom, and Tim Lister. *Peopleware: Productive Projects and Teams.* New York: Dorset House, 1987.

Deming, W. E. *Out of the Crisis.* Cambridge, MA: M.I.T., Center for Advanced Engineering Studies, 1986.

Donaldson, Scott E., and Stanley G. Siegel. *Cultivating Successful Software Development: A Practitioner's View.* Upper Saddle River, NJ: Prentice Hall PTR, 1997.

Dorofee, A. J., et al. *Continuous Risk Management Guidebook.* Hanscom AFB, MA: SEI Joint Program Office, Carnegie Mellon University, 1996.

Doyle, Michael, and David Straus. *How to Make Meetings Work.* New York: Jove Books, 1976.

Dymond, Kenneth M. *A Guide to the CMM: Understanding the Capability Maturity Model for Software.* Annapolis, MD: Process, Inc. US, 1996.

Engel, Lewis, and Tom Ferguson. *Hidden Guilt.* New York: Pocket Books, 1990.

Epstein, Donald M., with Nathaniel Altman. *The 12 Stages of Healing.* San Raphael/Novato, CA: Amber Allen Publishing and New World Library, 1994.

Fagan, M. E. "Design and Code Inspections to Reduce Errors in Program Development," *IBM Systems Journal,* no. 3, 1976, pp. 182–210.

Fairley, Richard E. *Software Engineering Concepts.* New York: McGraw Hill, 1985.

Fonteyn, Margot. *Autobiography.* New York: Warner Books, 1977.

Fowler, Kimsey, Jr. "SEI CMM Level 5: A Practitioner's Perspective," *CrossTalk: The Journal of Defense Software Engineering* 10, 9 (Sep. 1997), pp. 10–13.

Fowler, Priscilla, and Linda Levine. *A Conceptual Framework for Software Technology.* CMU/SEI-93-TR-31, Pittsburgh, PA: Software Engineering Institute, Carnegie Mellon University, December 1993.

Fowler, Priscilla, and Stan Rifkin. *Software Engineering Process Group Guide.* CMU/SEI-90-TR-24, Pittsburgh, PA: Software Engineering Institute, Carnegie Mellon University, September 1990.

Gause, Donald C., and Gerald M. Weinberg. *Exploring Requirements: Quality Before Design.* New York: Dorset House, 1989.

Gilb, Tom. *Principles of Software Engineering Management.* Reading, MA: Addison Wesley Longman, 1988.

Grady, Robert B. *Successful Software Process Improvement.* Upper Saddle River, NJ: Hewlett-Packard Company/Prentice Hall PTR, 1997.

Hayes, Will, and David Zubrow. *Moving On Up: Data and Experience Doing CMM-Based Process Improvement.* CMU/SEI-95-TR-008, Pittsburgh, PA: Software Engineering Institute, Carnegie Mellon University, August 1995.

Herbsleb, James, et al. *Benefits of CMM-Based Software Process Improvement: Initial Results.* CMU/SEI-94-TR-13, Pittsburgh, PA: Software Engineering Institute, Carnegie Mellon University, August 1994.

Hickman, Craig R., and Michael A. Silva. *Creating Excellence: Managing Corporate Culture, Strategy, and Change in the New Age.* New York: New American Library, 1984.

Hillier, Fredrick S., and Gerald J. Lieberman. *Introduction to Operations Research,* 3rd ed. Oakland, CA: Holen-Day, Inc., 1980.

Hofman, Bruce, Gayle Bertossi, Kim Caputo, and Karen Reineke. "Experiences From Performing Interim Profiles," 7th Software Engineering Process Group Conference, Boston, MA, May 1995.

Hofstadter, Douglas R. *Gödel, Escher, Bach: An Eternal Golden Braid.* New York: Vintage Books/Random House, 1979.

Hohmann, Luke. *Journey of the Software Professional: A Sociology of Software Development.* Upper Saddle River, NJ: Prentice Hall PTR, 1997.

Humphrey, Watts S. *A Discipline for Software Engineering.* Reading, MA: Addison Wesley Longman, 1995.

Humphrey, Watts S. *Managing Technical People: Innovation, Teamwork, and the Software Process.* Reading, MA, Addison Wesley Longman, 1997.

Humphrey, Watts S. *Managing the Software Process.* Reading, MA: Addison Wesley Longman, 1989.

Ibrahim, Rosalind L., and Iraj Hirmanpour. *The Subject Matter of Process Improvement: A Topic and Reference Source for Software Engineering Educators and Trainers.* CMU/SEI-95-TR-003, Pittsburgh, PA: Software Engineering Institute, Carnegie Mellon University, May 1995.

ISO 9001. *Quality systems—Model for quality assurance in design/development, production, installation, and servicing.* Second edition. Geneva, Switzerland: International Organization for Standardization, 1994.

Juran, J. M. *Juran's Quality Control Handbook,* 4th ed. New York: McGraw Hill, 1988.

Juran, J. M. *Managerial Breakthrough: A New Concept of the Manager's Job.* New York: McGraw-Hill, 1964.

Katzenbach, Jon R., and Douglas K. Smith. *The Wisdom of Teams: Creating the High Performance Organization.* Boston: McKinsey & Company, Inc., Harvard Business School Press, 1993.

Kepner-Tregoe, Inc. *Project Management.* Princeton, NJ: Kepner-Tregoe, Inc., 1987.

Kuhn, Thomas. *The Structure of Scientific Revolutions,* 2nd ed. Chicago: University of Chicago Press, 1970.

LaMarsh, Jeanenne. *Changing the Way We Change: Gaining Control of Major Operational Change.* Reading, MA: Addison Wesley Longman, 1995.

Lawson, Joan. *The Principles of Classical Dance.* New York: Alfred A. Knopf, 1980.

Leonard-Barton, Dorothy. "Implementation as Mutual Adaptation of Technology and Organization," Research Policy 17, 5 October 1988, pp. 251–267.

Loomis, Mary E. *Dancing the Wheel of Psychological Types.* Wilmette, IL: Chiron Publications, 1991.

McWilliams, John-Roger, and Peter McWilliams. *DO IT! Let's Get Off Our Buts!* Los Angeles: Bantam Prelude Press, 1991.

Moore, Geoffrey A. *Crossing the Chasm: Marketing and Selling Technology Products to Mainstream Customers.* New York: Harper Business, 1991.

Norman, Donald A. *The Design of Everyday Things.* New York: Doubleday/Currency, 1990.

Olson, Tim, et al. A *Software Process Framework for the SEI Capability Maturity Model.* CMU/SEI-94-HB-1, Pittsburgh, PA: Software Engineering Institute, Carnegie Mellon University, 1994.

Olson, Tim, and Neal Reizer. "Defining and Tailoring Processes That Work," 9th Software Engineering Process Group Conference, San Jose, CA, March 1997.

Osterweil, Leon. "Software Process: A State of the Art Report," 14th International Conference on Software Engineering, Melbourne, May 1992.

Osterweil, Leon. "Software Processes Are Software Too," 9th International Conference on Software Engineering, Monterey, CA, 30 March–2 April 1987. Los Alamitos, CA: IEEE Computer Society, 1987.

Paulk, Mark C., et al. *Capability Maturity Model for Software, Version 1.1.* CMU/SEI-93-TR-24, Pittsburgh, PA: Software Engineering Institute, Carnegie Mellon University, February 1993.

Paulk, Mark C., et al. *Key Practices of the Capability Maturity Model for Software, Version 1.1.* CMU/SEI-93-TR-25, Pittsburgh, PA: Software Engineering Institute, Carnegie Mellon University, February 1993.

Pryzyblinski, Stanley M., Priscilla J. Fowler, and John H. Maher. "Software Technology Transition," 13th International Conference on Software Engineering, Austin, TX, May 1991.

Rogers, Everett M. *Diffusion of Innovations,* 3rd ed. New York: The Free Press, 1983.

Rozum, James A. *Concepts on Measuring the Benefits of Software Process Improvements.* CMU/SEI-93-TR-09, Pittsburgh, PA: Software Engineering Institute, Carnegie Mellon University, 1993.

Sashkin, Marshall, and Kenneth J. Kiser. *Putting Total Quality Management to Work: What TQM Means, How to Use It, & How to Sustain It Over the Long Run.* San Francisco: Berrett-Koehler Publishers, Inc., 1993.

Schein, Edgar. *Organizational Culture and Leadership.* San Francisco: Jossey-Bass, Inc., 1985.

Schneiderman, Ben. *Designing the User Interface: Strategies for Effective Human-Computer Interaction*, third edition. Reading, MA: Addison Wesley Longman, 1998.

Scholtes, Peter R., et al. *The Team Handbook: How to Use Teams to Improve Quality.* Madison, WI: Joiner Associates, Inc., 1988.

Senge, Peter M. *The Fifth Discipline: The Art and Practice of the Learning Organization.* New York: Currency and Doubleday, 1991.

Senge, Peter M. *The Fifth Discipline Fieldbook: Strategies and Tools for Building a Learning Organization.* New York: Learning Organization, 1994.

Shaw, Brian. *First Steps in Ballet.* London: Octopus Books Limited, 1980.

Smith, Kenwyn K., and David N. Berg. *Paradoxes of Group Life: Understanding Conflict, Paralysis, and Movement in Group Dynamics.* San Francisco, Jossey-Bass, Inc., 1987.

Sorell, Walter. *Dance In Its Time.* Garden City, NY: Anchor Press/Doubleday, 1981.

Tushman, Michael L., and Philip Anderson. "Technological Discontinuities and Organizational Environments," *Administrative Science Quarterly* 31 (1986), pp. 439–465.

Wakulczyk, Marek. "NSSF Spot Check: A Metric Toward CMM Level 2," *CrossTalk: The Journal of Defense Software Engineering* 8, 7 (Jul. 1995), pp. 23–24.

Wakulczyk, Marek. "Success Is Not Accidental: CMM Level 2 in 2.5 Years," *CrossTalk: The Journal of Defense Software Engineering* 10, 9 (Sep. 1997), Web Addition.

Weick, Karl E. *Sensemaking in Organizations.* Thousand Oaks, CA: Sage Publications, Inc., 1995.

Weick, Karl E. *The Social Psychology of Organizing.* New York: Newbery Award Records, Inc., 1979.

Weinberg, Gerald M. *Quality Software Management: Volume 1, Systems Thinking.* New York: Dorset House, 1992.

Weinberg, Gerald M. *Quality Software Management: Volume 2, First-Order Measurement.* New York: Dorset House, 1993.

Weinberg, Gerald M. *Quality Software Management: Volume 3, Congruent Action.* New York: Dorset House, 1994.

Weinberg, Gerald M. *Quality Software Management: Volume 4, Anticipating Change.* New York: Dorset House, 1997.

Whitney, Roselyn, et al. *Interim Profile Development and Trial of a Method to Rapidly Measure Software Engineering Maturity Status.* CMU/SEI-94-TR-4, Pittsburgh, PA: Software Engineering Institute, Carnegie Mellon University, March 1994.

Wiegers, Karl E. *Creating a Software Engineering Culture.* New York: Dorset House, 1996.

Yamamura, George, and Gary B. Wigle. "SEI CMM Level 5: For the Right Reasons," *CrossTalk: The Journal of Defense Software Engineering* 10, 8 (Aug. 1997), pp. 3–6.

Yourdon, Edward. *Decline and Fall of the American Programmer.* Englewood Cliffs, NJ: Prentice Hall/Yourdon Press, 1993.

Zubrow, David, et al. *Maturity Questionnaire.* CMU/SEI-94-SR-7, Pittsburgh, PA: Software Engineering Institute, Carnegie Mellon University, 1994.

Index

System/Software Requirements

The CD-ROM works with all of the following system configurations:

Windows 95 with Microsoft Word 6.0, Microsoft Excel 5.0, and Microsoft PowerPoint 4.0

Windows 95 with Microsoft Word 7.0, Microsoft Excel 5.0, and Microsoft PowerPoint 7.0

Windows NT with Microsoft Word 6.0, Microsoft Excel 5.0, and Microsoft PowerPoint 4.0

Power Macintosh System 7.5.5 with Microsoft Word 6.0, Microsoft Excel 5.0, and Microsoft PowerPoint 4.0